The Comfort Women

The Comfort Women

Japan's Brutal Regime of Enforced Prostitution in the Second World War

GEORGE HICKS

W · W · NORTON & COMPANY
New York   London

Copyright © 1994 by George Hicks

First American Edition 1995
First published as a Norton paperback 1997
All rights reserved

Printed in the United States of America

The text of this book is composed in Times New Roman 327
with the display set in Trump Mediaeval
Composition and manufacturing by the Haddon Craftsmen, Inc.
Book design by Jacques Chazaud

Library of Congress Cataloging-in-Publication Data

Hicks, George, 1936–
        The comfort women : Japan's brutal regime of enforced
    prostitution in the Second World War / George Hicks.
            p.   cm.
        Includes bibliographical references and index.
        1. Comfort women—Asia—History.   2. Service, Compulsory non
    -military—Asia.   3. World War, 1939–1945—Women—Asia.   4. Sino
    -Japanese Conflict, 1937–1945—Women.   5. World War, 1939–1945—
    -Asia—Atrocities.   6. Sino-Japanese Conflict, 1937–1945-
    -Atrocities.   I. Title.
    D810.C698H53   1995
    940.54'05082—dc20   95–2162
        ISBN 0-393-03807-6
        ISBN 0-393-31694-7 pbk.

W. W. Norton & Company, Inc.
500 Fifth Avenue, New York, N.Y. 10110
www.wwnorton.com

W. W. Norton & Company Ltd.
Castle House, 75/76 Wells Street, London W1T 3QT

    7 8 9 0

Contents

Contents

Acknowledgments

I had never heard of the comfort women until the fiftieth anniversary of Pearl Harbour, in December 1991. Some Korean women, who were taking the Japanese government to court, made the front pages of the international press. The Japanese government flatly denied any knowledge or involvement, and argued that the so-called comfort women were privately organised camp followers. Was this a lie? If so, how could it be nailed?

I asked Les Oates, a retired senior lecturer in Japanese in Melbourne, Australia who is rarely at a loss on matters Japanese. Of course he knew about the comfort women. As a war veteran he had even seen them in Southeast Asia in 1945.

Since Les and I had already worked together on a couple of books involving Japanese sources on Southeast Asian history, there was no doubt that he could swiftly translate and hammer into shape the most arcane Japanese language material. The problem was that, unlike with our other books, we didn't have any sources—in any language. Although there is a huge literature in English on the Pacific War, we could find no mention in it of the comfort women.

I then contacted another old friend, Professor Akira Takahashi of the University of Tokyo. Through him I soon met Ms Yumi Lee, whose family was originally from Korea, but had lived in Japan for three generations. Through her contacts in activist circles she was able to collect practically everything that had been written about the comfort women. She found about 80 per cent of the material (much of it exceedingly obscure) used in the writing of this book. Without Yumi Lee and Les Oates I could never have got started.

I needed someone to help from the Korean side. Professor Chalmers Johnson kindly introduced me in Seoul to Professor Hye Kyung Lee, who translated reams of Korean material into English and found virtually all the photographs used in this book.

In the Philippines, attorney Romeo T. Capulong, a legal adviser to the Philippine comfort women, gave me good advice and a vast amount of material on the local scene. In Indonesia, another human rights lawyer, Adnan Buyong Nasution, introduced me to several Indonesian women, and gave me the background to the local story.

In Malaysia, Haji Mustapha Yaakub of UMNO Youth Malaysia, gave me the Malaysian background and introduced me to Madam X, a refined, gracious and above all courageous woman who told me her story in calm but horrific detail.

From the other side of the world, in the Netherlands, Theo van Boven, Professor of International Law at the University of Limburg, kindly faxed me valuable material. Bart van Poelgeest, scholar, archivist and author of the Dutch government's report on forced prostitution, sent me his official report and a major article he had written about the Dutch victims.

No-one can write on this subject without being in debt to the continuing research of Professor Yoshimi Yoshiaki, an historian at Chuo University in Tokyo. It was Yoshimi who first found the 'smoking gun' which forced the Japanese authorities to admit to military involvement in the comfort women issue, in effect admitting that they had been lying for decades. Yoshimi generously sent me unpublished Japanese military records proving Japanese military involvement.

Thanks to David Jenkins of the *Sydney Morning Herald*, we found other incriminating evidence which Professor Yoshimi had always assured me must exist. In the Australian Archives in Melbourne, Australia, the decrypted messages sent by the Japanese Chief of Staff of the 1st Southern Expeditionary Fleet on 18 August 1945 (three days after the surrender) reads: 'On 1st August the personnel employed in connection with Japanese naval comforts at Singapore were appointed civilian employees of 101st hospital. Most of the girls were made auxiliary nurses. Other commands under 1st Southern Expeditionary Fleet are to conform.' As the Allies moved in, the Japanese attempted a cover-up by disguising comfort women as nurses. Finally, on 20 August at 1915 hours (just before they surrendered), the Japanese Civil Administration Department from Makassar, Indonesia once again ordered that comfort women were to be attached to local hospitals as nurses and 'when this message is understood, burn it'.

This Southeast Asian cover-up helped to obscure the nature of the system. For almost forty years the truth was hidden. Living victims were too intimidated to challenge the might of the Japanese state. All documentary evidence appeared to have been burnt. Then, slowly, fragment by fragment, witness by witness, victim by victim, the truth emerged.

I dedicate this book to Madam X and the other hundred thousand or more victims of Japanese forced prostitution in World War II.

George Hicks
Melbourne
August 1994

Note on names, institutions and exchange values

The east Asian names in this book are as written in East Asia: the family names first followed by the personal names. Korean and Chinese personal names are made up for the individual using meaningful or symbolic words. They almost always consist of two words: for example, Ok Ju. While the Western style has usually been to link up the two words with a hyphen to indicate it is a personal name, it is never written that way in the original languages. Hence the two-word personal names in this book are not hyphenated. Similarly, Japanese personal names are preceded by the family name which is the style used here: Miyazawa Kiichi rather than Kiichi Miyazawa, which is the reverse of Western practice.

The most notorious institution during the Pacific War was the *kempeitai,* or Japanese military police. The *kempei,* or military police officers, had absolute power, and the gross brutality associated with the Japanese Armed Forces was often the work of the *kempeitai.* The very name struck fear into those who heard it, often including the Japanese soldiers themselves.

Besides the normal duties of keeping order in the Army the *kempeitai* had the additional role of combating 'subversion'. In a sense they were the Army equivalent of the Special Higher Police, or Thought Police, with a lower level of ideological sophistication.

A standard rendering of monetary values is impossible because of the extreme instability of exchange rates and prices during the Depression and the war years. Exchange rates at any given time bore little relation to purchasing power. The most relevant guide to current values is to compare prices with a Japanese serviceman's monthly pay rates in 1943: Superior Private ¥9; Sergeant (middle NCO range) ¥30; Lieutenant (middle company officer range) ¥94; Lieutenant Colonel (middle field officer range) ¥310. Combat zone allowances roughly doubled these rates of pay and naval rates varied only slightly from Army rates. The minimum regular civilian wage at this time was about ¥100 per month while nurses were paid ¥90.

Introduction

The plight of comfort women was not of major concern to the powers fighting World War II. Nor has it proved of interest to its historians. There is no monument to the unknown comfort woman as there are monuments everywhere to the unknown soldier.

It has taken half a century for these women's ruined lives to become a human rights issue. There were thirty years between Japanese journalist Senda Kako's groundbreaking discovery work, and the setting up of hotlines in Tokyo, Kyoto, Osaka and South Korea, to encourage women to come forward.

From the late 1980s, women's groups in Korea and Japan began to organise to force the issue on to the political agenda. The first ex-comfort women began publicly to testify to their ordeals. In story after story, what has slowly and painfully emerged is a picture of a large-scale, officially-organised system of rape by the Imperial Japanese Forces. Thousands of women, from young village girls to older professionals, an estimated 80 per cent of them Korean, were part of the comfort system across Asia.

Kim Hak Sun was the first former comfort woman to announce she was willing to publicly tell her story, as part of legal action against the Japanese government. Her example gave others the courage to join her in a class action which was launched in the Tokyo District Court on 6 December 1991. The women are demanding compensation, as well as Japanese government admission that force was used to recruit them. Their case is moving slowly on.

An Asia-wide movement is also emerging on the issue. Asian governments have to varying degrees supported women in their own countries. But because many countries are dependent on Japan for aid and investment, such support can be less than wholehearted.

In February 1993, a group of Japanese scholars called on their government to break a long taboo and allow school history books to cover atrocities committed during Japan's colonial rule in Korea, from 1910 to 1945. Until now, the Education Ministry has kept any reference to comfort women out of the nation's textbooks.

As the women continue to speak out, this deliberate historical blindness will become harder to sustain. Their stories will become part of the larger story of World War II.

Madam X and Mun Ok Ju

Madam X, at that time a young Chinese girl living in British Malaya, recently described to me in Cantonese how she became a comfort woman:

Some time in January 1942, the Japanese occupied Kuala Lumpur—but all that seemed remote to us. We were safe in our little village. No Japanese would bother us there. Then one day in February 1942, two lorries full of Japanese soldiers came into our village. I remember it was February because it was on my mother's birthday. How did the Japanese find our village? They were led there by a thirty-year-old traitor. How could he do such a thing, directing the Japanese soldiers to our village?

I was cooking at the time and was unable to escape. The armed soldiers moved quickly through our village, cutting off all hope of escape. Three soldiers with rifles came to our house while the rest fanned out through the village. They burst in and grabbed me. My parents tried to rescue me but my father was kicked in the head. Blood went everywhere. I struggled as hard as I could, but I got kicked in the head too. I still have that scar. See? Then my panties were ripped off and one of the soldiers undid the front of his trousers. While the others held me down, he stuck his thing into me. I had no idea what he was trying to do. I knew nothing about the facts of life. I was only fifteen and hadn't even had my first period.

It was agonizing. Blood came out. They did it on the kitchen floor, right in front of my parents and brother. Three soldiers did it to me in turns, and then they took me out and put me in one of the lorries along with some other girls from my village. My brother was put in the other lorry and taken away. We never saw him again. As I was being put in the truck, my parents rushed out to try and rescue me. My father was trailing blood from his wound. For the next three years, I was constantly haunted by that last vision of my parents, especially my father's blood on the ground.

Then I was taken to a big two-storey bungalow in Jalan Ampang. Six Japanese officers who were living there raped me again. I was crying for my parents and bleeding from my head wound and also from down below. But the officers there did the same thing to me again. I couldn't sleep or eat and thought all the time of my parents and brother. After a short while in the bungalow, they took me to the Great Eastern Dance Hall, which I think was also in Jalan Ampang. The dance hostesses had all become comfort girls. Those girls could all speak fluent English. The same thing happened to me in the Dance Hall as in the bungalow. Then a month later, they took me to the Tai Sun Hotel opposite the Pudu Jail in Jalan Pudu.

There I had a big room with a double bed. I got two simple meals a day and there was a cleaner who changed the sheets daily. I was forced to have sex with ten to twenty men a day. As a result I was continuously raw. Red raw. Sex was excruciating. Oh, you have no idea how painful it was! You couldn't imagine it! But I had to be gentle and serve every soldier well. If I didn't perform well, I would get beaten. Some of the men would be drunk and beat me anyway. One man, although drunk, stayed inside me his whole allotted hour. It was unbearable—but I had to bear it.

Mun Ok Ju was originally from Taegu in southeast Korea. Born in 1924, one of four children of parents who were casual workers, she had had only three years of schooling before starting work at ten, first as a housemaid, then in a cottage workshop making footwear. In 1942, when wartime conditions made employment hard to come by, and when she was eighteen, she was approached by a local man with the Korean name of Song and the Japanese name of Matsumoto. He offered her 'a good job in a restaurant, in a warm country though some distance away'. He wore a smart Western-style suit, with tie and leather shoes, which marked him out as either a professional, or some sort of agent of the Japanese regime. Koreans then were under pressure to adopt Japanese names and ways, and Ok Ju adopted the name Fumihara Yoshiko. The real lure was the good salary which would enable her to send money home to help her impoverished family—an important consideration in a society where Confucian values of filial piety were deeply important.

Together with a group of seventeen girls aged between fifteen and twenty-one, Ok Ju was taken to the nearby Korean port of Pusan, then shipped to Rangoon in Burma, lodged in the hold. Her fellow passengers included more than 200 girls in the care of ten men of Matsumoto's type. Most were expecting to work in restaurants, canteens or similar surroundings. The Korean women only saw the servicemen who shared the passage to Burma when they emerged to defend the ship from enemy air attack.

In Rangoon the women had their first definite indication that they were to become comfort women. Some Koreans enlisted in the Japanese Army told them that they had 'made a big mistake'. The shock proved too much for one of the girls, who drowned herself. The others were taken away in batches of fifteen to twenty. Ok Ju's group was sent to a comfort station in Mandalay. Ok Ju had to service more than thirty men a day in a cramped thatched hut partitioned by hanging mats which did not quite reach the ceiling.

Her 'comfort station' was called the Taegu Inn, and was situated some distance from the Army barracks, without the close supervision reported in some areas. But the women were not allowed to leave their quarters without a leave pass issued by Divisional Headquarters, of the same kind as issued to troops. This was given once a month to groups of five or six, in her case marked 'Fumihara Yoshiko and party of . . .', the hours being indicated and strictly checked.

At a time when a private's pay was about ¥15 (Japanese yen) a month, the fee per visit was ¥1.50 for privates, ¥2 for non-commissioned officers, ¥2.50 for junior officers and ¥3 for senior officers. At the reception visitors would receive on payment a ticket, which they would then hand to the comfort woman.

The collected tickets were handed daily to Matsumoto. Once a month, he would pay the women half the equivalent value. But out of this sum they had to buy such items as food to supplement the very basic rations supplied, clothing, tobacco and occasional liquor 'when needing relief'. Ok Ju saved a total of ¥15,000, but this consisted entirely of tips. She deposited this in the field post office, being entitled to do so by her paramilitary classification.

Health measures included a weekly disinfecting of the rooms and a venereal disease inspection by the unit medical officer. If infected, the women were not admitted to go to hospital as occurred in some areas, but were allowed to rest in their rooms during treatment. A sign, 'No entry this week', would then be placed at their door. Unlike the procedure in some areas, they were obliged to maintain service during menstruation, using absorbent cotton and frequent douches. On one occasion Ok Ju attempted during menstruation to refuse service to a drunken non-commissioned officer, who accused her of lying, and threatened her with a sword. With the defiant spirit not uncommon among Koreans, she attempted to disarm him and in the struggle he received a fatal cut—easily done with that formidable weapon. She was court-martialled but acquitted on grounds of self-defence. Some of the Japanese themselves remarked: 'He was a nasty drunk, always abusing the comfort girls. Got what he deserved!'

After six months in Mandalay, Ok Ju's group were transferred in small boats to the coastal town of Akyab, close to the Indian front. They were joined by their unit a few days later. They remained there for about a year, during which Matsumoto left and the Army took over operation of the four comfort stations. Two of these housed Japanese women, one house being reserved for officers. While there Ok Ju received a leg injury from bomb shrapnel, leaving lasting effects. She had further spells in Prome and Rangoon. During this time she apparently provided additional forms of entertainment, as she remembers both Japanese and Burmese songs popular at the time. Finally she and others were transferred to Ayutthaya in Thailand, where they were given a month's training as nursing assistants to handle injections, bandaging, pulse and temperature taking, and malaria treatment. They had to improvise uniforms, but had the Red Cross insignia on their caps. Ok Ju worked at the Ayutthaya Field Hospital for the last few months of the war, without any news of the military situation. Finally a weeping NCO broke the news of Japan's defeat, adding that the Koreans would now become independent.

As remittance facilities were available in Thailand, Ok Ju had sent ¥5000 home. The rest she had left in her Japanese account. It turned out to be impossible to visit Japan, since the Red Cross repatriation ship sailed direct to Inchon. Of her group of seventeen from Taegu, twelve had survived, the others having been lost through suicide, illness and shipwreck.

The hidden story emerges

It was the sight in a wartime photograph of two women wading across a river with their skirts tucked up and their luggage perched on their heads, which first caught Senda Kako's journalistic interest. Walking alongside the women was a grinning soldier. Senda asked a former war correspondent who these women were; he was told they were 'Korean Ps'. He still failed to understand. It was explained they were Korean 'comfort women', a term also new to him. The correspondent then told Senda about the system of providing women for the sexual comfort of soldiers in war zones. Senda reflected on their tragedy. Since his informant knew little about the comfort system as a whole, Senda began to investigate for himself.

It was 1962. Senda had come across the photograph while doing some research on the war for the Japanese-language newspaper, the *Mainichi Shimbun*. The photograph of the comfort women had been among a collection of 25,000 censored wartime photographs.

Since 1962, much has surfaced about the system of providing women for the 'comfort' of the Japanese Armed Forces. The issue raises afresh the question of Japanese reluctance to acknowledge wartime atrocities. The comfort system consisted of the legalised military rape of subject women on a scale—and over a period of time—previously unknown in history. Comfort women were in the vanguard of the Japanese Forces. Accounts are given of how the women would arrive with the ammunition—and sometimes even before essential military equipment.

It took Senda two years to track down authentic information. In Fukuoka on the Japanese island of Kyushu, he found the brothel-keeper who had provided the first officially-sanctioned comfort station near Shanghai in China in 1938. He also found the army doctor, Aso Tetsuo, who had examined the women for venereal disease and pronounced the younger, less experienced Korean girls, unsurprisingly, healthier than the accompanying Japanese prostitutes.

His preliminary contacts persuaded Senda to continue his investigations. For many years he researched and wrote about the comfort women in relative obscurity. Although his work was translated into Korean, for a long time the subject made little impact in South Korea, the part of the divided Korean Peninsula that has had the most contact with Japan since the war in the Pacific. Since 1910, the Korean Peninsula had been a Japanese colony, with Koreans regarded as Japanese subjects. During the 1930s and 1940s, Korean women were shipped all over the Japanese Empire, which for a brief period stretched from the Siberian border in the north, to Burma in Southeast Asia, encompassing Micronesia and the Solomon Islands in the Pacific.

The comfort women were, however, not exclusively Koreans. Women from other Japanese-occupied territories were also forced into sexual servitude, as the case of Madam X shows. This became increasingly clear from the early 1990s onwards, when media attention prompted a growing number of former comfort women to reveal their stories. Their overall numbers will probably never be known, even if Japanese authorities were to reveal all available official documents, for the women did not even rate a category of their own in army manifests. The first batches of women shipped from Nagasaki to Shanghai were listed as so many units of 'war supplies'. While such categorisation could have been an attempt at concealment, this seems unlikely given the highly pragmatic approach the Japanese military took in providing for the sexual comfort of its men. There were also unambiguous regulations for the operations of comfort stations, which began to be revealed.

The only approximation of statistical data on the comfort women comes from the hotlines set up in 1992 to collect information about comfort stations and comfort women, in Tokyo, Kyoto and Osaka. At about the same time, South Korean women's groups also set up similar hotlines but the information gathered was mostly on individual cases, 155 in all. The only generalised data to emerge from the Korean hotlines were analyses of age and location: 80 per cent of comfort women were aged between 14 and 18. As for destinations, 31 per cent went to Manchuria, 14 per cent to Taiwan, 7 per cent each to Saipan, Osaka, Singapore, Taikachin (in China), and 4 per cent each to Kyushu, Nagoya, Nanking, Hokkaido and Tientsin in northeast China. The remaining 2 per cent went to 'other Pacific islands', a reference to Micronesia.

During the month or so that the hotlines were in operation in the three Japanese cities, all callers were asked a standard set of questions, so a degree of sampling was achieved. Among the Tokyo callers, who were the most numerous, 79 referred to comfort stations in China, 56 to Manchuria, 36 to Southeast Asia, 22 to the Western Pacific, 23 to Japan and 6 to Korea. In Kyoto, 65 callers referred to China (including Manchuria), 4 to Korea, 2 to New Guinea (meaning Rabaul), 4 to the Netherlands Indies (Indonesia), 8 to the Philippines, 3 to Burma and 2 each to Malaya, Thailand, French Indochina, Japan and Taiwan. In Osaka, where many calls would have been pre-empted by the earlier phone-ins in nearby Kyoto, 25 referred to China, 7 to the 'southern islands' (meaning Southeast Asia and Micronesia) and 2 to Japan. Although not all callers answered all questions, the areas where comfort women were found were obviously widespread, covering all territories occupied by the Japanese between 1930 and 1945.

The data also revealed a wide range of nationalities. In Tokyo, Koreans were mentioned by 175 callers (of whom 78 had encountered only Koreans), while 86 callers mentioned only Japanese women. Smaller numbers mentioned Taiwanese, both Chinese and indigenous, 'Manchus' (meaning the non-Chinese ethnic groups); mainland Chinese, Indonesians (who were also in New Guinea), Dutch, Burmese, Malays, and White Russians (in Manchuria). In Kyoto, 68 mentioned Koreans, 40 Japanese, 29 Chinese, 5 Filipinas, 2 each White Russians, Taiwanese and Vietnamese, and 1 each Dutch, Malays, Eurasians, Indonesians, Thais and Burmese. The Osaka callers described Koreans as most numerous, with others being Chinese or Southeast Asian women.

In the Kyoto survey, approximate figures for women in particular places were given in over 60 cases. Some respondents indicated various combinations of Japanese, Korean and Chinese women, frequently with an overall total of about 15 in any one place; 40 instances are cited of groups consisting only of Koreans, usually with between 10 and 20 in one place. In some cases there were fewer than 10, but groups of up to 80 women are also recorded. Figures for 'only' Japanese and 'only' Chinese comfort women in a particular location are given in 16 and 11 cases respectively, with 40 the largest number in any one place—for both Chinese and Japanese. The Osaka survey did not obtain comparable figures.

The Kyoto survey also asked what terms were used to describe the establishments where the comfort women operated. It found that most respondents were equally divided between 'comfort station' and 'P house', with one instance of 'WC' and one of 'brothel'. Two were called 'pompon houses'—a term which came into common use in post-war American-occupied Japan. There is only one reference to women being called by the official term, comfort women (*ianfu* in Japanese), the more common usage being 'P', coupled with the nationality. Sometimes the latter was in slang form, such as *Chan-P* for Chinese and *Chom-P* for Koreans. It has been suggested that the slang 'P' derives from the English initial of the word 'prostitute', but it is more likely that it comes from the vulgar Chinese term *p'i*, for vagina. It should be noted that the use of the terms 'P' and comfort women was confined mainly to the military, while 'comfort women' was not so much a euphemism as a form of officialese.

Although no figures are available for the total number of women involved in the comfort system, an approximate estimate can be made using various ratios that have been cited for troops to women. This is not, however, a satisfactory basis, because of the large variations from place to place and time to time. Nonetheless, data from the Tokyo phone survey do correlate roughly with known troop numbers in the areas mentioned, and ratios of troops to women in China were obtained for every year from 1937—45 although each referred to a different area. In four cases, the ratio of troops to comfort women was 50:1; in others, the ratios ranged from 35:1 to 100:1. The average ratio overall was just over 50:1.

A ratio of 29:1 is frequently quoted. This may have been the ideal, but the findings do not support it. According to Japanese wartime figures, the ratios for the Kwangtung Army based in Manchuria and China were between 35:1 and 45:1, whereas estimates by hotline informants ranged from 35:1 to 100:1 for China. One of the first five relevant official Japanese documents to be uncovered mentions 1004 women for the 21st Army, which would have numbered 40,000 to 50,000 troops. This implies a ratio of between 40:1 and 50:1. Commonsense suggests that ratios as high as 30:1 are unrealistic. As will be described, when forced, the women serviced 30 men a day, so a ratio of 30:1 would imply that each soldier had sex virtually every day—unless a number did so twice a day—which is equally unlikely and never reported. Apart from the question of the libido required, Japanese soldiers could not have afforded daily sex, given military wages and the fees charged for using the comfort women.

If we assume a ratio of 50:1, then the total of some 7 million troops from all theatres of war indicates that there would have been about 139,000 comfort women at most. If the wartime death rate among them is taken to be about one-sixth, or 23,000, then some 116,000 comfort women might be expected to have survived their ordeal. Reducing this figure by 50 per cent to allow for death due to old age or illness since the war suggests there could be around 58,000 surviving comfort women. Yet, surprisingly, until recently the numbers of comfort women who had come forward could be counted on the fingers of one hand.

Deception and abduction

What makes the comfort system particularly repugnant is not just that the women were shipped throughout Japanese-occupied territory, right up to the frontlines, to face the same dangers as the soldiers. What is even worse is that the women were for the most part duped, abducted or coerced into sexual slavery.

Although Japan had a system of licensed prostitution before the war, the majority of the comfort women were naïve young girls drafted into the comfort system against their will. While some Japanese officials took the trouble to get the women to sign an 'agreement', the widespread lack of comprehension of what this entailed made such 'consent' a sham. Recruitment like Ok Ju's falls into the mode of deceptive enticement. Private individuals were involved, who were either seeking their own fortunes, or had been hired by the Japanese authorities to find women. As the Japanese military's demand for women grew, direct recruitment through the police or local government became more common. Such official recruitment was part of the labour draft for war industries, and provided a convenient cover for recruiting comfort women. Under the strengthened National General Mobilisation Regulations, Korean girls were seized in virtual slave raids, while nearer the frontlines local girls like Madam X were also seized for sexual servitude.

After the war, the fate of the comfort women was very varied. Madam X and Mun Ok Ju were among the minority who made it home and were able to resume a more or less normal life. Many more remained in the post-war version of the comfort system, providing sexual service to yet more soldiers, in different uniforms. At the other extreme, many comfort women did not survive the war, succumbing to illness, enemy action or death at the hands of Japanese troops as part of the habitual practice of mass suicide in defeat. A few others chose to remain in the former occupied areas, some even marrying local men and merging into the local population.

Today psychiatrists and psychologists recognise the trauma suffered by rape victims often prevents their integration into society. Not surprisingly, most comfort women appear to now lead a perilous emotional existence, made all the more distressing by the perceived necessity to remain silent over the decades following their horrific experiences. Their strong sense of isolation, and alienation from their society, has been described by some victims as more unbearable than their original ordeals. Beneath the façade of a typical grandmother minding her adopted daughter's house and son, Madam X remains unable to relinquish her fear of sex and hatred of men, which extends even to her foster-son-in-law and perhaps also to her grandson. As with many comfort women, she was unable to bear children, and continues to suffer a variety of physical problems linked to her years of sexual slavery.

An injustice unavenged

Unlike other World War II atrocities, such as the Nazi massacre of the Jews or the Japanese abuse of prisoners of war, it has taken half a century for the officially sanctioned and organised comfort system, involving the continuous rape of thousands of women by Japanese troops, to become public. Feminists suspect that this massive abuse of women might, indeed, never have been seen as an atrocity at all had not some brave women spoken out. Exploitative treatment of women is still the norm throughout most of the world, especially in the two countries most involved, Japan and Korea. Prostitution rackets in places like Thailand and the Philippines involve younger and younger victims, as men from many countries attempt to avoid AIDS by using barely pubescent girls.

The comfort women issue could perhaps not have been dealt with earlier. The changing attitudes of women, and towards women, in Asia were an essential precondition. Then as now, rape was never an easy charge to sustain. Given the high moral value attached to chastity, the comfort women invariably emerged from their wartime experiences defiled, yet unable to accuse their abusers. They had everything to gain by keeping silent and everything to lose by making accusations. From the patriarchal point of view, it was seen almost as a kindness to the comfort women to pretend that this systematic brutalisation had never taken place.

That local operators and recruiters collaborated in the comfort system was another good reason for silence. Many of them continued after the war in the same line of work, often using the former comfort women who, for economic reasons, were unable to break away from them. Until the late 1980s South Korea was also ruled by a succession of military men who did not countenance citizen demonstrations or lobbying of any kind. The passing of military rule and the relaxation of strictures against democratic speech have both helped to promote an increasingly vocal feminist movement. This has brought issues such as sex tourism and the comfort women's plight into the open as political issues.

In his epilogue to a major list of sources on comfort women, *The Emperor's Forces and Korean Comfort Women*, Korean activist Kim

Il Myon states that he has not compiled the listing for mere 'sensation seeking', but in the hope of contributing to the still incomplete tasks of social progress. He summarises these as the liberation of workers, women and colonies. But all the research, rhetoric and war memoirs were as nothing until the women were prepared to come forward and speak out against their exploitation. Since the late 1980s and the early 1990s, aided by feminists and other activists, increasing numbers of former comfort women have been condemning their wartime abuse and demanding redress from the Japanese government. It was not until the comfort women rose to cry out, that researchers and activists could change the subject into an issue. Their courage made possible such landmark initiatives as the 1991 Tokyo lawsuit and the 1992 Asia Solidarity Conference on comfort women in Seoul.

The saga of the comfort women is not just about a wartime atrocity which has remained unpunished. The issues involved with how the perpetrators of the comfort system almost got away with their crimes highlights how the exploitation of women—and children—for profit from sexual service continues today.

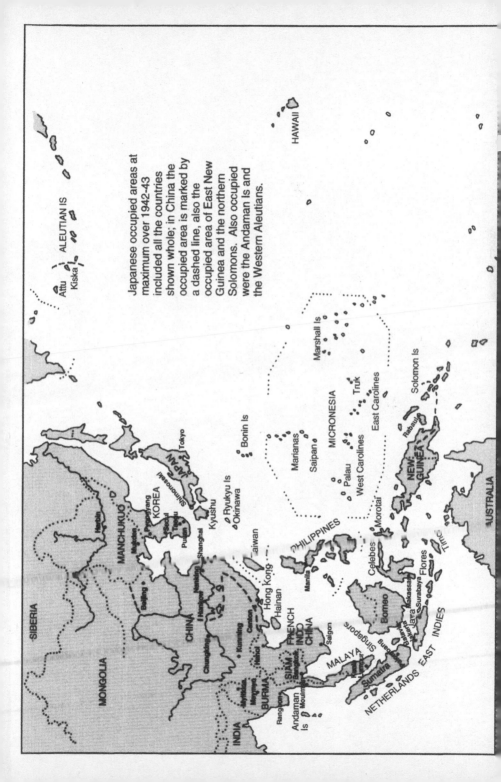

Japanese occupied areas at maximum over 1942-43 included all the countries shown whole; in China the occupied area is marked by a dashed line, also the occupied area of East New Guinea and the northern Solomons. Also occupied were the Andaman Is and the Western Aleutians.

The Comfort Women

1. Mars and Venus

Wartime exploitation of women for sexual service is part of a long and inglorious tradition. Other armies had had similar systems before the Japanese.

The feudal Japanese approached prostitution with an openness which made famous the pleasure quarters of cities such as Kyoto, Osaka and Tokyo. In the mid-eighteenth century, the Floating World, or the pleasure quarters, in Edo (as Tokyo was then called) were famous as 'the nightless city'. Glamorised by artists and writers, the wealth of erotic literature and art disguised the slave-like conditions in which the women worked.

Geishas were differentiated from common prostitutes by their rigorous training as musicians and genteel entertainers. The provision of sex was only rarely part of a *geisha's* evening's entertainment. She tended to be attached to one man at a time. In 1872, Japan had prohibited bondage and restricted prostitution to a voluntary contract system, whereby women were employed by licensed brothels on the basis of a loan, usually to their families, to be worked off over a period of years. Although such contracts were free in the legal sense, there was often a strong economic compulsion, with prostitutes often being described as 'security' for loans.

In pre-war Japan, prostitution was state-organised, with the women licensed and subjected to medical inspections. In the late nineteenth century and at the beginning of the twentieth, Japanese travelling prostitutes or *karayuki*, were to be found in many parts of Asia, including areas which later became Japanese-occupied territories. The export of women for sexual service was therefore not a new idea for the Japanese.

Before the era of Japanese influence in Korea, prostitution had followed a pattern common to many pre-modern societies. It was associated either with upper class courtesans on the Chinese model, or a more plebeian, pseudo-familial type, with marriage to or adoption by pimps.

Among the Japanese systems imposed on the Koreans when the peninsula came under Japanese influence in 1904, was an attempt to put prostitution on a more orderly basis, starting with the setting up of a Floating World or red light district in Seoul. After total annexation in 1910, licensed prostitution was introduced. The new system, controlled by the Japanese military-political police, or *kempeitai*, was a characteristically Japanese system. There was meticulous registration, and provision for medical checks and reporting of infection. However, as a health measure the licensing system was less effective in Korea than in Japan, probably because medical services were less developed. In 1921 a comprehensive check found that over half the licensed and unlicensed prostitutes were infected with venereal disease.

Given the well-organised and open nature of prostitution in Japan, it was logical that there should be organised prostitution in the Japanese Armed Forces. Although the institution of military prostitution was universal, few historians have chosen to deal with it. Meirion and Susie Harries' monumental history of the Japanese Army, *Soldiers of the Sun*, refers to the phenomenon several times in passing, evidently without considering it worthy of particular attention. The Allied Forces were themselves involved in the repatriation of comfort women after the war. The term 'comfort girls', generally regarded as a quaint oriental euphemism, was well known. There was a tendency to equate the comfort women with the regimental brothels or 'camp followers' associated with other armies, and to be seen at military bases everywhere, almost from time immemorial.

Fighting men and sex

Mars and Venus have gone hand in hand throughout military history. This image may sit oddly with the conventional heroic picture of fighting men, but it is comprehensible to anyone with first-hand experience of combat, or a prolonged spell of life in uniform. Combat, especially under modern conditions, has been justly described as the most stressful environment possible, apt to produce what one Japanese Army medical officer described as 'temporary derangement'. Combat aside, any ex-soldier will remember the obsession with sex in a community of men—the fittest of their generation in the prime of life, in a confined and regimented situation—deprived of usual social and emotional outlets.

More or less institutionalised means have always been found for catering to this primitive sexual need. For the armies of history, much smaller in size than those of today, and fighting more leisurely campaigns, there were the camp followers.

The Roman Empire, with its far-flung army, had a comfort system remarkably similar to that of the Japanese military. Roman society was, of course, founded on a system of slavery which made life more comfortable and pleasurable for the élite, but less so for those at the bottom of the pile. Slavery ensured a regular supply of captive females for the military brothels which were attached to every Roman garrison or campaigning army. The task of these Roman comfort women was to provide sexual services at all hours of the day and night, as well as to do traditionally female chores such as nursing, washing and cooking. The only way a sex slave could improve her lot was to catch the eye of someone powerful or rich enough to pluck her from the common herd for his personal use.

Other armies followed suit. During the sixteenth century, the Spanish Duke of Alva's army, when invading the Netherlands with the Armada, was followed by '400 mounted whores and 800 on foot'. Henriques' voluminous *Prostitution and Society*, quoting from a German military science text, the *Kriegsbuch* of 1598, gives an illuminating account of the function of camp followers. Like the Roman system, it anticipated the type of organisation found in the Japanese Armed Forces:

> When a regiment is strong in numbers, then the camp followers are also not few. There should be appointed by the Colonel an official, able, honest, sensible warrior, who has helped in battle and attack. He should have his own Lieutenant and Second-Lieutenant, when the gang of camp followers is strong in number. He should have captains' pay and his Lieutenant and Second-Lieutenant as arranged, for such an officer must know how to order and lead such troops, just as ordinary or straying troops have to be kept in order and led . . . Under the officer for the harlots is a provost, whose duty it is to establish peace and order. When he cannot make peace by other means, he has a conciliator about the length of an arm, with which he is authorised by their masters to punish them.

With the change to armies of mass conscription in the nineteenth century came greater problems in maintaining order, controlling venereal disease, and preventing desertion. The scale and nature of military prostitution were transformed. Military authorities recognised, to varying degrees, its relevance to such problems as keeping troops more contented and tractable, forestalling the danger of rape among civilian populations, and controlling disease. The impoverishment and social dislocation of the earlier phases of the Industrial Revolution meant there was generally an ample supply of women for military prostitution. The extent of organisation and openness varied according to prevailing moral attitudes in different societies. However, as military histories are invariably concerned with either military science or national glory, military prostitution is rarely comprehensively recorded.

Of the British Army in the nineteenth century, Henriques remarks:

> The British soldier, unlike his continental counterpart, has never had his sexual needs provided for in this country. It has been otherwise overseas. It is probably true to say that Venus has been in constant attendance upon Mars wherever the British soldier has served in our once far-flung Empire, both in an official and an unofficial capacity.

The best-documented example of prostitution for the British Army comes from a House of Commons Commission of Inquiry into the Indian Army, in 1893. The circumstances which led to the inquiry resulted from the *Contagious Diseases Act*, in force from 1866 to 1886. This provided for the compulsory periodical examination of women suspected of suffering from venereal disease, something adopted when it was discovered that the disease rate in the British Army was more than three times that of the better-regulated French.

The published report of the Commission of Inquiry details British military prostitution in India which, like the Roman system, anticipated many later Japanese practices. The Indian Army was distributed in distinct settlements called cantonments, each with an attached 'bazaar' where Indians performed all the services required of a settled community. The bazaar included a prostitutes' quarter where the women displayed themselves on balconies. They were recruited mainly from the lower ranks of the prostitute-pimp caste, usually supervised by a resident procuress paid from their earnings. There were some women of other origins, including occasional Europeans, but the fee for a visit was higher than a labourer's daily wage. The minimum age of the women was fourteen, with most between seventeen and eighteen.

Until 1888 a register of prostitutes was maintained. There was a system of compulsory medical examinations, and the regiment paid each woman one rupee a month for soap and a towel. Even after these formal arrangements were abolished, the system continued on a voluntary basis, and the women often followed the regiments between cantonments. As one witness put it: 'If we had no women the men would have been all over the place and we do not know what offences might have been committed.' According to another: 'When the soldier is drunk he occasionally beats and otherwise ill-treats the women. But the women themselves make singularly little complaint on this score.'

The Commission of Inquiry concluded that there was 'no shadow of foundation' for rumours of compulsion in this system. But when the report appeared it became impossible to maintain it. It was superseded by a more fluid system involving greater participation by the growing numbers of European and Eurasian women in India.

The world wars provided various arrangements for prostitution. A vivid glimpse of conditions in World War I is provided in *Ettie: A Life of Ettie Rout*, the biography of pioneer New Zealand feminist, Ettie Rout by Jane Tolerton. She formed a volunteer sisterhood to help nurse 'sick and wounded colonials' in Egypt. On arrival there she was appalled by the combination of 'sergeants, syphilis and sand'. The New Zealand commander had tried to combat disease by issuing Metchinoff's ointment as a prophylactic, but his men usually sold it to the locals to treat lice. In England, Rout found the prostitution situation still more acute. As she expressed it: 'If they will have women—and they most certainly will—give them clean women.' Having failed to dissuade her countrymen from sex tours to their favourite haunt, Paris, she made an arrangement with a responsible madame there to specialise in New Zealanders, and to use a prophylactic kit designed by Ettie herself. Although she became a legend among New Zealanders of her time, she is not mentioned in her country's official war history, and her books on birth control were banned in her home country.

Information on the German Army's prostitution facilities during World War II is found in Seidler's *Prostitution, Homosexuality, Self-Mutilation: Problems of German Public Hygiene Control 1939–45*. Military brothels were established in the key zones of occupied areas as auxiliary installations, under orders from central command. Local commanding officers were made responsible for equipment, supervision and supply. The motive was hygiene control in the light of German experience in World War I, when there had been two million cases of venereal disease in the German Army alone. Inspections during World War II were conducted by local doctors under the supervision of Army medical officers. In Western Europe, existing brothels were reserved for German Army use, while in Eastern Europe women were sometimes given the choice of compulsory labour or prostitution.

Regulation was characteristically meticulous. On the walls of every room were three notices: 'Use a condom—danger of venereal disease!' 'Memorise your partner's registration number!' and 'Disinfect after intercourse!' A routine order issued in Bucharest indicates business hours as 1400 to 2300. Medical orderlies and military police would be on duty from 1300 to 2400 to control disturbances. No more than ten soldiers could occupy a waiting room at once. Queuing outside was forbidden and vehicles could not be parked in front of buildings in use.

In the case of the Allies, scattered references to British 'regimental brothels' and French 'military field brothels' are sometimes encountered, but no systematic information on them is available. In general, the only sources on the subject of military-related prostitution are personal memoirs, fictionalised treatment in novels like Norman Mailer's *The Naked and the Dead*, or television dramas like *China Beach*. An isolated reference to an organised brothel in a United States military context occurs in China, where the commander of a Sino-American air force was so concerned with the rate of infection from brothels in Kunming that he brought in twelve healthy Indian prostitutes—an arrangement eventually vetoed by his superior. Although United States forces have often adopted *ad hoc* health precautions in brothels adjacent to their bases, notably in South Korea, no greater degree of military intervention has occurred.

The Japanese rationale

Superstitions are universal in armed forces. The Japanese had some which were linked to sex. They included the belief that sex before going into battle worked as a charm against injury. Amulets could be made with the pubic hair of comfort women, or from something belonging to them. Sexual deprivation was believed to make one accident-prone. Sex also acted to relieve combat stress and, particularly in the Japanese case, the savage discipline endured by the troops. In his book *The Emperor's Forces and Korean Comfort Women*, Korean Kim Il Myon, although bitterly critical of Japanese colonialism and militarism, shows a realistic understanding of the ordinary Japanese private or naval rating:

> To soldiers in the frontline, ever surrounded by the sound of guns, wrapped in smoke stinking of death and not knowing when death would come . . . a visit to a comfort station was no doubt the only form of relief. It was the only kind of individual act in which one was 'liberated'. Theirs was a prison-like existence, subject to random, arbitrary punishments by mad dogs of NCOs, their eardrums daily ringing from blows. The comfort station was where they were at least temporarily 'liberated' from the savagery of the unit. It was their 'oasis'.

Some sources indicate that the practice of visiting comfort women was ritualised by the Japanese, especially before a unit was to leave for the front. The common rationale was that men without previous sexual experience should have intercourse at least once before death. A man who remained aloof from this recreation became an odd man out—a serious matter in military psychology. In one recorded case a man who had never visited a comfort station was forcibly taken to one by his comrades, who then watched through holes in the wall as he was chased around the room by the woman. The Japanese rationale is expressed in a War Ministry circular:

> It is not necessary to emphasise how much the environment influences troops' psychology and therefore the promotion of discipline. Thus care must be taken in regard to suitable living conditions and comfort facilities. In particular the psychological influence received from sexual comfort stations is most direct and profound and it must be realised how greatly their appropriate direction and supervision affect the raising of morale, the maintenance of discipline and the prevention of crime and venereal disease.

The crippling of whole battalions by venereal disease was not unknown, and the Japanese took such a threat seriously, since they had learned the hard way. In 1918, Japan had taken part in the Siberian Intervention initiated by the Western powers against the revolution in Russia. Between then and 1922, the equivalent of one division of seven was incapacitated by venereal disease. This object lesson is frequently quoted as either justification for, or explanation of, the systematic establishment by the Japanese of military-controlled comfort stations.

The health of the soldiers was a matter of particular concern between 1937 and 1939, since the Japanese Armed Forces were then
conducting their most protracted overseas campaign, the drive to
take military control of China. A report by Dr Aso Tetsuo (Suzuki
Yuko 1991), who was a medical officer at the Shanghai base hospital,
probably helped to lay the foundations for later policy guidelines on
the best sources of healthy comfort women. Since his background
was in gynaecology, Dr Aso was opposed to the system of licensed
prostitution. In early 1938, he was instructed to examine about 100
women who were to work in a 'recreation centre'. At first he assumed
that they were attached to the canteens service, and might be suspected of some infection from the troops. On being confronted with
a group of about eighty young Korean women and twenty more mature Japanese, however, he came to realise the reason for the examinations. With the assistance of another medical officer, seven medical orderlies and two nurses, he carried out the required inspection in
the deserted school where the women were assembled. His surviving
report was written the following year as a submission to a conference
on venereal disease prevention:

> Those to be examined were 80 women from the Peninsula [a term for Ko-
> reans often used to avoid reference to nationality] and 20 or so from the
> Homeland [Japan proper]. Among those from the Peninsula, there was
> very little indication indeed of venereal disease, but those from the Home-
> land, although free of acute symptoms at present, were all extremely dubi-
> ous. In age, these were all past 20, some approaching 40, and had already
> spent a number of years in prostitution. Those from the Peninsula pre-
> sented a pleasing contrast, being in the main younger and unsophisticated
> . . . Care needs to be taken with the more jaded type of woman, whom I
> have repeatedly examined for syphilis and found clearly branded with a
> past history of venereal disease by the scars of bubo excisions on the
> groins. These are really dubious as gifts to the Imperial Forces.

Karayuki such as those examined by Dr Aso continued to be recruited as comfort women, so the risk of infection from them remained. But available numbers soon proved inadequate, given the
vastly expanded scope of the war and the increase in men in uniform.
There was little attempt to recruit Japanese women who were not
from a background of professional prostitution, partly because they
were needed at home to replace men in farming and factory work,
and partly because the troops' morale would suffer if they realised

their own sisters were being forced into prostitution. The emphasis was increasingly placed, then, on recruiting non-professional Korean women—by any means possible.

The context of prostitution: Japanese expansionism and the growth of militarism

The systematic exploitation of Korean women all over the Japanese Empire as comfort women was an adjunct to the second and more uncontrolled phase of Japanese expansionism in the Fifteen Years War. This term was often used in Japan to refer to the events between 1931 and 1945. It was made possible by what Kim Il Myon calls 'a counter-current to the early twentieth century tide of liberation' in which the beginnings of democracy were crushed by ultra-nationalists and the military.

In the 1920s the convention was established that the Prime Minister should command a majority of the elected House of Representatives. Although under the then Constitution the Emperor was empowered to appoint any of his subjects as Prime Minister, his 'transcendent' status placed him at a remove from the political process. He had to rely on the advice of his elder statesmen as to who, in any given situation, had the political resources to function effectively in the key position of Prime Minister.

By the late 1920s, the two major liberal parties, financed by the *zaibatsu* combines, and with nationwide networks of voter support, had become the major focus of the political process. For a time power alternated between them. This system had corollaries, such as a measure of recognition of trade unions and a wide range of freedom of expression, as well as a foreign policy based on coexistence in the League of Nations, and concomitant reductions in military potential. The Washington Pact on arms limitation and preservation of the status quo in the Pacific was accepted. This was known as Shidehara Diplomacy, for the leading Foreign Minister of the time, who re-emerged after the Pacific War as Prime Minister.

Japan's initial military and industrial build-up of the late nineteenth century (known as the Meiji Restoration after the Meiji Emperor, the grandfather of Emperor Hirohito), had been stimulated by the campaign to abolish the 1858 five-power 'unequal' treaties. These followed the pattern of those imposed on China. While Japan succeeded in projecting itself into modernism, China was to weaken almost to semi-colonial status, a prey to the ambitions of Japan, a country with one-tenth its population.

If Japan's expansionism had been part of the nineteenth and early twentieth century phenomenon of the Western powers' rampant imperialism, as the only Asian power it was unable to pursue further ambitions in the face of concerted opposition from the West. The opposition to allowing Japan a rightful place as an equal among the big powers took on a racial dimension in the 1920s. This bred resentment and fed Japanese insecurity, which in turn pushed its extremist military factions towards greater aggression.

An earlier phase of Japanese expansionism, at the turn of the century, had led to the acquisition of Taiwan (then known as Formosa), Korea (Chosen), and southern Sakhalin (Karafuto), as well as a League of Nations mandate in Micronesia. These successes had been due, in part, to British backing, Britain being the only leading Western colonial power with whom Japan had an alliance. A pact had been signed in 1902, the two nations brought together by the threat of Imperial Russian expansion in East Asia. Having confronted Russia in the Crimea and the approaches to India, Britain became alarmed by the Russian acquisition of the maritime province of Manchuria. The Russians obtained the concession of an ice-free port in Korea, which the Japanese regarded as 'a dagger pointed at the heart of Japan': the stage was set for the Russo-Japanese War of 1904.

This was to be the first war in which an Asian power successfully took on a Western one. Its outcome was a strategic foothold in Manchuria for Japan. From there she was later to threaten China. Colonial-type treaty rights similar to those enjoyed by the Western powers were obtained in China, especially in Manchuria. The Japanese—British alliance lasted throughout World War I, yielding the Micronesian mandate for Japan.

When the Russo—Japanese War broke out in 1904, the Japanese Army had already secured Korea. Once Chinese and Russian influence was removed from the peninsula, the Koreans themselves failed to mount any cohesive national resistance to the Japanese takeover. This took the form, at first, of conversion to protectorate status, and later of annexation. The Korean royal family was intermarried with the Japanese aristocracy. The *Yangban* ruling class, modelled on Chinese mandarins, proved (just as did its Chinese prototype) incapable of reorganising Korea as a modern state.

Having experienced such spectacular success in competition with its Western rivals—in contrast to the fate of the two ancient Asian civilisations of India and China—Japan quickly developed a profound contempt for other Asians. This was intensified by a reaction against its traditional veneration of India and China as the sources of Buddhism and classical learning. Some elements in Japan did, however, remain attached to tradition, and developed a Pan-Asian ideology based on Japan repaying its ancient cultural debt by leading a struggle for Asian liberation. For a time, at the beginning of the twentieth century, Pan-Asianists gave concrete assistance or refuge to revolutionaries from China, India, the Philippines and elsewhere. But patronising and paternalistic attitudes gained ascendancy, and their program was eventually distorted by ruling circles into the theme of the Greater East Asian Co-Prosperity Sphere, the declared aim of the Pacific War.

The dominant elements in Japan had, in any case, always rejected the spirit of Pan-Asianism in favour of participation in the Imperialist Club. The classic statement of this perspective is to be found in an article titled 'Abandoning Asia and Joining Europe', written in 1885 by the prominent theorist of modernisation, Fukuzawa Yukichi, founder of Keio University, and co-founder of one of the two major pre-war parties. The article (Takeuchi Yoshimi 1963), written to refute Pan-Asianism, is still cited in the context of the comfort women, as well as other issues.

> Although our country is situated at the eastern edge of Asia, the spirit of our people has already abandoned Asia's hidebound ways and embraced Western civilisation. We have here two unfortunate neighbour countries—China and Korea. Although their people in former times shared with Japan a similar nurturing in Asian-type doctrines and customs, now, either because of some difference in race or because of some difference of mode within that inherited education . . . these do not comprehend the path of national reform . . . In framing present policies, we have no leisure to await their awakening and together revive Asia . . . We cannot treat them with special consideration just because they are our neighbours, we must treat them just as Westerners do.

Among Koreans there was naturally some resistance to being treated as Japanese colonial subjects. There were widespread demonstrations for independence in 1919, amounting almost to an abortive uprising. Korea was then under a military regime ruthlessly administered by the *kempeitai* under a Governor-General, General Terauchi Masatake. During the 1920s, Korea benefited to some degree from a liberal trend in Japan, resulting in a less arbitrary civil administration headed by a leader from the moderate wing of the Navy, Admiral Saito Makoto, later assassinated by extremists in Japan.

Developments in Korea and Japan were wrecked, however, by a combination of domestic and international crises brought on by the Depression of the 1930s. The economic dangers facing Japan made the solutions offered by military men attractive, if not irresistible. The seizure of Manchuria and the creation of the puppet state of Manchukuo in 1931, were entirely the initiatives of young turks in Japan's China-based Kwantung Army. There was no authorisation from the liberal Japanese government of the time, or even from the War Ministry. The action was portrayed as an emergency measure to protect Japanese treaty rights; in fact it was designed to secure Manchuria's rich resources, to stimulate the Japanese economy under Depression conditions, and to develop a secure base for further expansion into China.

The wave of popular enthusiasm and Right-wing conspiracies which followed what was tantamount to an Army coup, induced the Japanese authorities to recognise Manchukuo. Immediately, there was a flood of Japanese officials and private fortune hunters into northeast China. These included a rising generation of new industrialists, favoured by the Army over the established *zaibatsu*, as well as small-scale operators moving to wherever the best pickings were to be found. In the later recollections of a *kempeitai* officer:

> Many of these were disreputables who had gone broke in the home country and wormed their way into the favour of corrupt military and *kempeitai* officers through bribery. Such traders included a proportion of Koreans.

Prostitution inevitably followed this influx. The Manchukuo authorities maintained a licensing system as a health measure. In Manchuria many women of Chinese and White Russian origin were available, supplemented, often willingly, from Japan. To many, there was the promise of what seemed a welcome 'release' from their cramped and depressed lives in Japan. Indeed, business was so much better in Manchuria that debts which would have taken years to pay off could be settled in six months, allowing women in this line of work to start their own brothels. It even became necessary to draw lots for permission to leave for Manchuria. There was also a psychological bonus: women who were usually despised were now admired for their courage in moving to a war zone, enabling them to think of themselves as patriotic.

Large numbers of Koreans were also enticed into such service. As in the colonies of the Western powers, many Koreans, especially those from the upper classes, took advantage of opportunities offered by collaboration. They served in the armed forces, in the police or civil administration, or in semi-official bodies such as the Japanese-sponsored Women's Association. Many of these organisations, though later reviled as 'remnant forces from Japanese imperialism', continued for some time as a force in post-war South Korea. There were few alternative trained and cohesive entities capable of countering 'the Communist threat'. Korean complicity in the traffic in comfort women is sometimes cited as a reason for Korea's failure to bring the perpetrators to book after the Pacific War.

In Japan, meanwhile, the success of the Manchurian adventure was generating Right-wing radicalism and expansionism. The able leaders of both parties were assassinated, leaving their followers in disarray, unable to contest the return of military men to the ruling élite. Right-wing terrorism occurred on a dramatic scale, and pro-war cliques in the Armed Forces strengthened. The parties continued to retain a share of Cabinet posts, however. In 1937, in the last pre-war election they still vastly exceeded the far Right and pro-military parties in electoral support and—unlike the situation in the European Axis countries—there was no popular mandate for the military forces.

In the panic following an attempted coup by Army dissidents in 1936, however, the Armed Forces had recovered an earlier privilege: they nominated their respective ministers from the active list. The Army subsequently used this privilege ruthlessly as a veto on Cabinet formation. Eventually, by capitalising on growing international conflict and developing a network of collaboration in bureaucratic and financial circles, the Army came to dominate the whole political process. Its formal legal basis was derived from extensions to the National General Mobilisation Law, passed in 1938, when it was recognised that the war in China was likely to be protracted.

Military control at grassroots level was exercised through a network of local bodies called 'neighbourhood associations' in Japan and 'patriotic teams' in Korea. There was strict censorship of the means of expression and action by the Special Higher Police (whose role was to act as 'thought police'), and the *kempeitai*. Indoctrination through the media and the education system was so intense and pervasive that the few who had sufficient independence of mind to present problems for social control were easily suppressed.

Ideological conditioning centred on a much-intensified cult of the divine Emperor as head of the nation-family and fountainhead of absolute authority transmitted down through all forms of social organisation. Divinity in the Shinto sense has different connotations from the Western concept, being animistic and immanent rather than theistic and transcendent. Thus the Emperor was not viewed as infallible; rather the concept of his divinity implied that loyal service to him guaranteed success. To this day the actual personal role of Emperor Hirohito during the war remains a matter of debate. On the one hand, it seems clear that neither he nor any other single authority had decisive control over the intense factional rivalries both between and within the Army and Navy, as well as in other organs of government. On the other, he was by no means free of involvement in political and military machinations. Although the Emperor remained a silent figure when presiding over most of the formal top-level Imperial Conferences throughout the war, he had considerable input into preparatory discussions and manoeuvres.

Determining the precise locus of responsibility is a problem common to large Japanese organisations. It should be noted that the person of the Emperor is often strongly emphasised as a tangible focus of resentment by Koreans as well as Japanese radicals, whether socialist or feminist.

There were good psychological reasons for a focus on the divinity of the Emperor. The Japanese contempt for other Asians, based on the contrast in their respective recent achievements, was deepened by the cult of the Emperor, with its implication that all Japanese shared in his divinity. All others were excluded.

Koreans, especially, were placed in an ambiguous position. They were officially included among the 'Emperor's children', so as to secure their loyalty. At the same time they were deprived of even the limited civil rights available under the old Japanese Constitution—such as voting for the Diet's Lower House—unless they lived permanently in Japan.

Assimilationist policies, aimed at incorporating the Asian peoples within a Japanese colonial identity, were strengthened in Korea and also in Taiwan as the crisis of the 1930s deepened. Korea presented the larger problem in view of its long-standing cultural and historical identity. The island of Taiwan (Formosa) was a frontier region, settled in recent centuries by southern Chinese, and with a considerable non-Chinese aboriginal population. In both countries the development of education, hitherto scarcely available to the mass of the people, was based on the Japanese language, especially at more advanced levels, with local languages allowed only limited scope.

In 1941, Japanese administrators in Korea began a campaign, still much resented to this day, to induce the general adoption of Japanese names. A plausible reason advanced for this was the small number of existing surnames, actually clan names on the Chinese pattern. This meant that sub-groups had to be distinguished by places, such as the Kyongju Yis and the Chinhae Kims. But assimilation was the ultimate aim, and Korea was flooded with four-character slogans such as 'Japan and Korea of common ancestry' (historically largely true but not genuinely relished by either side), 'Korea and Japan indissoluble', and 'All viewed with even benevolence'.

In Taiwan, the adoption of Japanese names was purely voluntary, even requiring permits. As in Korea, military service was at first also voluntary, beginning with porters in 1937 and extending mainly to paramilitary service from 1942. The assimilationist campaign was so successful that a later source on Taiwanese comfort women relates that many Taiwanese on military duties only realised, on reaching the mainland, that they were ethnic Chinese, not Japanese. Similar scripts and physical characteristics, limited literacy and the multiplicity of Chinese dialects made this degree of confusion possible.

The Japanese state religion, Shinto, an integral part of the education system, was also widely promoted, through a network of local shrines. As in Japan, this religion was not designed to rule out adherence to other beliefs, which were tolerated and even sometimes sponsored, as long as they did not oppose the state creed. There was some harassment of Christianity when incompatibility was suggested, but on the whole, a distinction of function was accepted. In Korea, on the outbreak of war in China in 1937, the state religion was strengthened by the adoption of a public ritual of reciting a three-fold oath, known sometimes as the 'subject oath':

1. We are subjects of the Imperial State and will serve it with loyalty.

2. We subjects of the Imperial State will co-operate with mutual devotion and strengthen our solidarity.
3. We subjects of the Imperial State will nourish endurance and discipline and thereby enhance the Imperial Way.

The Japanese Armed Forces pre-war, and in Occupation

The Japanese Army which had been organised during the Meiji Restoration was by the 1930s a national army, with the men drawn from across the country and from all classes. This was different from other sectors of Japanese society, which were organised on rigid hereditary class lines. The Army was, however, for the most part made up of peasants for whom, despite its brutal discipline, it was a step up from their rigid stratified civilian life and struggle for survival.

The Navy tended to have better-educated men than the Army, and its officers, from the upper echelons of society, approximated the *samurai* class. The viciousness for which the Japanese Armed Forces later became infamous was the work of the Army, which had the larger share of Right-wing extremists, the Navy tending to have a stronger moderate faction. But in both wings of the Armed Forces the extreme authoritarianism of the Emperor cult found its ultimate expression. The Emperor under the Constitution was the Commander-in-Chief of the Armed Forces, and was treated as having a direct, intimate relationship with them which bypassed the authority of the civil government. The Armed Forces were described, more than any other organ of state, as the Emperor's 'children' or his 'limbs'. Even the comfort women themselves must have been psychologically affected by this setting. According to the accounts assembled by Kim Il Myon, they generally found it effective in countering violent behaviour from troops to plead that they also were 'children of the same Emperor'.

In the *Imperial Rescript to the Armed Forces*, issued by the Meiji Emperor, is found the classic statement of the Forces' ideology. They are enjoined to 'regard your superior officer's orders as Our orders', so that these retained a sanctity at all levels in what is described as the 'aesthetic of the Imperial Forces' warriors'. They overrode any other consideration of reason or morality, in the drive to victory or death. It may be noted here that instructions on comfort women were not described as 'orders', the usual formal term, because of the convention that orders in this sense had to be equated with the Emperor's will. This meant it was felt improper that such undignified matters as comfort women should be dealt with on this level. Another term, strictly meaning 'notification', is usually found in the context of comfort women. It was also applied to other ambiguous matters like the euthanasia of wounded soldiers who could not be evacuated, so as not to imply that the Emperor would order his own men's death.

The ideology of the Armed Forces further envisioned an organic harmony where there should be no need for factional division or arbitrary oppression of the lower ranks by the higher. Such ideals were, however, by no means the daily reality. The Army and Navy were far from being in harmony, and within each service there was intense factional rivalry. This made it possible for the more militant to act independently; they led Japan into a disastrous war it could not hope to win. Not only were the privileges and status of rank jealously maintained, but these formal structures were further subdivided among cliques relating to place of origin, distinctions of seniority by length of service, or between professionals or draftees.

Military training was designed to secure instant obedience. It was a brutal, highly disciplined system, with each man responsible for the actions of his colleagues. Far beyond the rational requirements of discipline, domination was constantly expressed and enforced, without regard to any due process, by arbitrary blows or beating with spiked belts or boots. Sometimes a pair of subordinates would be ordered to punish each other with blows and, no matter how they might try to pull their punches, the constant tension of the milieu could easily spill over into something more serious, breeding more resentment for the future. Many pretexts could be found to inflict such punishments, like having a dirty rifle, described as something 'entrusted to the soldier by his Emperor'. Punishment could even be meted out for using language that did not accord with military jargon or for being 'too squeamish' on search and destroy expeditions into areas harbouring guerrillas. Perhaps even more unendurable was punishment designed to humiliate, such as forcing a man to crawl between beds imitating the call of a 'warbler in the valley', to climb up a pole and imitate a cicada, or to run on the spot while holding a spike between his forehead and a post.

Practices of this kind naturally produced an intense pecking order or what one Japanese critic has called a 'transfer of oppression'. This was not confined to the Armed Forces, but was visited in turn on any others who might fall under the mercy of any element of it. So the populations of occupied countries or prisoners-of-war were vulnerable. So also, of course, were the comfort women, although their sexual services might normally be expected to provide sufficient emotional outlet.

One medical officer, required to report on causes and remedies for the 1937 Rape of Nanking, involving mass rapes of the female population, indiscriminate acts of arson, pillage, looting and massacres on an unbelievable scale, produced some illuminating observations. He noted (Nishino Rumiko 1992) that 'battle neurosis' could be triggered by both the stress of combat, and sudden relaxation after it. He emphasised that the provision of alcohol and comfort women was unsatisfactory as a remedy for stress, and recommended limitations on alcohol, together with the provision of more wholesome recreation, such as sports and cinema. He also recommended the weeding out of undesirable characters, and more frequent relief from combat.

Japanese authorities did develop such additional facilities in settled areas. For the most part, however, logistical problems led to continued widespread reliance on comfort women as the standard measure for relieving the tension of combat, or military life generally.

2. The flesh market

The first comfort stations under direct Japanese military control were in Shanghai in 1932, following vicious clashes between Japanese troops and the Chinese. One of the commanders involved in the Shanghai campaign, Lieutenant-General Okamura Yasuji, confessed, 'though with embarrassment', in memoirs published in 1970 (Suzuki Yuko 1992), that he was the original proponent of comfort stations for the Army. After 223 reported rape cases by Japanese troops, he sought a solution by 'following local naval practice', and requested the governor of Nagasaki Prefecture to send a contingent of comfort women to Shanghai. Rape reports then fell off markedly, providing a rationale for the subsequent expansion of military prostitution.

These comfort women were made up of Koreans, not from the Korean Peninsula but from the North Kyushu mining area of Japan, where there was a Korean community. Their sending implicates not only the military, but also the Home Ministry, which controlled governors, as well as the police who were later to be collaborators with the Armed Forces in the forced recruitment of comfort women.

After some years of an uneasy stalemate in China, the Marco Polo Bridge Incident near Peking in July 1937 escalated skirmish by skirmish, incident by incident, into all-out war. It was barbarous and vicious. The Japanese Army swept into Shanghai, with three-and-a-half million people the largest Chinese city, and occupied it. In December, the Army converged on Nanking, the capital of China then under the Nationalists, or Kuomintang, led by General Chiang Kai Shek. The Japanese took the city in an orgy of death and destruction.

Following the Rape of Nanking, the Japanese authorities were compelled to take stock. They were concerned because this bloodbath had failed to break Chinese resistance. Rather, it had stiffened it. There was also a hostile international reaction. As one of the measures introduced to improve discipline, and set up a long campaign, the comfort station plan first mooted in Shanghai in 1932 was revived. The Shanghai Special Service Branch, normally in charge of undercover or subversive activities, asked contacts in their parasitic trading community to obtain as many women as they could by the end of 1937. There was no shortage of money. As in 1932, their agents resorted to the North Kyushu mining area but found few brothels there willing to release inmates for work in China. They recruited a few Japanese *karayuki* who had worked off their loans and were free to travel. The agents then took the step of enticing young girls from the Korean mining community, with substantial advances of pay, to accept what were made out to be cooking or laundry jobs for the Army.

This group of women from Kyushu was employed in a comfort station situated between Shanghai and Nanking, under direct Army operation. The station was described as a 'recreation centre', the official term, comfort station, not becoming established until some time later. Dr Aso, the Army medical officer who had first examined the women, preserved some photographs of the Shanghai station, as well as regulations posted up for users' guidance. The station consisted of ten barrack block-like huts, together with a supervisor's hut, all enclosed by a fence. The huts were divided into ten small rooms, each numbered and with a separate door. This was to be a prototype for the design of many subsequent comfort stations.

The posted regulations set out the whole procedure, including the hours of opening, the length of each visit, and the scale of fees. They also banned intercourse without a condom. These regulations also became a prototype, though were often much elaborated when comfort stations became more widespread. They were first published in 1969 by Ito Keiichi in his *Soldiers' History of the Army* (Kim Il Myon 1976), one of many studies he published on previously unrecorded intimacies of Army life.

The Army units around Shanghai and Nanking co-ordinated their use of the station by rostering days for the issue of 'comfort station leave passes'. The Army maintained the customary contract system with the group of Kyushu women, advancing ¥1000 which was to be worked off. The women were supplied with standard Army rations.

This early system of direct operation by the Army did not persist as the normal model for comfort stations, although it did occasionally recur in forward areas. In a more settled environment such as Shanghai, direct military operation of the stations soon came to be considered unnecessary and inappropriate. Firstly, the establishments of private operators were easily accessible, doing their best both to meet the standards required by the authorities, and to provide a more attractive service for the troops. Secondly, contempt was likely to be invited from international observers for an Army running prostitution services. The emerging pattern became one where the internal operation of comfort stations was left to private operators, on the principle of 'each to their own'. These civilian operators were given paramilitary status and rank, while the Armed Forces retained overall supervision and provided support in transport and health services as required.

In some cases the initiative in setting up the stations came from the Armed Forces. In others, private operators applied for permits. In some of these latter cases the operators were former officers whose term of service had expired, and who now hoped to use their military experience and contacts to finance their retirement years. These varied arrangements led to elaborate and detailed systems of regulations. (These are discussed more fully, by area, in Chapters 4 and 5.)

While the operation of comfort facilities came to be left to private enterprise, the recruitment of comfort women was increasingly taken over by officials. There is very little surviving documentation of this process, however, compared with that concerning the functioning of the system. Whereas Japanese officials no longer deny the existence of comfort stations, forced recruitment, and official complicity with the recruitment process, remains to a large extent anecdotal.

The women's own stories, highlighted throughout this book, contain ample references to the recruitment process. Critics of this anecdotal evidence tend to take the position that comfort women, with an eye to financial compensation, have been motivated to claim victimisation and deny voluntary participation. The most commonly-cited argument against voluntary participation is the traditional strength of the ideal of chastity in Korea. As Kim Il Myon states, this ideal was so formidable that Japanese police would refrain from searching women's quarters, even when a subversive was suspected to be hiding there. On the other hand, it could be argued that the ideal of chastity would also prevent women from publicly admitting their pasts. While total veracity cannot be expected from any historical source, there can be no doubt that a militarist regime such as pre-

vailed in Japan in the 1930s and 1940s was fully capable of excesses
such as deception and even slave raids. Overall, the picture that
emerges from the case histories appears fundamentally reliable.

From village to comfort station: recruitment

The numbers and sizes of comfort stations were linked to the
strength of Japanese units in an area. Because of this, Korea itself
does not appear to have had many comfort stations, even though it
was the main source for the recruitment of comfort women. Japanese troops in the Korean Peninsula were thinly spread, since it was
remote from active war zones. Its main importance was as a transit
area.

As in Japan, troops in Korea would for the most part have used
the licensed prostitution system which, when it was abolished in 1947
under the United States administration, involved 2124 prostitutes in
South Korea. There are only brief mentions of comfort stations in
Taegu and Yongdo, with one fuller account from a North Korean
woman who was forced into service in the far northeast. This was a
strategic area, being adjacent to the short Soviet frontier, and rather
remote from normal amenities. She recalls having to visit units in
mountain areas as the need arose.

In Japanese society, then as now, there was status consciousness
linked to ethnic origins. This probably had a bearing on where the
majority of the comfort women came from. On the scale of Japanese
preference, Koreans were ranked after Japanese and Okinawans;
then came the Chinese, and lastly Southeast Asians, who tended to
be darker-skinned. Where available, Japanese prostitutes were preferred for the officers, even though these women were often considerably older, more jaded, and more likely to be diseased. At the same
time, they were more capable of social chit-chat—an echo of the *geisha* system. Japanese prostitutes were more likely to be assigned to
the safer base areas.

These distinctions had official recognition. Comfort station fees
were set according to the ranks served, often further influenced by
the ethnic groups to which the women belonged. In accounting for
the numbers of comfort women, it must be borne in mind that pref-
erences relating to nationality and ethnicity were often more blurred
the further from East Asia the comfort stations were located. If there
were no women from the preferred ethnic groups, there were always

native women—and even women interned in POW camps—to exploit. What really mattered, after all, was that they had the required female bodies.

A major obstacle to obtaining a clearer picture of the recruitment process in Korea has been the shortage of official records of draft procedures. All such documentation was systematically destroyed at the end of the war, as was the case with all confidential material that could be used as evidence in war crime trials. The complicity of collaborators who connived at the deception involved in recruiting the thousands of women required by the comfort system also makes it less likely that documents casting light on the recruitment process will become available.

As the Japanese Armed Forces increased and military demand for comfort services grew, prostitution on a voluntary basis became insufficient. Given the poverty and scarcity of jobs in the rural areas, deceptive offers of well-paid work sounded attractive and provided sufficient lure. When such tactics did not yield sufficient numbers, direct recruitment through police or local government became more common. Here again, there was often an element of deception. The concurrent drafting of women to provide labour for war industries disguised the recruitment of comfort women. Finally, women were seized in virtual slave raid conditions under the much strengthened National General Mobilisation Law.

Yo Bok Sil and Yi Sang Ok

In 1938 when Yo Bok Sil was seventeen, she was seized at home by Japanese officials and forced on to a truck. Her sick father tried to prevent her abduction but received a beating for his pains. All the other girls had fled from her village, but along the way about forty were rounded up from other areas. Together with another seven seized by the police in the town of Naju, Cholla South Province, they were put aboard a goods train under the guard of ten soldiers. They were 'treated like criminals', with any who tried to escape being beaten.

After a three-day journey they reached Tientsin where there were about 1000 Korean women in national costume. They were taken off in different directions, in groups of about fifteen. Of Bok Sil's group, half accompanied troop movements, while her half were lodged in a Chinese house in rooms about five square metres in area, with earthen floors spread with rush matting. The rooms were curtained off with straw mats. Behind these, they had to service soldiers.

Like other virgins, Bok Sil resisted with all her strength, but was violently deflowered. She ended up covered in blood while screams sounded from the adjoining rooms. After this first night trauma, the whole group discussed suicide, and two of them hanged themselves in their rooms. The others, including Bok Sil, resigned themselves to their fate.

There were weekly medical inspections. For meals, utensils were brought from nearby deserted Chinese houses, and the women ate in the Army cookhouse. They had to service thirty to forty men daily, the largest number coming on Sundays when the men were off duty. Occasionally men stole in at night. The comfort station was close to a combat area, and on one occasion Bok Sil was injured in the leg by shrapnel from an exploding shell. This injury took six months to heal, but she had to resume work from the fourth month.

She never lost hope of escaping. There was little chance of this, in view of the stricter guard kept after the suicides. Late in the war, however, a Korean interpreter with the *kempeitai* helped her and two other women to escape, ensuring their safe passage by train by accompanying them in his *kempeitai* uniform. They reached Pyongyang and were there when the war ended.

From the age of thirty-four Bok Sil cohabited with a man for three years. But she felt unable to conceal her past from him, and since she was unable to have children, she found him a replacement and then left. In recent years she has been living on meagre welfare payments. She feels that she might have been better off had she died in the war. She wonders why the Japanese did not similarly draft Japanese women for such service, and how they would feel if some other nation had seized their own women.

Yi Sang Ok was born in Inchon. She belonged to a large family of independent farmers. She began school at the age of eight, but her elder brother prevented her continuing on the grounds that there was no need for girls to go to school. So she ran away and stayed with her aunt in Seoul. When she grew older she took casual work as a housemaid in various places. At fourteen she was working for one Kim Un Sik, who seemed to be running some kind of employment agency for girls, since he regularly sent them to different places. One day, one of his employees offered to find work for Sang

Ok in Japan. She was attracted by the idea, and on his instructions boarded a ferry at Pusan with twenty other girls, supposedly bound for work in a scrubbing brush factory. She was the youngest.

After about a week in Shimonoseki, they boarded a ship, and over a month sailed via Yap and Saipan to Palau Island. There Sang Ok and her companions were taken by truck to a comfort station housed in a long barrack building managed by a Japanese couple. There were twenty rooms, without either blankets or mattresses, but spread with matting of some plant material.

Soldiers began coming from about 4 or 5 p.m. When she tried to refuse service, she was beaten so savagely her hearing was permanently impaired. She was also stabbed with a bayonet. The manager-couple had an office by the entrance where the soldiers paid. Sang Ok had no idea what the fees were, since she received only the fixed rate of ¥30 a month. The men brought their own condoms and the women visited a medical officer once a week.

Sang Ok remained in Palau until she was twenty-three. Then heavy fighting forced her and her companions deep into the jungle, where they were forced to live off edible plants, snakes and frogs. They were eventually rounded up by United States Forces and sent home via Singapore. Sang Ok could not trace her family, but cohabited with a widower ten years older than she and brought up three step-children. Over recent years both her *de facto* husband and her step-son have died, and she has been living on welfare, combined with casual work such as caretaking.

The effect of this law was to put Japan and her colonies on a total war footing in terms of economic and social control. The National Labour Service Association was also set up under its provisions. Although originally passed in 1938, the law was used for the comprehensive exploitation of Koreans only from late 1942. As one source puts it (Yoshida Seiji 1983):

> By the time the Chinese and southern fronts had reached a stalemate in late 1942, almost all able-bodied men had either been conscripted into the Armed Forces or drafted for the war industries, so that out of a total ethnic Japanese population of 70 million, over 10 million were mobilised for war purposes. Not only men but women also, including girls throughout the country who were students or members of youth organisations, became workers in war industries such as the Women's Voluntary Service Corps.

About a year into the war with America, the situation became unfavourable and national general mobilisation reached its limits. Labour
shortage became acute in the construction of bases, airfields, roads, har-
bours and the like, essential for the prosecution of the campaign both at
home and in the occupied areas, and military operations were impeded.
So the Imperial government adopted as national policy the utilisation of
the human resources of the Korean Peninsula and drafted Koreans by the
issue of Cabinet and ministry ordinances.

The Women's Voluntary Service Corps was ostensibly (and, to
some extent, actually) directed towards labour service in essential
war industries. The women were, however, sometimes diverted into
prostitution and the Women's Voluntary Service Corps became so
identified with it that the women who actually did work in factories
have been reluctant to acknowledge their membership of the Corps.
This has made the task of estimating the number of comfort women
even more difficult.

Before the institution of the General Mobilisation Law, a procedure had grown up which is described as 'official mediation'. Kim Il
Myon quotes what happened when a Korean member of the police
force visited a village to recruit young women for what was then
called the Women's Patriotic Service Corps. His hopes for promotion depended on success in such operations. The Korean policeman
first gave a speech in poor Japanese on Japan's sacred mission in the
conflict, including the promise that, if the people of the Peninsula
played their part in achieving Japan's inevitable victory, they would
share equally in the glory of the people of Japan. Since the villagers
had very limited understanding of Japanese, his speech had to be interpreted for them by an assistant, probably provided from the village office. The policeman could probably have made a much better
speech in his native Korean, but this procedure was adopted because
it was more awe-inspiring. Finally he read out the names of five village girls reported to have been recommended as suitable 'volunteers'.

It did not escape notice that these 'suitable volunteers' happened
to be the more attractive girls of the locality. It was still assumed,
however, that they would be required only for duties like laundry or
sewing. The policeman promised that the work would earn them
good clothes and money, reminding the girls that if they did not
show up at the train station at the appointed time the next day, the
kempeitai would investigate the reasons why. Invoking the dreaded

kempeitai was usually the clinching argument.

Daughters of the landlord class and local officials were normally spared war work or enforced prostitution, because the Japanese authorities relied on their families to control the rural population. The only exceptions were when members of this class showed signs of encouraging resistance movements. A Japanese primary school teacher reports (Jugun Ianfu 110 Ban Henshu Iinkai 1992) that she was instructed to choose a number of her more senior pupils for labour draft, specifying that these should come from poorer families, who would be more acquiescent for financial reasons. The limited educational opportunities available to Koreans, especially females, meant that a promise of special training was often an effective inducement to enter the Women's Voluntary Service Corps. The Korean school system under the Japanese was designed to cater for all children of Japanese residents, but only for Korean children showing exceptional ability. Overall, Koreans accounted for only one-third of staff and students, and the use of their own language was restricted.

Recruitment seems to have been mostly from the lower classes who were likely to be illiterate. The resulting character of the Korean comfort women corps is clearly indicated in a thorough and fairly objective study of a comfort station carried out late in the war by a United States psychological warfare team, on the northern Burma front. It describes the comfort women as averaging twenty-five years of age and being

> uneducated, childish, capricious, and self-centred. They were not beauties by either Japanese or Western standards. They would only talk about their own personal concerns and, though sedate in the presence of strangers, could be coquettish on gaining some familiarity. (United States Office of War Information 1944)

The women said that they disliked their occupation and would not discuss it—nor their families. They believed that dropping propaganda leaflets on Korea was a good idea, but did not wish the Japanese to receive reports about them. Surviving photographs of this group have a certain pathetic appeal and, combined with the American report, convey the impression that their personality type helped them cope with the experiences they had faced better than some others might have fared.

Of others taken, young schoolgirls were not spared. Indeed, the school system was used as a source of recruits. Professor Yun Chung

Ok, the central figure of the South Korean women's group which has been working to bring the comfort women issue on to the international agenda, was one of those saved by foresighted parents. In 1943, she was a first-year student at Ehwa Women's College in Seoul, Korea, the forerunner of the university where she later taught. As the draft was gradually being extended among unmarried women, many of the students began to leave school to rush into marriage. This was a widespread tendency, with various motivations. Sometimes the prospective bridegrooms' families were willing to meet the girls' wishes, since this would offer the hope of an heir in case the son, drafted for military or labour service, did not return. Many girls were also willing to marry the crippled or handicapped who were unfit for service. After the war such marriages often ended in divorce.

At Yun's school, to save their students from disappearing, staff assured parents that their daughters were safe. But soon afterwards all parents were required to affix their seals to a statement of willingness to comply with the National General Mobilisation Ordinance. Yun's parents then removed her from school, saving her from joining a war industry or becoming a comfort woman.

Despite the prevailing official secrecy and the deceptive means of recruitment, knowledge of the comfort system gradually spread. Attempts at evasion, sometimes successful, as in Yun's case, often proved futile. One example of the spread of such information is given in the Korean Government-General's *Special Higher Police Monthly Report* for October 1939. It describes how an ex-comfort woman who had returned from Nanking was imprisoned for seven days for 'spreading harmful rumours'. She had been describing how comfort women in frontline areas had been compelled also to perform military-related duties, and that these had been so dangerous she would refuse to return there. Reports a few months earlier record the imprisonment for four months of a woman for gossiping about a bride who had married to avoid a draft of unmarried women. Her body oil was allegedly to be extracted for use in aircraft. Another was sentenced to seven days in gaol for charging that a girl had been bought for ¥17 from her parents, for blood and oil extraction for use in Manchuria. It is possible that rumours of this kind were echoes of the highly secret operations of the notorious Unit 731, which was carrying out a program of human experimentation for biological warfare purposes in Manchuria.

Slave raids and frontline military efforts

If other methods failed, there was always the slave raid. One such raider was Yoshida Seiji, who in 1983 published his wartime experiences, *My War Crimes: The Forced Draft of Koreans*. On graduating from Tokyo University in 1936, Yoshida was appointed to a post in the administration of the client state of Manchukuo. A few years later he was transferred to Army Headquarters in Nanking, as a War Ministry administrative officer in charge of military transport in the Shanghai area. He noticed that each regiment had at least one comfort station, usually with a few Japanese women of more mature years, and twenty to thirty younger Koreans. The more senior officers had special clubs with luxurious *geisha*-type entertainment.

In Shanghai at the time there was an underground Korean resistance movement calling itself the Korean Provisional Government affiliated to the Chinese Nationalists, and led by Kim Koo. On one occasion, after clearance by his superiors, Yoshida arranged an air passage to Hankow for a group of Korean 'medical staff', who later turned out to be members of this movement, apparently including Kim Koo himself. Yoshida was made the scapegoat and court-martialled for 'assistance to the enemy in wartime', an offence which could carry the death penalty. Instead, he was sentenced to two years in the Nanking military prison.

On his return to Japan in late 1942, he was appointed to the newly-formed National Labour Service Association, and given the task of co-ordinating conscript labour throughout the country. His post was mobilisation department head in Shimonoseki, a city at the western extremity of Honshu, and the regular port for sea links to the Korean port of Pusan. Yoshida's main duty was to control the flow of conscript labour to essential industries by order of Army and Navy headquarters in western Japan, particularly to the mines in the region. Much of the draft was handled through the regular network of police and the Korea Government-General's organisation. In cases of urgent demand, however, Yoshida describes how he himself led 'slave-raid' expeditions which recruited thousands of male labourers and about 1000 women for comfort duties.

In frontline areas, where the logistics of recruitment were less organised, officers and soldiers led raids on the civilian population and prisoner-of-war camps. Madam X, the young Chinese girl living in Malaya recounted in the interview quoted in the Introduction how she was seized by soldiers invading her village, raped in front of her parents and then taken with several other village girls to a comfort station in Kuala Lumpur, where she worked as a comfort woman until the war ended in 1945.

Ma Fe Yabut Santillan

In the Philippines, Ma Fe Yabut Santillan was eighteen years old, and helping her mother to run a small *carinderia* or food stall in Manila, when the Japanese Occupation began in 1941. Their food stall was near to the place where a Japanese garrison was stationed. She told her story in Calica and Sancho (1993):

A few months after the Japanese came, some Japanese officers came to our *carinderia* and demanded that they be allowed to eat without paying. My mother and I agreed so as to avoid any untoward incident. After the initial contact with the Japanese, the officers began to eat regularly in our *carinderia*. It was there that I met Captain Sakuma. He . . . always told me that he liked the dishes we cooked for them.

Captain Sakuma liked my cooking so much that a few months later he came with three soldiers and demanded that I work in the garrison as a cook. I and my mother protested. This made Captain Sakuma angry and he shouted at me and demanded that I go with them . . . he took hold of me and slapped me. My mother was kicked for coming to my assistance.

I agreed finally to go to the nearby garrison. There I was taken to a small room where I found two other girls, one of whom told me I would be treated like a maid in the morning. But at night I would have to be a 'wife', to serve the sexual needs of the Japanese.

The next morning, I was ordered to prepare breakfast for Captain Sakuma. I prepared bread, fried eggs and coffee and brought it to him. He was already seated in the mess hall of the building. He was very appreciative. He thanked me and praised me for the breakfast I had prepared. Later I was ordered to wash his clothes.

Later that night my ordeal started. I was very tired and was lying down on my bed when Captain Sakuma entered our room. When Dessie and the other girl saw him, they kept quiet and lay on their sides, facing the wall. Captain Sakuma motioned to them to keep quiet. I got up and sat on the bed without saying anything. He went straight to my bed and sat beside me.

He started touching my hair and told me to be a good girl. At first I did not move, but when he started kissing me, I shoved him aside and he fell on the floor. I stood up and tried to run but he was able to hold my arm, and then he slapped me. He shouted 'cura, cura', and then kicked me in the chest. It was very painful and I almost lost consciousness. He then pulled me and shoved me down on the bed. He started tearing my dress. At this time I did not make any resistance because I was afraid he would hurt me more. He then took off his shirt and pants and lay beside me.

It was my first time and that experience really caused me so much pain. I kept on crying while Captain Sakuma was using me. He kissed me on my lips, cheeks, neck and breasts. He was acting as if it was his first time to 'use' a girl. It made me feel so dirty. After a few minutes, he forced himself into me. After he was through, he stood up and picked up his clothes. He took my blanket and covered my naked body. I was then crying. He told me I was a good girl and that I should remain as such . . .

All throughout my stay in the garrison the same thing happened. I cooked for and prepared the needs of Captain Sakuma in the morning, while at night he would lie beside me and force me to make love with him. I did not put up any resistance every time he would have sex with me, because I was afraid of being hurt. After he was through, I would go to the [lavatory] and douche myself.

Captain Sakuma abused me for almost two years. During this time whenever he had visitors he would offer me to them as part of the entertainment. Eventually I was able to make my escape with the help of a cousin. My mother asked him to rescue me.

The Semarang cases: sex slavery

The only cases of forcible seizure for rape and prostitution which led to war crime trials involved Dutch women internees in central Java, in Indonesia. The Batavia Military Tribunal was held in 1948. The focus of the activity that led to it was an officer cadet school at Semarang, commanded by Lieutenant-General Nozaki Seiji. A staff officer, Colonel Okubo, proposed solving the problem of venereal disease among the cadets by using European women from the nearby internment camps. He apparently expected volunteers to be sufficient. General Nozaki agreed to the plan, subject to the permission of the Resident, and headquarters in Jakarta. Okubo was assured by the Resident that verbal permission would be adequate. During a visit to Jakarta he obtained the agreement of the Chief of Staff, on condition that a concrete plan was drawn up, and declarations of willingness obtained. Okubo instructed his adjutant in Semarang to draw up a plan for four comfort stations, one of which was to be reserved for the cadets.

The final detailed arrangements were left to a young captain, who worked with those who were to become the four comfort station operators, and the police, to recruit the women. Nozaki later stated that to his subsequent regret, he kept no check on proceedings, other than to inspect accommodation in the cadets' club, a week after it opened.

The captain's team of recruiters went to four camps in Semarang, and two in nearby Ambarawa. They began by drawing up lists of eligible women, generally meaning single and healthy, aged from seventeen to thirty-five. The reactions to the recruiters' efforts varied, according to the attitudes of the camp administrations and those of the internees. At one extreme, as at Camp Lampersari, opposition was so concerted that the Japanese backed down. At the other, in the words of one of writer Shirley F. Huie's informants, the attitude was: 'Let them go, it will be better for the rest of us.'

In one camp, Gedangen, some of the more mature women volunteered, either to spare younger girls or hoping for better conditions outside. The recruiters were, however, not satisfied with the available choices, and attempted to recruit others by force. They met desperate resistance from the internees who, armed with bamboo sticks and lengths of pipe, were able to force the Japanese to make do with volunteers. Some forcible recruitment is also mentioned at Halmahera camp, but details are clear only for the two camps Ambarawa Four and Ambarawa Six. These formed the basis of the war crimes trials.

Evidence before the Batavia Military Tribunal described how, on 23 February 1944, two Japanese military personnel and six civilians descended on Ambarawa and took a register of all women aged from 17 to 28. They recorded names, ages, homelands, marital status, and whether or not the women had children. Three days later, nine women were removed to Semarang and, together with others from nearby camps (apparently 35 in all), were forced to sign declarations of willingness. They were offered 50 guilders each in advance, which they refused. After a rough medical check, they were distributed among four comfort stations: the *Shoko* (Officers' Club) for cadets, the *Semarang Club*, the *Hinomaru* ('sun disc') and *Futabaso* ('new buds').

The women were forced into service from 1 March 1944. Two attempted to escape, one of whom, on recapture and torture, committed suicide by slashing herself. Another attempted suicide by drinking quinine. Another of the women described how, on arrival at the *Futabaso*, she was immediately taken to a room by a drunken officer, who eventually raped her. He was followed by five others. This pattern was repeated each day in the nauseating surroundings of a house without ventilation or drainage. She finally suffered a nervous breakdown and was admitted to a mental hospital.

Meanwhile the numbers required for the Semarang comfort stations were made up by the seizure of about 100 local women, Indians and Chinese as well as Indonesians. They were inspected at the *Shoko* club, many being pressed into service despite mass protests by their families. Seventeen of them were taken via Surabaya in eastern Java to a comfort station at an airfield in Flores, Eastern Indonesia. Reports from other sources have implied these were all Dutch women, but the Dutch account does not support this. As usual, the ethnicity and nationality of the comfort women were ill-defined.

One witness from the *Shoko* told how she was so worn out after servicing four men that she refused a fifth. At this the Japanese proprietor struck her and threatened to send her to a brothel near the Army quarters, where she would have to handle fifteen men daily. She became hysterical and fainted. After ten days in isolation she was deemed to have recovered, and forced back to work.

Another witness was among the seven women taken from the Halmahera camp. After signing the usual declaration she was sent to the *Hinomaru* comfort station. Her first client was a civilian, whom she tried to deter by claiming she was menstruating. He raped her regardless. From then on she had daily to service five Japanese, military or civilian, until her release.

A further account comes from a woman who had been living outside the camps. She was then eighteen and lived with her family in Jakarta. In April 1944 she was ordered to report to the local police station and register herself and her nineteen-year-old sister. In the police station there were already about 100 European, Chinese and

Javanese young women. All but twenty were eventually sent home. Those remaining included the witness. After refusing an offer of money, they were forcibly removed to Semarang. There, along with seventeen others, she was lodged in the Hotel Splendid and forced to service Japanese officers. One, claiming to be a doctor, injured her by placing an object in her vagina. She was later taken via Surabaya to Flores. No further details of her account are given in the materials released at the war crime trials.

Shirley F. Huie in *The Forgotten Ones*, a compilation of accounts of internment life in Java, quotes a diary-based account of the seizure at Ambarawa Six, from the Dutch Commandant's secretary:

> It was seven girls and two married women. I have their names. They did not go voluntarily. Mothers tried to fight to protect them but were beaten back. They were taken off in a truck. Three months later, on 11 May, they were brought back and reunited with their families. They talked about it and the stories are not nice . . .
> They did not have therapy when they were reunited with their mothers and were kept separately in the camp. It puts a stigma on you. God knows the impression it all left on these young girls. The sister of my friend in Holland is all right. She is married to a very understanding man and has three lovely boys. No one outside the family knows about her camp experience.

The release of the Dutch women came about through the transfer of the internment camps from the Home Ministry to the Army, from 1 April 1944. A captain was appointed to look into the matter, and a camp doctor put him in touch with a woman in Halmahera camp who was protesting against her daughter's seizure. The captain asked for instructions from Headquarters in Jakarta, where Colonel Odajima had just arrived from Tokyo on an inspection tour. He interviewed the mother and decided that all involuntary comfort women should be released. He made this recommendation to the General Headquarters for Southeast Asia in Saigon, which ordered Nozaki to release the women in Semarang. Nozaki claimed afterwards that as a result of rumours of compulsion, he was already considering this, and was ashamed that his intentions had been anticipated by the order from Headquarters.

Most of the women were transferred to Kota Paris in western Java, together with others from elsewhere in Java, including Bandung. The mothers of some of the women were able to join them. According to Keetje Ruizeveld, who was released with the Bandung group, there were more than 100 Dutch women in the camp in Kota Paris who had been forced to become comfort women. Her reason for going public was to reveal that many more women were forced into comfort stations than the thirty-five women mentioned in the Semarang case.

Jan Ruff

One of the victims in the Semarang case, Jan Ruff, has given a vivid public account of her experiences. She is among the few non-Korean comfort women to talk about her trauma. Her case was not cited in the Dutch war trials because she had left Indonesia by that time. Since the prosecution had sufficient witnesses available, she was not called on to testify. Unlike the trial witnesses, who gave evidence anonymously, Jan Ruff chose to give public testimony in support of the Asian women campaigning for redress from Japan.

Soon after the war she married an Englishman, and since 1960 has been living in Adelaide, Australia. She had kept her experiences secret from all except her husband. She decided to break her silence on learning of the Asian women who were beginning to speak out:

> When I read their stories and saw them on television, I knew they wanted a Western woman to speak up as well.

She began by giving her two daughters copies of a notebook filled with her writing, and asking them to read it. The notebook told in graphic detail her experiences as a war rape victim.

On 9 December 1992, in a public auditorium in Tokyo, Jan Ruff first told her story to the world. This public hearing was organised by the Japan Lawyers' Association, the Dutch Foundation for Honorary Debts, and various interested citizens' groups. One woman each from North and South Korea, China, Taiwan and the Philippines also participated. In comparison with accounts by the Asian women, Jan Ruff provides more detail concerning the violent processes of seizure and 'breaking in'. The briefer accounts of the Asian women affirmed the prevalence of such methods. On the other hand, Ruff gave virtually no particulars of the functioning of the comfort station. This was, perhaps, because of both the comparative brevity and the traumatic intensity of her ordeal. These did, however, affect the whole of her subsequent life in a manner comparable to the experience of many other comfort women.

In February 1944, Jan had been interned in Ambarawa Camp Six for nearly two years, with her mother and two younger sisters. She was then twenty years old. On returning to barracks from camp duty one day, she found herself ordered to line up in the compound, together with all single girls aged seventeen and over. The girls were apprehensive during inspection by a group of Japanese soldiers, who 'marched up and down, sneering, pointing, and touching'. Finally all except ten, including Jan, were sent away. They were ordered to pack a small bag of belongings and board some trucks waiting at the gate. With the guards watching them pack, Jan made sure to include a Bible, prayer book and crucifix for spiritual support. Jan's fellow camp inmates tried to resist the girls' removal but, as in most such cases, this was to no avail. The ten girls were joined by six others from an adjacent camp.

On reaching Semarang, Jan was among seven ushered into a large house by an officer who seemed to be in charge. She does not mention any of the known names of the four military brothels in Semarang, knowing this one only as the *House of the Seven Seas*, but the description suggests the *Shoko* club. Each girl was shown her own bedroom, but that first night they huddled together in one big bed, praying, too afraid to sleep. They were left undisturbed.

The next day they were assembled in the living room and told explicitly what their duties were to be, with warnings against trying to escape. When the girls protested they would rather die than submit, the Japanese pointed out that they were helpless captives, and if they did not obey, their families would suffer. Next day the front room was converted into a reception area, and the girls' photographs were taken. They tried to make these as uninviting as possible. A Japanese woman arrived to help with the proceedings, inspiring in the girls a spark of hope that she might sympathise with their plight. But they met with no sympathy from her. That night the girls were paralysed with a fear which Jan says has never quite left her. Sometimes it returns with a special intensity, burning through all her limbs, she said. She led the group in prayer until, one by one, they were dragged off to the bedrooms, fighting and kicking. Jan hid under the dining room table until she was hauled out by a 'large, fat and bald' officer she knew by the name of Mihashi:

> I kicked him on the shins. He just stood there laughing. My fighting, kicking, crying and protesting made no difference. I screamed 'Don't, don't' and then in Indonesian, *'Djangan, djangan'*. He pulled me up and dragged me into my bedroom, while I continued to fight him.

He drew his sword and began tracing its point on her flesh. She fell to her knees, asking God to forgive her her sins.

> Mihashi tore at my clothes and ripped them off. As I lay there naked on the bed, he slowly ran the sword over my body, up and down, up and down. I could feel the cold steel touching my skin as he moved the sword over my throat and breasts, stomach and legs. He played with me like a cat plays with a helpless mouse. Then he started to undress. He threw himself on top of me, pinning me under his body. I tried to fight him off and kicked and scratched him, but he was too strong. The tears were streaming down my face as he raped me. It seemed as if he would never stop. To me, this brutal and inhuman rape was worse than dying.

After he left she ran to the bathroom 'to wash all the dirt, the shame and hurt off my body'. Other girls were doing the same.

> We washed ourselves as if it could wash away all that had happened to us. I dared not go back to the dining room and decided to hide myself. I hid in a room on the back verandah. My whole body was shaking with fear. 'Not again, I can't go through this again,' I thought.
> After a while the angry voices and footsteps came closer, and I was dragged out of my hiding place. The night was not over yet, there were more Japanese waiting. The terror started all over again. I never realised suffering could be so intense as this. And this was only the beginning.

Jan's job was to service officers who, in theory only, took their pleasures in the evening:

> In the daytime we were supposed to be safe, although the house was always filled with Japanese coming and going, socialising, eyeing us up and down. Consequently we were often raped in the daytime as well. As soon as it was getting dark, the house would be 'opened', and a terrible fear would burn up my body. Each evening I tried to hide in a different place, but I was always found, then dragged into my room, after severe beatings.

An attempt to make herself unattractive was unsuccessful, and may have well increased her erotic appeal:

> One morning I decided to cut off all my hair and make myself look as unattractive as possible. I cut my hair until I was quite bald. 'No one would like me like this,' I thought. But of course, it did not help me one bit. The rumour spread that one of the girls had cut off all her hair, and it turned me into a curiosity object.

The reaction of the 'clients' in their enjoyment of their victims' behaviour defied prediction. Jan relates that every time a Japanese raped her she tried to fight him off. She 'hit out strongly and delivered mighty blows, kicks and scratchès and injured the Japanese quite often'. As with her first assailant, Mihashi, one forms the impression that many clients may have preferred this kind of sado-masochistic drama to tame submission—something of which Asian women might have been more aware. But finally Ruff was warned that if she persisted in fighting she would be 'moved to a brothel down town for soldiers, a brothel for native girls where conditions were worse'. This threat was not carried out.

Jan was soon to realise that, from the manageress to the doctor, everyone they saw was part of the comfort system:

> One day a Japanese doctor arrived at our house. Immediately I thought that he would be able to help us. Surely, as a doctor he would have compassion for us. I requested to speak to the doctor. But he showed no interest, no signs of compassion or apology. In-stead, the doctor ended up raping me on the first day of his visit.

Not only rape but also exhibitionism appeared to be among the doctor's pleasures:

> In the days leading up to the doctor's visit, a gynaecological type of equipment had been installed in one of the rooms on the back veran-dah. From now on we were to be examined for any possible disease. Each time the doctor visited us he raped me in the daytime. The door of the doctor's examination room was always left open, and to humiliate us even more, any other Japanese were allowed to look on while we were being examined. The humiliation was unbearable . . .
> More anxiety came when I realised that I was pregnant. I was absolutely terrified. How could I give birth to and love a child con-ceived in such horror? Like pillars of strength the girls gave me their support and they advised me to tell our Japanese woman guard that I was pregnant. I approached the woman, and as an answer to the problem she produced a bottle full of tablets. I could not kill a foe-tus, not even this one. It would be a mortal sin if I did. I continued to refuse the tablets. Eventually they were forced down my throat. I miscarried shortly after.

One expedient the girls tried in an effort to at least slow down the pressure of service was to encourage the officers to play cards with them, a form of subsidiary entertainment sometimes mentioned in comfort stations. One officer sympathised and actively co-oper-ated in playing cards for hours to stall the others: 'Every minute of delay was important, because as soon as one officer finished with us, another would be waiting.'

Ruff was eventually released and taken to the Kota Paris camp with the other seized internees, where they were reunited with their families. She estimates their stay in the brothel as at least three months, which generally agrees with the evidence of other Dutch witnesses. During those three months, she says:

> They had taken everything away from me, my self-esteem, my dignity, my freedom, my possessions, my family. But there was one thing that they could never take away from me. It was my Faith and my love for God . . . it was my deep faith in God that helped me survive all that I suffered at the brutal, savage hands of the Japanese. I have forgiven the Japanese for what they did to me but I can never forget.

Just before internment Ruff had taken her preliminary vows towards becoming a nun. Her experiences were deemed by the Church to preclude her from becoming one, even though she had been anything but a willing party to her ordeal. After her later marriage, she had three miscarriages and was only able to sustain a pregnancy following extensive remedial surgery. One lifelong effect of her experiences is that the mere act of getting into bed at night brings back her fear. Nor has she ever been able to enjoy intercourse with her husband to the full—a fact she bitterly resents.

3. Sex in a war zone

Although in theory Koreans and Taiwanese were regarded as Japanese nationals, in practice the Japanese professional prostitutes fared better as comfort women. They tended to be kept in the more secure base areas, and made available to the higher ranks, while Koreans were pooled and sent to the frontlines.

In his study, Kim Il Myon makes several observations on Korean and Japanese comfort women. He generalises about the majority Koreans and the minority Japanese, taken to be about 80 per cent and 10 per cent of the total. He characterises them rather stereotypically as being, respectively, younger and older, amateur and professional, deceived and voluntary, sincere and superficial in both technique and sentiment, naïve and jaded, and intended for men as against officers. Like their menfolk, the Japanese women tended to look down on lower ranks. Even when they were obliged to give them service, it was not particularly enjoyable for the men, who felt them to be condescending. Since the Japanese women were professionals, they were skilled at faking sexual arousal, which would bring a fast reaction from the client and a quick conclusion to the encounter—the woman's real purpose. Greenhorn soldiers would be under the illusion that a woman had found them attractive. Koreans, on the other hand, were much more spontaneous in their reactions—at least until they tired from a quick succession of visits. Kim suggests this would set in from about the fifth.

When Japanese women were serving in forward areas, however, and dealing with men who might die at any time, they would tend to develop a patriotic consciousness, combined with some sympathy for the men's situation. This attitude would earn them some respect. This was still further strengthened when the women encountered a unit from their home locality, infantry units being largely formed on this basis. A 'classic example', according to Kim, was a comfort station of over twenty women from Kyushu, stationed for some years with a unit of similar background on the Soviet border. There such a degree of familiarity developed that the situation, it is said, resembled a collective marriage. In such a case the women would be able to limit the number of clients they served, if too exhausted or raw.

In the case of Korean or Taiwanese comfort women, an encounter with men from their own localities is also described as being welcome—though there was less likelihood of their developing a patriotic spirit. Yamatani Tetsuo, in researching his 1979 film on comfort women, *An Old Lady in Okinawa: Testimony of a Military Comfort Woman*, found evidence in Okinawa that some of the Koreans identified with Japan; this he attributes to the partial success of assimilationist education. But in most cases they were judged apolitical, given their background. Where Kim Il Myon quotes soldiers' comments appreciative of Koreans, the reference is to their greater freedom from disease, their youthful vigour and their 'tightness', compared to which some Japanese *karayuki* made them feel like 'a carrot in the Pacific Ocean'. Sometimes when Japanese women were reserved for officers, the latter would still seek out Koreans, annoying the men, who regarded the Koreans as their private preserve. This type of relationship would bring a response from the Koreans, who felt themselves in competition with the Japanese, and who would do their best to retain the soldiers for themselves.

Kim Il Myon follows his observations on ethnic differences with generalisations about Chinese comfort women. According to him, they fall into three main types. First were those who were destitute as a result of war and had no other means of support. Second were those who were seized in the course of punitive search and destroy expeditions, and forced into comfort stations. Third were cases of women volunteering to serve as a means of spying for the Chinese Army. Close relationships with the soldiers were more rare in the case of Chinese because of language difficulties, but they did occur. On a number of occasions, this led to desertion by Japanese troops and defections, mainly to the Chinese Communists. Such Japanese deserters often became propagandists, later contributing to the postwar Communist movement in Japan. Korean deserters joined Kim Il Sung's guerrillas, forming the nucleus of the future North Korean regime.

The situation in China was extremely tortuous, with regional rivalries, and tensions between Nationalists and Communists and the sometimes ambiguous pro-Japanese regime of Wang Ching Wei. Some further light on these complexities, and on spying by comfort women, is provided by a post-war novel written in Taiwan by T'ang Te Kang, entitled *War and Love*. It claims to be based on testimony by ex-comfort women, and certainly agrees with the general picture drawn by Japanese sources. It portrays Wang Ching Wei's 'false army' as aiding the development of comfort stations, largely for their own monetary gain, and its involvement in smuggling to the unoccupied areas. In the later stages of the war, the Japanese Army in China is described in the novel as sinking into dissipation, 'infected with Chinese-style vices'. Amid scenes of corruption, great tragedy and heroism were, however, played out.

The main action of the novel is set in an unnamed 'mountain zone', with three classes of comfort stations. The highest is the Imperial Army Comfort Station reserved for Japanese only and meant to be staffed by Japanese, though many of its women were actually Chinese from the region north of the lower Yangtze, traditional home of courtesans, wearing Japanese costume. The next class was the Chinese and Business Gentlemen's Club for 'false army' soldiers and traders with the Japanese. Here the staff were all Chinese. At the bottom came the Army and People's Reception Station, with primitive facilities and short visits.

The novel's story concerns only Chinese characters associated with the middle-ranked house. Its proprietress had been a Japanese-speaking professional in Shanghai. The Chinese staff are described as having been mostly 'seized, bought, deceived or drafted', though some had come voluntarily. The story of the proprietress is intertwined with that of a refugee from Soochow, originally employed in the lowest class of brothel but moved up to the middle-class house when this ran short of staff. Then the more attractive from the lowest-class house were used to make up the numbers. She forms an attachment with a guerrilla client disguised as a 'false army' soldier, and they both flee when the *kempeitai* begin to uncover espionage activities. The rest of her tragic story concerns the civil war leading up to the Communist victory.

The drift of the story supports the view that one motive for the intensive use of Korean women was the fear of espionage by indigenous women.

Breaking the women into the job

In the numerous cases where the women had been recruited under false pretences, initiation into the job would have been as devastating for them as a major battle for a soldier. One graphic and stark account of such an initiation is given in *Memoirs of a Korean Comfort Woman*, published under the name of Kim Chun Ja by the Modern History Research Society of Japan, in 1965 (Kim Il Myon 1976). Nothing is known of Kim Chun Ja's identity, but her accounts are among the more detailed of the earlier 'war reminiscence' literature.

Kim Chun Ja

Kim Chun Ja's account begins when, with four other girls, she was pressured to volunteer for the Women's Patriotic Service Corps. They were handed over by the officiating policeman to a middle-aged Japanese couple, to be taken by train to Seoul. On arrival, as they were walking to an inn, the man warned them to keep close together, since there were many 'wolves' in the streets, and if they became separated, 'anything could happen'. On the way they stopped at a clothing store and each was bought a two-piece Korean costume, as well as a Japanese-style cotton kimono and undergarment. Next they were bought a range of cosmetics. The man told them he was giving them these things even before they had done any work, because he had great expectations of them. They were, of course, pleasantly excited, as well as thrilled by their first visit to a large city. But they were also puzzled as to why such things were needed in the Patriotic Service Corps. When one of them asked, the man explained: 'These are your weapons. You must take good care of them, like the soldiers with their guns and bullets.' On enquiring of her duties, the woman of the couple told Kim Chun Ja that these would be no hardship. Their job was to make themselves pretty, and comfort the soldiers. 'You see, the soldiers are tired from the long war. They are very pleased if you make a pretty show and welcome them. That's the job of the Patriotic Service Corps.' 'Do you mean that we sing and dance for them?' asked the innocent woman. 'Well, something like that' was the reply.

The women were then taken to dinner in a restaurant, during which they were given Japanese names. As usual these were based on the Japanese pronunciation of the Chinese characters for their Korean names, with some modifications to make them sound natural. Kim Chun Ja was renamed Kanei Haruko, the last word being written in exactly the same way as Chun Ja. Finally they were taken to a secluded Japanese-style inn. The woman explained that this was usually reserved for Japanese, and 'Peninsula people' were not admitted. They were, however, able to stay there on her recommendation, because of the duties they were to perform. She then took them to the bathhouse, where she personally scrubbed them thoroughly. She made appreciative remarks on their bodies, commenting on one in particular that she would become the most popular girl in the unit.

Next they were dressed in sets of Japanese bathrobes, and taken to a room where five Army officers were drinking. Shyness kept the women at the entrance until their guide urged them in, telling them that these were the top officers of the unit, with whom they were to work. The girls were to learn their names and recognise the officers, 'so that they would be well looked after'. They had to begin by serving them *sake*. The woman assured the top officer that any one of the girls would make certain he would have a successful war, and return safely, in triumph. Although the girls would not have understood the implications at the time, this alluded to the superstition that deflowering a virgin before combat would act as a charm against injury or death. He replied that he would 'try it out'.

Before long each of the girls was seized in a well-practised grip, 'like sparrows caught in an eagle's talons', and dragged screaming to separate rooms. Chun Ja describes how she was ordered to undress her captor, who 'stared at her, despite his drunkenness, with eyes as sharp as a leopard's'. She took off his clothes until only his loincloth was left. She needed special urging to make her remove this, and when she did she was transfixed at what it revealed. He joked that she seemed to be falling for him—but she was not to be alarmed because there were others in the unit a lot bigger than he. It was then her turn to disrobe, and as she did so she had a vision of her parents bidding her farewell. She asked their forbearance, since this was what Patriotic Service must mean.

Once she was naked, her captor gave her a thorough inspection and pronounced her fit to provide ample comfort to the men of his unit. He then proceeded to break her in with an initiation lasting four hours. He forced her into endless variations as she wept with grief, pain and shame. The same sort of treatment was repeated over the following three days, the girls being rotated among the men. They were told: 'With soldiers, like horses, the first spell of testing and training is most important. If they are not properly toughened right from the first day they're no use at all on the battlefield.' From this, the women came to realise what their future life would be. Their pudenda grew swollen and inflamed, and they were constantly attempting to gain relief by applying cold towels.

Finally the girls and the supervising couple were put aboard the last goods car of a troop train headed for China, 'like contraband', since they were not officially part of the unit personnel. The last part of their journey was by truck. It was not long before troops were lining up for service. The arrival of such a contingent was customarily announced by large character notices along the line of: 'Amazon force arrives today. Going all out to give service.' There are references to men spontaneously ejaculating in the queue or even masturbating, so that they would not suffer premature ejaculation when their turn came.

Sometimes the 'breaking in' was not done until arrival at the unit where the women were to work. This would give the women's controller a good opportunity to curry favour with the commanding officer or other such dignitary by offering a 'taste of virginity', another version of the 'law of the first night', as it was known in mediaeval Christendom. Systematic training in tricks of the trade followed. The women would be taught to address the proprietor-couple as 'father' and 'mother'. They were not to become excited or over-exert themselves during work, or they would soon be worn out. Above all, they were not to become attached to any particular soldier but should treat all equally. This principle was also laid down in official regulations, but was frequently infringed. The women were at the same time taught to match their style of service to the type of client. They were to take a leisurely approach to older men, to praise the sexual technique of officers, and to bring some suggestion of a less mercenary, more romantic approach to young and unsophisticated soldiers.

Among the tricks of the trade the women were taught was one to strengthen their thigh muscles for heavy service by walking with a coin held between their buttocks. They were shown how to douche with a 'pump-like water-pistol' or, alternatively, if business were too brisk, to keep balls of cotton wool soaked in disinfectant by the bedside for hurried application between visits. Authorities everywhere were insistent that troops use condoms, and regularly issued them where possible. Nevertheless, they could run short in difficult areas, and there are various references to their being washed for re-use. Naturally the system fell short often enough, and infection or pregnancies resulted. Kim Il Myon records that if babies resulted, the Korean women would pay Chinese families to look after them, and were sometimes able to reclaim them later. Unlike the Japanese women, with their professional background, the newly-recruited Koreans would take something like three months to adjust and make the best of their unbearable situation.

Comfort women on campaign

China and Manchuria were the main arenas where the comfort system developed, always accounting for the great majority of comfort women. The invasion of Manchuria of September 1931 was followed by piecemeal penetration of northern China and Inner Mongolia, through the establishment of local puppet administrations culminating in all-out war from 1937. Over the following three years, Japanese forces occupied most of the northern plain and the navigable stretch of the Yangtze River, as well as all ports on the coast, and other lines of communication. There were nearly 1.5 million troops involved in the Chinese theatre, and some 690,000 in Manchuria.

The more extreme conditions of the comfort system tend to be better documented. They provide expression of anti-Japanese feeling or, more practically, strengthen claims for compensation. It is, of course, impossible to make any sort of statistical estimate of the extent of various degrees of brutality, but it is clear that acute abuses were widespread. The character of the Japanese Armed Forces is shown by their other well-documented excesses. Added to this were the conditions of the war, the environment and the weather. One grim observation relates that when comfort women, as well as others, died in the Manchurian winter, the ground would be too hard to dig, so bodies were left in the graveyard until the thaw. This usually meant abandoning them to the wolves.

Service nearer the front was the harshest for the women. They were lodged in humble huts or makeshift barracks on the edge of tropical jungle, or surrounded by the bleak loess plains of northern China. They were obliged to relieve men fresh from combat, or tense patrols 'with bear-like bulk, dulled gaze, and insistent grip'. Visits from the officers were still more repulsive. With their overpowering arrogance, they treated even their own men as an inferior species. How much worse must they have treated Korean comfort women! They were also apt to evade payment, as if the world were theirs by right.

What the women dreaded most were visits by bodies of troops in transit. A stable attachment to one particular unit would at least tend to limit the volume of service required, and perhaps improve the chances of developing some degree of fellow-feeling. But in the case of transients, the demand would not only increase in volume, but also in intensity. Such troops would often be headed for action, and would regard this as possibly their last chance for sex. After a quick succession of such visits, the woman's performance would become mechanical. The men would regard this as poor service or coldness. This could lead to violence. The women might then fall back on the assimilationist formula that they were also 'children of the same Emperor'. This is reported as generally effective in calming men down.

Sometimes in such harried conditions, the women could be dazed or even faint, so that they would lose count of their clients, or fail to keep the tickets which formed the basis of calculating their share of the takings. This would give the proprietor the opportunity to cheat the women of part of their dues. The more professional Japanese, who had the more concrete goal of working off contracts, sometimes kept a check by making marks on the wall for each client. The Koreans, at least to begin with, were more trusting. Kim Chun Ja's memoir relates how she calculated the number of men she had served each day by the sum given her by the proprietor when camp curfew time came, and the stream of men receded like the tide. In principle, her share was two-thirds of takings. Whether what she got was due her is a moot point.

Another risk from transit units was that the women sometimes lost their belongings to thieving soldiers who believed that such female objects would act as a charm in deflecting bullets. The loss of a garment or footwear could be a hardship in a remote area where these were hard to replace. The women would have had to rely on the proprietor to buy more—another opportunity to make money out of the women.

Kim Chun Ja notes that during her two years of service in northern China, the only occasions when she was sure of an undisturbed night, when officers were usually free to call, was on the eve of a 'death-defying expedition'. This was a visit to the advanced fortified posts known as pillboxes. They were designed to monitor or counter guerrilla movements.

To provide occasional sexual recreation, a couple of comfort women would be sent with a supply run. They would be issued with a pistol each to use against guerrilla attack, and were instructed how to reserve the last bullet for suicide, if this were necessary to prevent capture. At the pillbox a comfort room would be set up in a cell otherwise used to hold occasional prisoners. The whole garrison would take a turn before the return of the supply convoy. During the women's absence, it is said, the proprietor would sometimes perform a magical popular Shinto ritual to ensure the women's safe return. Whatever his personal feelings, the women represented a substantial financial investment to him. Their replacement would be a problem in a frontline area.

Another occasion of particular hardship was a division-scale mobile operation. Then all the comfort women assigned to a force would have to accompany it. One of the largest of these was the Honan Operation, a search and destroy campaign designed to suppress guerrilla activity in the province of Honan in China. It was largely successful, but at a huge cost in both effort and destruction. Kim Il Myon quotes a description of the comfort women on that operation:

> At a position some metres away from the rearmost ranks of the force, a large number of women were lined up in a rank, bearing armbands inscribed 'Patriotic Service Corps'. They all wore military uniforms and seemed uncomfortable from the pressure of the uniforms on their breasts . . . They walked silently in a tight group behind the supply train, with the desiccated yellow dust blowing on them. They were prostitutes assigned to the force. The march continued for fully ten days. On the tenth day they reached a hamlet called Yangchiat'un, with the flow of the Yellow River spreading vast and sluggish before them.
>
> On arrival, the women, with feet bleeding from the long forced march, came under the supervision of the sergeant in charge of canteens, who chose the most attractive one to serve the officers. As he instructed her: 'This is the same as being in the frontline. You never know when the Eighth Route Army [Communist] guerrillas will attack so you must always be prepared. You will now look after the officers and will have to work even harder than before for our country.' He taught her how to bow in greeting to each officer and again in thanking him after the service was

completed. The sergeant himself would earn points for the quality of service given by the women under his care.

The first session was with an officer of very solid build, aged about thirty, who nodded her in the direction of a thin army mattress. She, of course, was not allowed to show any sign of exhaustion or lethargy from the long march. On completion, he did make a curt expression of appreciation and she thanked him as instructed. She then had ten minutes to rearrange herself for the next officer.

A former medical officer in Manchuria, during a post-war phone-in program, recalled the mobile railway comfort stations used there. He noted that they were guarded by Japanese and Korean *yakuza* and that some travelling circus girls had also been pressed into service. In his medical examinations he found that some women tried to conceal venereal disease symptoms by applying iodine.

One former soldier recalled that, while he was there, a comfort station near a divisional headquarters by the Soviet border bore only the unit name on its entrance, without any other explanation. Troops there were only allowed to visit it from their third year of service. Men in their first year were largely occupied in the servile role of personal batmen to officers, while the second year men were subject to the widespread practice of collective punishment for the desertion of one of their number.

According to the soldier, even the more senior men used the comfort station rather infrequently. The atmosphere of close military supervision provided little relief from daily tension, even though no other form of outside recreation was available. This meant that the women had a more leisurely life than usual—more so on one occasion when the unit was fully occupied in water-borne exercises. Then comfort women were noticed fishing in the river not far away.

A few more first-hand eyewitness accounts gathered by Kim Il Myon help to fill in the picture of comfort women on campaign:

A military truck was coming towards us, kicking up yellow dust over the North China plain. On board were women wearing multicoloured kerchiefs—red, yellow, blue. Among them, as they cautiously approached us through the minefield, was one who had a gunshot wound in the arm. They seemed to us like angels descended from heaven. There were more than ten of them, most from Korea, those from Japan being from Kyushu. The force was very excited, after being separated from women for so many months. There were 10hx4f000 or more troops.

Sex there was pitiful. There was a row of barrack-type buildings and on entering one there was just one mattress. It was filthy after soaking up the sweat and grease of thousands of men. The women would lie on it and sleep with only a single chemise. Japanese, Korean and Chinese comfort women were all in the same condition.

One night I slipped away to the comfort station. After chatting for a while to the proprietor, I paid the fee for the night and entered the woman's room. She was a small, dumpy woman who handled the business quite mechanically, as if it were bothersome. There was no charm whatever, no different from relieving oneself in the lavatory.

She looked only eighteen or nineteen and there was nothing erotic in her fragile limbs, which did not look fully developed and imparted a pathetic impression. During the action she only rubbed her cheek a little but made no sound and showed no agitation. She did not even breathe harder. She did not seem to know how to perform. It was unsatisfying and pitiful. That part of her body, like an unripe fruit, had not lost its hardness and I had the illusion I was ravishing a child. I came very quickly, without any sense of rapture.

Given the conditions in which such intercourse took place, the purely functional nature of the encounter could not be disguised. Said Madam X of her own experiences:

They never asked for a massage, and nor did they give or expect anything in the way of foreplay. We didn't even have to strip naked. We only had to undress from the waist down. After each man I would go to the bathroom and wash myself. When a lot of soldiers had a day off at the same time, we would be terrifically busy; there would be a long line of soldiers waiting to be serviced. If a soldier exceeded his allotted time then Mamasan would knock on the door and tell him his time was up. I would never dare tell him. The officers could keep us all night.

Time out in a comfort station

To give a more complete picture of the women's lives, Kim Il Myon presents a picture of 'life in the intervals of the sex-hell'. In theory, workers were allowed two days off for menstruation, with notices to this effect being stuck on the doors to their rooms, or circulated in daily routine orders. Medical officers could also authorise time off for other health reasons. There are reports of comfort stations being closed on one day of each month, and there were also irregular periods of inactivity associated with troop movements. But the most frequently mentioned break was a weekly half-day when medical examinations were held. The Korean women, being younger and of largely rural background, are described as more likely to pursue some sort of activity rather than simply lounging around. In the early hours of the day before visits began, doing laundry was common, given the distinctive Korean custom of wearing white clothing. Otherwise the women might play card games, with several packed into one of their small rooms for a game. Said Madam X:

> I never played cards or any other type of game with the soldiers. The only games we played were with the other girls. When there were no soldiers wanting to be serviced we would sometimes get together and play blind man's bluff.

Sometimes the women were allowed to shop. Its most common purpose was to obtain ingredients to make *kimchi*, the Korean dish of Chinese cabbage pickled with garlic and chilli. All the ingredients for *kimchi* were easily obtained in China and most other places, but *kimchi* itself was not. Chillies might also be added to other rations that were available. The sight of peppers drying in large bunches under the eaves was the most obvious sign that a house was a comfort station staffed by Koreans.

Newly-recruited Koreans would for some time have few interests other than speculating on the possibility of escape. They had little conception of geography, and would view boats passing on the Yangtze with the idle fancy that they might escape on one sailing for Korea. As they grew more resigned and accumulated some money, they often developed an interest in making life more comfortable. They began to accumulate furnishings.

According to a United States psychological warfare report on a comfort station in northern Burma, there had been no shortage of necessities there for most of the time. There had also been many luxuries, like gramophones. The women had been included in sports meetings, picnics and parties, and it was more than likely that the troops would have welcomed female companionship on such occasions in addition to the women's primary function. In other areas, a photograph of comfort women at a sports meeting in Taiwan survives. All types of organisations in Japan during the war insisted on physical exercise for their staff.

The movement of comfort women outside their posts was strictly controlled, as was that of the soldiers themselves, though details varied according to rules set by the officers in charge. In some instances the women were allowed out in the company of officers; others had to have a pass or be chaperoned by a guard or their proprietor. In Iloilo in the Philippines, one comfort station had an area where the women were allowed to take walks. Where conditions were more harsh, or the chances of merging back into the indigenous population excellent, the women were kept virtual prisoners, as in the case of some Filipinas. In Indonesia, one woman recounts how she, her sister and other Indonesian comfort women were kept virtual prisoners in all the camps she was in for four years. They were not allowed to converse with the male forced labourers on pain of execution for the men, if caught in the act.

Sometimes mail could reach comfort women, care of their units in settled areas. In correspondence with home, mention of their true occupation was mostly avoided. One field post office non-commissioned officer in Hupei, China, recalls handling mail for an area containing 2000 comfort women. It was collected every second month. He incidentally mentions being invited to a party celebrating a comfort woman's completion of service. She was then twenty-eight and had entered the profession ten years earlier, in Japan. Understandably, she seemed worn out.

Love and kindness

Among so many accounts of crudity, harshness and hardships, are a number of cases, related both in Kim Il Myon's book, and in other testimony, of personal empathy and even esteem between comfort women and servicemen. Personal relations were strongly discouraged, both by comfort station proprietors, as in Kim Chun Ja's case, and by military regulations. Rule 1 of the appendix on discipline in the Serviceman's Club Regulations, set out by unit Yama #3475, reads:

> The concept of common possession of the female staff is to be consistently applied throughout and the concept of special appropriation is strictly prohibited.

Such a rule would have been framed with an eye to the possibility of disorder through jealousy. Given the potential for varied emotional responses, particularly under conditions of extreme stress, rule making was not always successful. Professor Yun Chung Ok, the pioneer activist on behalf of comfort women, recognises this in an account of her visit to Rabaul:

> Even amid such a terrible life, Korean comfort women and young airmen, at a time when a mission meant death, seem to have experienced something like a raw encounter between fellow human beings.

She quotes an account of a comfort woman weeping aloud when a favoured soldier did not return, and offering flowers to his name, written on a piece of paper stuck in a corner of her room.

Ito Keiichi, author of *Soldiers' History of the Army*, also mentions cases of women going into mourning and refusing to work for up to a month on hearing of the death of a favourite soldier. During two years working in the supply section of a unit headquarters near Nanking, Ito says he became a kind of general counsellor to comfort women in the area. He noted how particular ties formed from time to time. When a favourite soldier was moved to the front the woman would still try to send messages or gifts or to receive messages, and might form another attachment to a local soldier who could help in such ways. He would often obtain news for her or visit her when ill with gifts. Apart from such particular arrangements, giving tips, souvenirs or presents to the women was widespread, says Ito. Sometimes these consisted of objects plundered in punitive expeditions, or from looting.

There are also reports from three widely scattered areas of women sharing clients, and agreeing not to accept each other's regulars. A former auxiliary *kempei* recalls that the Korean women in Ichang, China, maintained such a code, refusing a man who had received another woman's services, with the words: 'You're so-and-so's client.' Sometimes one might decline a fee from a favourite soldier, who would reciprocate with presents of Japanese sweets or buns, suggesting a personal rather than a commercial relationship. The narrator speaks of sensing a certain nobility in the women, although on occasion he had to restrain one who was violently drunk. This was later explained as caused by her brooding on the deceitful way in which she had been recruited (Nishino Rumiko 1992).

In a comfort station in Shantung, China, if a man made a single visit to one woman, the others would refuse service with the words: 'You're Nobuko's client, aren't you?' They are described by the observer as very strict in observing the code. It could, of course, only prevail in the case of small units stationed in one area for a long period, when all members would be recognised, and newcomers easily identified.

In a Navy comfort station in Penang, a former young officer speaks of a 'quasi-love' psychology between women and men, explaining that 'in the single building it was not possible to change the woman whenever visiting—not that the regulations prevented it'. In fact, they encouraged it. Officers could arrange with proprietors to take their women out on social occasions, and they, too, sometimes offered presents. The narrator himself was given a watch, and he always viewed the women as 'fellow human beings, lovers or mother figures. That was where I experienced my youth. Indeed, that was all I had of it.' This seems a common reflection of the generation. This young officer ended the war in the Andaman Islands, ill with malaria, returning home as the only male among 1300 'female paramilitary' (Nishino Rumiko 1992).

Madam X still speaks kindly of some of her clients:

> A number of men became regular customers and in some cases we became good friends. Hamabe-san was a regular who really liked me. He used to bring me chickens and other good food, and he was in tears when he was transferred. Some of the soldiers who gave me an emotional farewell were on one-way *kamikaze* missions.

There are a few records of some special relationships. Korean Sim Mi Ja relates some terrible experiences, but also tells of two men who at different times befriended her over quite long periods (Ito Takashi 1992). One was the commanding officer of the camp where she was first inducted as a comfort woman who, for the first eight months until his transfer, spared her having to service other men. Six years later, at the end of the war, he rediscovered her and paid for her necessary medical treatment. He had meanwhile asked a local *kempeitai* officer to help her. He did something to lighten her daily drudgery by taking her to cafés and on trips to various units scattered across western Japan.

A former artilleryman in Manchuria recalls a Korean comfort woman wishing to become his mistress, since she was afraid she would be sterile and unable to marry in Korea. He became so fond of her that he planned to marry her and work for the South Manchurian Railway Company after the war—on the assumption that Japan would still be in control. His last memory was of her waving from a hill when his unit was transferred. Japan's defeat naturally blighted their further hopes.

Another soldier relates how, when visiting a comfort station on the Manchurian border with another man, a woman picked him out. He had his first experience of sex with her—a common situation—and thought of her as his 'first love'. He would visit only her, bring her presents, and bribe her proprietor to allow him to take her on excursions. 'I felt as if I were making a truly human contact, if only for a short time. When I visited them, I felt as if able to recover human feelings.' (Nishino Rumiko 1992)

These were the feelings that many soldiers were conscious of having lost in the military process of 'bastardisation'. As one puts it (Nishino Rumiko 1992):

> Before going to the war, we were good husbands, good fathers, good brothers. So why did we change so much in the war? The Forces were a prison. In particular, what every new recruit experiences is what is called 'arbitrary discipline'—being beaten day after day. If your lapels are soiled or your boots poorly polished or if your replies or attitude don't appeal to your superiors you get knocked around.

This dehumanising process ranged from all-pervasive, arbitrary abuse, the daily static, to the extreme 'testing of mettle', when soldiers had to execute prisoners by bayonet or sword.

One comfort woman speaking to the Council for the Matter of Comfort Women in Korea recalls an association with a Japanese officer so favourably that she is disposed to excuse the Japanese as a whole, instead blaming the Korean agents who recruited her, and the South Korean government for its long indifference. Known now as 'old lady Kim', she left home despite her parents' objections, in the hope of an easier life.

'Old lady Kim'

Kim was taken by a Korean proprietor couple via Shanghai for a spell of two-and-a-half years at the front. Second Lieutenant Izumi took a fancy to her, called her to his quarters and was able to arrange for her to accompany him wherever he moved. He taught her writing and arithmetic, and in 1940 finally arranged for her safe trip home with four other women. He then wrote to her twice monthly, declaring his love and promising to reunite with her 'after victory'. She wrote back and sent him comfort parcels. Defeat spoiled their plans and, ostracised by her fellow-villagers, she moved to Seoul and became a married man's mistress. She bore a son, who in turn gave her two grandchildren. She never revealed her past, but when the comfort women issue started to be publicised, she raised the matter with her daughter-in-law and niece. They tried to dissuade her from carrying it further, but she insisted. She found it a great relief to unburden her *han*, the constantly recurring Korean word for long-held rancour. Her approach, however, differed from that of the campaigning women's groups. She regards the Japanese government as now responsible only for compensating Japanese comfort women. She contends that the South Korean government should care for its own citizens.

4. The Shanghai Regulations and their variations

Although there is not much documentation on the draconian recruitment methods for the comfort system, there is plenty on the running of comfort stations. As Japanese film maker Yamatani Tetsuo, who made a documentary on comfort women in Okinawa, has pointed out in an article that appeared in *Asahi* Tokyo on 23 January 1992, the Japanese recorded everything. He notes this was partly because comfort stations were regarded by the Japanese as a normal amenity. In the case of United States Forces, by contrast, although they had ample sexual services in areas such as Okinawa, no formal arrangements were made, presumably because public opinion would not acknowledge their need.

The *kempeitai* in Manchuria and China kept registers of photographs of comfort women. The movements of the women were recorded on transport lists in terms of units of 'munitions' or 'canteen supplies', less perhaps from an attempt at concealment than from simple indifference to their humanity, or the absence of a better category. Little, if any, of this material would have reached Japan proper, being mainly intended for security purposes in occupied areas.

Regulations for the operation of the pioneer comfort station near Shanghai indicate the most basic requirements in a simple form, largely because it was operated directly by the Army. These Shanghai Regulations were first published in 1969 by Ito Keiichi, in his *Soldiers' History of the Army*. They represent a prototype. Many similar sets, often much elaborated, appeared later. As is usual in such sets, they are not numbered consecutively, but each is preceded by the number '1' to indicate all are essential. They run:

- Entry to this comfort station is permitted only to Army and paramilitary personnel.

- Visitors must pay at reception and obtain a ticket and condom.
- The ticket fee is ¥2 for NCOs, men and paramilitary.
- The ticket is valid only for this occasion and if not entering a room can be refunded. There is no refund once it has been handed to a hostess.
- On obtaining a ticket, the visitor is to enter the room with the number shown. The time allowed is thirty minutes.
- The hostess is to be handed the ticket on entry.
- Drinking alcohol in the room is prohibited.
- Visitors must leave immediately after their business is completed.
- Any who fail to observe the regulations or who infringe military discipline are to be ejected.
- Contact without the use of a condom is prohibited.
- Entry times: 10 a.m. to 5 p.m. for men, 1 p.m. to 9 p.m. for NCOs.

Subsequent regulations were more complicated because of the general shift to management by private operators, under the general regulation of the Armed Forces. An example of a general directive based on this policy is contained in a magazine article published in 1955 by former Commander Shigemura Minoru, 'The Units Called Special Personnel'. The directive, dated 30 May 1942, is from the Navy Ministry to the Chief of Staff, Southwest Fleet. It concerned the 'Second Dispatch of Special Personnel'. It contains a table listing destinations like Ambon, Makassar, Balikpapan and Surabaya, all in Indonesia, and Penang and Shonan [Singapore] in Malaya. The numbers of personnel for each are listed in two columns headed 'Restaurants' and 'Simple Special Personnel'. The latter are comfort women, while the former would also provide geisha-type service. Administration was generally similar for both categories, being described in terms applied to most enterprises under wartime conditions, as 'officially controlled and privately managed'. Accommodation was to be rented to the operators and, if appropriate, sold to them. Bedding and food were to be provided by the operators but the Fleet could assist where necessary. Hygiene for servicemen was the responsibility of the Fleet, and that for 'paramilitary' the responsibility of operators. The only distinction between categories was that, for 'Simple Special Personnel', the commander of each Force would be in direct contact. Otherwise, this was to be delegated. Fees were to be set at a rate to enable repayment of a contract loan within one year as standard, though this could vary according to circumstances. Special arrangements were to be made for officers and NCOs.

The Okinawa Regulations

The most complete set of regulations framed under such official guidelines, and available in the original Japanese, is that issued by the unit Yama #3475 published in 1990 in the Key Document Series on the Fifteen Years War. This was well before the discovery in January 1992 of officially incriminating documents in the Defence Studies Library by Professor Yoshimi Yoshiaki of Chuo University. Unit Yama #3475 had been part of Ishi Corps, 62nd Division, and the regulations were found in the Okinawa Peace Memorial Library, among the city archives. They have some features reflecting the situation in Okinawa, a variation of regulations framed in occupied areas.

These 'serviceman's club regulations', dated December 1944, start by covering much the same ground as the Shanghai Regulations. There is, however, some elaboration, and they are supplemented by numerous other points, reflecting later experience. The restriction of use to service personnel is amplified by a ban on visiting non-military brothels. A diagram is added to give the form for a permit to visit the club, to be dated and sealed for the Commander, Western Zone Garrison, and distributed by the Orderly Officer. Payment is to be in cash to the operator, with no credit allowed. Fees are ¥3 for officers, ¥2.50 for NCOs and ¥2 for privates, the time allowed being forty minutes for all—which, if adhered to, would make pressure on the women more endurable than in some other places. Time limits were to be strictly observed, and order observed on pain of withdrawal of permission to visit the club.

To the ban on alcohol was added a ban on any meals or parties, though a permit might be obtained for chess or similar games on the premises. There is a specific rule forbidding violence arising from dissatisfaction with the women's service. Condoms were compulsory and hours were privates from 12 noon to 5 p.m., NCOs 5 p.m. to 8 p.m., and officers 8 p.m. to midnight. Times were to be strictly observed, and service given on a first come, first served basis.

Many other provisions were added to these. Service was tax-exempt (in Manchuria a tax exemption slip was issued for each visit).

Medical examinations were held three times a month with a *kempei* in attendance. A form is set out for filling in the results for all the women. Any who were infected or who were not examined were forbidden to work until cured or passed as fit. Any illness was to be reported immediately. Treatment was to be given by local doctors, and the costs met by the operator. The latter was to pay rent, though the unit might help with this or any other issues involving local authorities. The club was closed on the eighth of each month—one of the examination days. A routine order from the same Ishi Corps cautions against causing distress to the women in medical examinations, as someone was reported to have done, staring at their faces and pudenda.

Rules governing the operators forbade undue profiteering or aiding a breach of discipline. They had to guard against espionage and avoid discussion of military matters. Accounts of all transactions were to be kept and made available for inspection. The club would be closed if rules were infringed.

Users of the club had to observe the rule quoted earlier regarding the women as a 'common possession'. They were also to maintain the dignity of servicemen. Lounging around outside the club or acting in any way likely to lose the respect of the local inhabitants were forbidden. The men were to line up for service within the club enclosure, and avoid violence, theft, or damage to the premises. Taking the women out of the club was not allowed, and the women themselves were not to walk outside the enclosure without permission, or enter the barracks or work places.

A few final rules set out details on co-operation between the club and the unit. In principle, the club was to be self-supporting, but the unit could offer help if needed. It could negotiate rental terms, for instance, something normally done through the police. It could provide materials or labour for rebuilding or repairs, but would have to be reimbursed. If there were difficulties with the women's rations or if these were inadequate to maintain health, the unit would help out.

The Nakayama, Toyama and Ch'angchou Regulations

Among documents discovered by Professor Yoshimi are two further sets of regulations on serviceman's clubs, issued by units in the Canton area in 1944. The units are the Nakayama Garrison and the

Toyama Unit. The latter's regulations are described as supplementary to those issued by the former. Both are briefer than the Okinawa regulations, and seem to presuppose some standard procedures.

The Nakayama Regulations again restrict the club's use to servicemen, and require payment in cash, which here meant the currency issued by the Wang Ching Wei regime. (In other occupied areas, a military scrip was in use until the end of the war.) The fee table is complex, since it differentiates by duration of service as well as rank. For thirty minutes, officers, warrant officers and paramilitary were charged 11 yuan, NCOs 9 yuan and privates 6 yuan. For one hour, the rates were respectively 17, 11 and 9 yuan, while for senior officers only, the charge for a stay past midnight was 40 yuan. A curiosity is that each time column is divided into two, headed 'prostitutes' and a synonym for '*geisha*'. The first is left blank, however, and figures entered only under the second. There is no doubt that these referred to comfort women, because there are separate regulations for another club which was purely a restaurant. The explanation for this terminology is probably Chinese influence. The Japanese term synonymous with *geisha* more clearly implies a prostitute in Chinese. If the comfort women here were Chinese, it was probably their preferred term for themselves.

Hours of service were, for privates, 9.30 a.m. to 3.30 p.m., for NCOs 4 to 8 p.m., and for officers 8.30 p.m. onwards 'while operating', which would be some time in the early morning. There are the same rules forbidding parties or admission if drunk or improperly dressed, with the threat of withdrawal of the privilege of attendance for infringements. Women could not be taken out. Anyone observing infringements was to report them. Espionage was to be guarded against. The unit adjutant was responsible for supervision, the paymaster for financial matters, and the medical officers for hygiene.

The Toyama Regulations vary only slightly. The main variation is a uniform hour's duration of service, for which privates were charged ¥8, NCOs ¥10 and personnel residing outside the camp ¥15. These last could also stay the night, for ¥40. The use of yen here may indicate military scrip. There was also a form to be filled in daily, listing each woman, her total takings, the number of clients under officers, NCOs and men, and the number of condoms used.

Another Defence Studies Library document recovered is a set of regulations which formed part of standing orders for units stationed in Ch'angchou, China, in March 1938. The chapter on comfort stations begins by defining their purpose as 'regulating military discipline by devising means of relaxation and comfort'. The days of service were to be rotated among the local units, with the note that temporarily stationed units would be specially serviced. Time was available to NCOs and men from 9 a.m. to 6 p.m., each being allowed an hour.

Here rates differed for ethnic groups: ¥2 for Japanese, ¥1.50 for Koreans and ¥1 for Chinese. Officers, who had separate premises, were charged double. Condoms were to be used, here exceptionally described by a term usually meaning 'gas masks', but meant to sound like officialese rather than slang. (The usual slang term was 'steel-helmets'.) Health inspections were to be held on Mondays and Fridays, from 8 a.m. to 10 a.m. The women were to hold current health certification. The comfort station was closed on the fifteenth of each month. General supervision was the responsibility of the *kempeitai* detachment.

The Manila Regulations

Large numbers of other more fragmentary materials relating to the regulation, control or accommodation of comfort stations have come to light, generally following the patterns established above. A *kempeitai* report on a comfort station in Tacloban in the Philippines, for example, shows charges broken down between 1.50 pesos for privates, 2 for paramilitary and NCOs, 3 for officers, and 5 for a night's stay. The set time was one hour. The nine comfort women and the proprietress were all Filipinas, and sometimes made the rounds to other units.

The most comprehensive set of such regulations available is an English translation of 'Rules for Authorised Restaurants and Houses of Prostitution in Manila', dated 1943, and included in an Allied (mainly United States Army) intelligence report on *Amenities in the Japanese Armed Forces*. The translator had the advantage of possessing the complete original booklet containing the regulations. They were particularly thorough, since Manila was such a major centre, and little disturbed for a large part of the war. The report also includes some shorter sets of regulations applied elsewhere in the Philippines.

In translation, the usual term for comfort station is rendered as 'house of relaxation'. This reasonably conveys the sense of the Japanese term, though it has not been adopted elsewhere. Terms for comfort women are rendered either as '*geisha*' or 'prostitutes'. A complex procedure is laid down for setting up a house, which was probably general, but is not spelt out elsewhere. The operator had to be a Japanese national (which would include Koreans and Taiwanese), with business experience. An application had to be submitted, together with a statement of business plans, an affidavit accepting the Army's authority and a personal history, each in three copies. Upon receiving permission, the applicant was to submit three copies of the personnel list, one copy each of personal histories, and three copies of applications for authorisation of the 'hostesses'. Similar procedures were followed for any changes of staff. Operators needed permission to close or suspend business. Conversely, the military authorities could stop the business, although in some circumstances compensation could be applied for.

The women could be re-hired at the expiry of their contracts. There was also a form for applying for permission to leave an establishment. In the case of misconduct, their 'right to practise' would be withdrawn. They were also to be repatriated if medically unfit to continue. Minors were not to be employed.

Half the takings were to go to the operators, who were responsible for daily living costs, while the women were responsible for clothes and beauty aids. They were encouraged to save but only to a limit of ¥30 a month. Their savings were to be recorded in regular business reports. Costs of work-related illness were to be halved between the woman and the proprietor, except that, if a medical officer certified that illness was due to overwork, the proprietor would bear 70 per cent of the cost. Responsibilities for health precautions were spelled out, including the provision of 2000 strength potassium permanganate solution or 0.5 cresol soap solution. The hostesses were to 'wash and disinfect the necessary portions of the house weekly'. Intercourse during menstruation was forbidden. Baths were to be taken daily and bedding kept strictly clean. There were the usual provisions for maintaining order, with a ban on 'violence or unreasonable demands'. Kissing hostesses was banned.

The Manila booklet contained fourteen forms covering the various procedures. Prices differed between Filipinas and Japanese (then including Koreans and Taiwanese), the former receiving pesos 1.50 for privates and pesos 2.50 for NCOs for forty minutes, and for the higher ranks, pesos 4 for one hour and pesos 8 for an overnight stay.

The Japanese received, respectively, pesos 2, 3, 5 and 10. Both daily and monthly business reports were required, as well as medical reports.

Also included in the United States Army report is a police report, dated 7 February 1944, on twenty-five clubs, mainly comfort stations but including some restaurants, circulated by the Manila Sector Line of Communications to operators, as a warning to improve their standards. Although some clubs were reported as satisfactory, it was felt necessary to point out that:

> Scant attention has been paid to hygienic rules and there are many cases of failure to take hygienic measures . . . Many managers are interested in nothing but their own profit and do their job with no other purpose. They exhibit no concern for the welfare of the *geisha*, maids or hostesses, nor bother themselves with their health or sustenance nor with such matters as bath facilities. Their selfish conduct requires restraint.

Out of 1183 women examined, 69 were found to be ill, though the illnesses are not specified.

It is clear in this example that despite the care devoted to the health regulations, practice rarely met required standards. The same doubtless applied to other aspects of the regulations. They were framed with some sort of regard to fairness or even humanity, since the set hours would have limited the women's work load. At the same time, such provisions as length of service and banning alcohol and violence suggest the sort of hardships which the women would face, and tend to confirm the horrendous experiences recounted by the comfort women themselves.

Above all, the regulations demonstrate how well integrated the women were with the Armed Forces, and how every kind of activity was subjected to the totalitarian 'national defence state'. Despite the acceptance of the need for comfort women to satisfy brute human needs, there is recurrent concern for decorum. In the Ishi Corps routine order, both troops and women are cautioned against public behaviour offensive to local people. Although the women could ride in Army vehicles to visit the island capital, Naha, they were not allowed to sit beside the driver. There was a delicate psychological balancing act involved. Even if soldiers needed the comfort of a sexual 'oasis' to ward off explosions of repressed tension, this form of relaxation could also lead to punishment.

Money matters

Differentiation in fees by ranks and nationalities did not reflect any great distinction in the nature of the services provided, because in comfort stations shared by all ranks the times allowed were much the same, at least according to the regulations. Much more significantly, they reflect the intense Japanese concern with hierarchy. This had developed historically, from Japan's distinctive interaction of Confucianism with feudalism. It proved highly durable, surviving the dramatic social changes of modern times.

One of the most frequent formulae used in declaring Japan's war aims was 'enabling each nation to obtain its proper place'. The different fees for different ethnic groups reflect this. The same applied to individuals within society, so that there were different fees for different ranks. Of course, when different ranks used the same facilities, they had to be segregated by time bands—men first, NCOs second and then the officers, with much more flexible hours, coming last.

The 1992 Kyoto phone-in survey of the comfort system gives the widest range of information on fees charged, including some cases where these are differentiated both for ranks, and for the nationalities of the women. The distinction seems to have been general, though most of the Kyoto callers only remembered the fees they themselves had paid or heard about. With regard to rank differentiation, the charges for officers, NCOs and privates, given by callers, varied: ¥2, ¥1.50, ¥1; ¥1.20, ¥0.80, ¥0.50; ¥1.50, ¥1, ¥0.80. For Japanese and Koreans respectively, charges cited were ¥1.70 to ¥1.50, and ¥1.20 to ¥0.80, while in one case both Japanese and Koreans cost ¥1.70, against ¥1.50 for Chinese.

In twenty-two cases local currency is mentioned, in the case of China the yuan, with one mention of 20 bahts; otherwise, currencies are unspecified. There are three cases given as 'free' or 'paid by the Army', six with Army tickets, and one a packet of cigarettes.

Given that the ordinary soldier's pay was ¥15 a month, the comfort women's earnings were in theory fairly high for the time. A former medical officer in Manchuria recalls that in his time there the comfort women were being paid the uniform wage of ¥800 a month. But whatever the regulations said, and however much their earnings could be in theory, the reality was that virtually all the money earned or saved by comfort women was lost. In some cases, they were expected to pay for their upkeep out of their earnings. The comfort station operators generally charged exploitative rates for essential supplies such as soap or clothing, if they did not rob the women outright of their tips and earnings. It was not difficult to cheat them, since many were illiterate or too broken by continuous rape to take a commercial attitude to the experience. Accounts were also kept mostly by the operators, and slips of paper easily lost or misplaced.

If the women were in the frontline or part of a campaign operation, there was little they could buy with their earnings, especially as they were often in military scrip, which became valueless at the end of the war. There were also cases of comfort women who received no payment of any kind. Some of those who were paid did save what they earned, and some were even able to remit the cash to their families. Others deposited the cash in a military savings bank. This was often confiscated, as in the case of Mun Ok Ju.

Ok Ju had not only remitted money to her family in Korea, but also deposited some of her earnings in a field post office. After the war, she found it difficult to get back to Japan to claim her savings. In 1991 while helping to prepare for the comfort women's lawsuit against the Japanese government, she checked on the fate of her deposits, in case this could strengthen her claim on the Japanese government. The records were traced to the relevant office in Kumamoto in Kyushu. They showed she had deposited, under the name of Fumihara Ok Ju, a total of ¥26,145, from June 1943 to September 1945. Interest brought her total credit to ¥50,108 by March 1965, when the account was closed in accordance with the Japan—South Korea Basic Treaty on Claims and Economic Aid. Under this, South Korea agreed that all claims on Japan by its citizens were settled by Japan's advance of $500 million in grants and soft loans.

Madam X says of her pay:

> The mama-san also took half of all the money we earned. The officers paid us the most. They had three stars and they came at night and paid us $4 [Straits dollars]—half for mama-san. In the beginning we were paid in the white man's money, but later we got more and more Japanese money, which at the end of the war became worthless. Some of the girls had savings of over ¥2000, but they lost the lot. Fortunately I had some Straits dollars as well as yen. We were paid first in chips or tickets, which we cashed at the end of the month. I never received any tips but at least in the

Tai Sun Hotel I was paid. In the first two places I was not paid at all. The ordinary soldiers were only allowed to stay one hour and had to pay $2 or ¥2. Some of them gave me jewellery, which they had stolen when they looted houses. Unfortunately I had to sell all the jewellery after the war in order to live because most of my savings were worthless.

Staying healthy

Health problems represented the most widespread hardship for comfort women throughout the occupied areas. Although standards of troops' behaviour towards them might vary, disease everywhere presented intractable problems—even when the authorities were disposed to offer treatment, rather than regard the women as disposable items.

The threat of disease was inherent in the women's occupation. Disease control was, after all, the most pressing motive for the setting up of the comfort system itself. Added to this were the health problems experienced by armies everywhere, and inevitable among large concentrations of men under improvised living conditions. As communications broke down during the later part of the war, malnutrition spread. Beri-beri was rife. Medical supplies grew more scarce and more likely to be reserved for personnel on combat duty. The tropics added a further range of diseases to those known in temperate zones, and the messages from the south requesting reinforcements of comfort women are an ominous indication of this. In the colder northern areas, on the other hand, tuberculosis was prominent as a cause of death.

For venereal disease, prophylaxis was standard procedure. Soldiers were issued with condoms, both at the unit when going on leave in case they were tempted to unauthorised sexual activity, and at the comfort stations. They were told to assume that every sex partner was infected. Said Madam X: 'Many but not all of the men used condoms. The condoms in those days were thick and crude, and some men refused to wear them.' Sometimes when the men were more than willing to use a condom, there were none available. Some comfort women reported the repulsive duty of washing and recycling used condoms. In each woman's room was generally installed a container of permanganic acid solution with a rubber tube for the men to wash their genitals after intercourse. The women were also expected to douche after each contact, though at rush hour the best they could do was wipe their pudenda with a pad of impregnated cotton wool. In some cases they used salt water, which was said to become clouded if they were infected with syphilis. They were also often injected with salvarsan or terramycin, either as a prophylactic or as treatment. The latter is usually referred to as '606' and is blamed to some extent for the sterility which later affected many comfort women. Damage to the reproductive system due to their work was also a factor in this. Lectures to the women on hygiene was a preventive measure.

The authorities for their part did everything possible to discourage the men from exposing themselves to the risk of infection. There were monthly inspections of the kind called 'short-arm parades' in some English-speaking armies, and severe penalties awaited any found to be infected. Such measures are avoided in some armies as likely to lead to concealment, but the Japanese Forces always leaned in the direction of severity. Venereal disease was described as a Class Three case, after wounds and other disorders, and penalties generally included a drop in rank, even for the unit commanding officer, if suspected of laxity in discipline or precautions. There might be spells of confinement in the guard-house or even beatings in the hospital for men with a long history of venereal disease. The island of Ch'ungming on the Yangtze was used for isolating serious cases, recalling the legend among Allied troops in Southeast Asia that there was an island where sufferers of the quickly fatal 'black pox' were sent to die. As often happened, some officers were able to evade penalties, and at a hospital in Surabaya in Java, were treated for venereal disease concealed under false names.

In the case of the women, infection would usually be detected in the periodical medical examinations. These varied in their efficiency, sometimes being conducted by medical officers with gynaecological backgrounds, but often by those less qualified. Sometimes these were medical orderlies who were only equipped to make a visual check for discolouration or pus. There are reports of women pleading to be passed as fit, rather than lose time in paying off their debts; in any case, inflammation would eventually make work impossible. Women found to be infected would be named in evening roll-call or daily routine orders. They would then become statistics in a highly-organised system of health reports.

A number of these reports survive among the recovered Defence Studies Library documents. They give the percentages of comfort women infected in units under the 21st Army in Canton. The figures are: 28 per cent among 159, 1 per cent among 223, 10 per cent among 192, 4 per cent among 122, 2 per cent among 41, and nil among 180. In a summary report prepared by the Medical Officer's branch of the 15th Division for January 1943, a breakdown is made between Japanese, Koreans and Chinese. The centres covered were Nanking, Wuhu, Chit'an and Chenchiang in China. Japanese totalled 1095, mainly in Nanking, of whom 20 'failed the inspection'. Koreans totalled 198, also mainly in Nanking, of whom 9 'failed'. Chinese totalled 820, outnumbering the others outside Nanking, and probably locally recruited, the number 'failing' being 55—perhaps because less effectively supervised.

There is also a report by a naval medical officer in China giving monthly figures from May to November for an unspecified year. For May, 4 women were reported as being treated in hospital out of 283 examined; for June 10 out of 328; for July, 24 out of 365; for August, 9 out of 380; for September, 6 out of 342; for October 10 out of 352, and for November 2 out of 228.

Another Defence Studies Library document was a report on hygiene made by the Government-General in Hong Kong, and dated 1942. In addition to cholera and beri-beri, the report noted that venereal disease was spreading, and that plans were being made to concentrate all comfort station operators in one area, for better control. The area chosen was in Wan Chai, which had been taken over entirely as a residential area for Japanese.

Treatment of the women for venereal disease was the basic policy, and seems to have been general in stable areas. There are, however, references to women being allowed to die untreated, or abandoned or even killed. According to one story, a woman was shot through the vagina. Where treatment was not given, folk remedies were sometimes tried, such as concoctions of garlic, dandelion or obscure local herbs. Conditions of formal treatment, where given, varied between military and civilian hospitals, North China railway hospitals, or free clinics for all types of prostitutes in Manchuria. When the women had to pay for treatment, this would consume much of their earnings. If they were on a loan contract, the amount would be added to their loan, which seems to have been the practice in the Japanese licensed brothel system.

Some types of disorders were unresponsive to treatment. These included endometritis or vaginitis. Treatment was attempted with potassium permanganate wash. Urethritis was very common, though generally curable by a week's rest, which was generally allowed. Even then some women would wish to return to work earlier, for the sake of earnings or remittances home. The Manila Regulations indicate that medical officers could diagnose whether illness was due to overwork, in which case the proprietor had to bear most of the cost of treatment. Staff could also be suspended or dismissed for acting improperly or breaking regulations. There is occasional mention of seriously ill women being allowed to return home, such as one who suffered from opium addiction and prolapse of the uterus. In her case a special *kempeitai* permit is mentioned as required.

Catching a disease was not the worst thing that could happen to many of the women; pregnancy was. Their reaction was often of horror, and suicide was not unheard of. Certain savvy mama-sans prevented such a possibility by dosing the women with herbal concoctions, while others forced pregnant girls to abort using pills. There are also accounts of women carrying their babies to term, while presumably continuing to service the men. Other women were operated on to 'stop menstruation', so presumably they were sterilised. Many of the women in any case later became sterile from a combination of disease and trauma to their reproductive systems.

Says Madam X:

> Fortunately, I never got VD. One of the girls did and I heard that she was taken away and beaten to death. The rest of us remained quite healthy. Given our hectic sex life, I don't understand how we remained healthy. Maybe we were just a bunch of young country girls living off our youth.

This influential photograph of comfort women crossing the Yellow River prompted Senda Kako's pathbreaking investigations. *(Dong-A Daily)*

Madam X in 1943 aged seventeen. This photo was taken by the Japanese and displayed in the Tai Sun comfort station along with those of the other comfort girls. This is probably the only such photograph to have survived.

A 1938 view of the first Army-run comfort station in the Shanghai suburbs. *(Dong-A Daily)*

Front entrance to the Army comfort station in Shanghai. The characters on the right read 'Welcome to Warriors for Victory in the Sacred War', while those on the left read 'Service by Japanese dianthi offering both body and heart'. *(Dong-A Daily)*

Regulations posted at the first regular Army-run comfort station in the Shanghai suburbs. *(Dong-A Daily)*

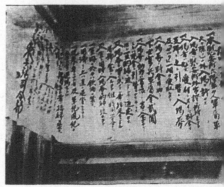

Soldiers lining up for service at a comfort station in Hankow, China.
(Joong Ang Daily)

Draftees to the Women's Voluntary Service Corps, some of whom
were sent to comfort stations. *(Dong-A Daily)*

Korean girls in the Women's Voluntary Service Corps marching between their dormitories and the factories, Nagoya, Japan. (*Dong-A Daily*)

Lee Jong Sook (Yi Chung-suk), a former comfort woman, when she was a twelve-year-old elementary schoolgirl. (*Joong-Ang Daily*)

Korean members of the Women's Voluntary Service Corps and their Japanese supervisor at a Mitsubishi war factory. (*Dong-A Daily*)

Comfort stations and surrounding area in Iloilo, Panay Island, Philippines.

This building was the Tai Sun Hotel in Kuala Lumpur, Malaya, where Madam X was kept from 1943–45. *(George Hicks)*

During the war this hotel was the Hinomaru comfort station in Semarang, Java. *(Utsumi Eiko)*

(ABOVE) Korean comfort women being interrogated by Allied Intelligence Myitkyina, North Burma, 14 August 1944. *(Dong-A Daily)*. (BELOW) American troops with comfort women in Okinawa. *(photographer unkno*

(ABOVE LEFT) Professor Yun Chung Ok, the pioneer investigator and activist. *(photographer unknown)*. (ABOVE RIGHT) Kim Hak Sun, the first comfort woman to come forward publicly, at the opening meeting of the Sisters of Hibiscus. *(photographer unknown)*

(BELOW LEFT) Yoshida Seiji, the Japanese official and author of *My War Crimes* in 1992. *(photographer unknown)*. (BELOW RIGHT) Professor Lee Hyo Jae, a leading Korean activist. *(photographer unknown)*

(TOP, FACING PAGE) The first three comfort women plaintiffs at the filing of the lawsuit in Tokyo, 6 December 1991. *(Dong-A Daily).* (BOTTOM, FACING PAGE) The two named Korean plaintiffs with comfort women activists in 1992. From left to right: Noh Chong Ja (plaintiff), Sim Mi Ja (plaintiff), Hwang Kum Ju and Kim Pok Tong. *(photographer unknown).* (ABOVE) Former comfort women demonstrate weekly in front of the Japanese Embassy in Seoul, Korea. *(photographer unknown)*

A 1992 Buddhist ceremony to console the spirits of dead comfort women. *(photographer unknown)*

5. The Empire of the Sun

If comfort stations were to be found wherever the Japanese flag flew during the war in Korea, Manchuria and China and far beyond, they were also found in Japan. The comfort system for the most part followed closely on the heels of the troops, and the progress of the war reveals the trail of the comfort women. Meanwhile, what was going on at home?

Japan

The presence of licensed prostitution with its established system of health precautions and maintenance of order, limited the role of comfort stations in the Homeland. Besides, as the war expanded, the bulk of men in need of comfort were away with the Armed Forces fighting in foreign lands. For the few without access to licensed facilities, a number of stations were established, often involving Korean women. By the time war broke out, there was already a long-established practice of getting Korean women to serve Korean labourers in Hokkaido development projects and Kyushu mines. Many of the civilian prostitutes in Hokkaido were reported to have been recruited by deception, which led to some suicides. This was the not-unknown phenomenon of 'white slavery', in early post-war years a term sometimes used to describe the Japanese military comfort system, as something of its workings were becoming known.

An intermediate case between the civilian and military systems emerged from documents found in the Hokkaido Development Memorial Institute at the same time as Professor Yoshimi's discovery of official documents linking the military to the comfort system in the Defence Studies Library. These were entitled 'Draft Guideline for Coolie Supervision', and were issued by the War Ministry in March 1940. They authorised operators to recruit Chinese and Korean women as part of 'welfare facilities' for Chinese drafted labour in Hokkaido, 'in consideration of their sexual needs'.

In Japan there are two houses still standing identified as having served as comfort stations. One is in Kashiwa, a country town east of Tokyo. Not a great deal is known about it, but it was pointed out to one of Professor Yun Chung Ok's women activists, Yang Ching Ja, by a local Korean resident who had been seized for labour draft in 1940, 'while shopping'. He saw the house in 1947 after it had been used as a comfort station by the local air base and *kempeitai*. Only later did he realise it might have contained Koreans, when he visited his family in 1964 and heard that a relative's daughter had been taken for the Voluntary Service Corps, but had never returned. He attempted to trace her, but was unsuccessful.

The second identified comfort station is associated with a much more notorious project, the construction of a vast underground bunker at Matsushiro in the central mountainous region near Mount Fuji. This was designed to accommodate the Emperor's household and central organs of government in the event of last-ditch resistance in the Japanese homeland. This contemplated last phase of the war was, with the usual optimism preserved to the very end in official terminology, described as the 'decisive battle for the Homeland'. This implied it would be so costly to the enemy that some form of compromise peace settlement would be reached, short of the 'unconditional surrender' demanded by the Allies.

Construction of the bunker went on from November 1944 until the eve of surrender in August 1945, when it was virtually completed. The immense task was mainly carried out by the Nishimatsu-gumi construction company, under Army supervision, with draft Korean labour under relentless pressure. One of the supervising engineers was a Korean, Kim Sok Ji. He is said to have been employed in this capacity only because his origin was not recognised, since he was an engineering graduate from Osaka and used the Japanese surname Mihara.

According to him, the bunker was built by 7000 Korean labourers housed in 152 barracks. There were deaths daily, as might be expected from intensive tunnelling with little attention paid to proper safety precautions. Total losses from all causes are estimated at 1000. There are later rumours that those who excavated the Emperor's own quarters were killed to preserve secrecy. At the end of the war, the breakdown of social restraints was demonstrated by the local villagers' wholesale plunder of the bunker's luxurious fittings.

The bunker's comfort station was housed in a refitted silkworm workshop rented by the police from its owner. He was told that a 'recreation room' was needed to avert molestation of local women by Korean labourers. The owner thought this term implied a 'good-quality' facility. It turned out to be a comfort station used not so much by Koreans but by the Army officers supervising the construction. Paid ¥100 a month rent, the owner describes the clients' behaviour as boisterous, leading to broken windows.

The proprietor was a Korean known as Haruyama, who brought four women from his homeland. They were joined by six more Koreans from northern Japan. The women never left the house, all their errands being attended to by a bouncer.

The whole question of Matsushiro and its significance has been publicised in recent years, by Yamane Masako, the half-Japanese daughter of one of the Koreans conscripted to work on the project. She remained in Japan when her parents moved to North Korea. Her exposures of the project fused with the Korean residents' finger-print boycott movement, protesting against official Japanese treatment of long-resident Koreans as aliens.

Professor Yun Chung Ok visited the bunker's former comfort station, and pressed for its preservation as a symbol of patriarchy and colonialism in their darkest manifestations.

Another reference to comfort stations in the last phase of the war comes from the reminiscences of a *kempei* who used comfort women as spies to obtain inside information on the morale and general conditions of troops in the Ninety-nine League Beach area on the eastern Pacific coast. This was with a view to making a realistic estimate of the prospects for the 'decisive battle for the Homeland'. There were three comfort stations in the area, housing sixty women, most being Japanese from the north, with some Koreans. Eight of them were selected on the basis of the usual meticulous records on their registers: character, health, family members, home environment, education, father's occupation, reason for family debt, level of literacy, and ability to keep secrets. The *kempei* obtained their co-operation as well as that of the proprietors, by offering to pay off their debts. He maintained contact by visiting them in the guise of a client and, in return for sound information, which he deemed to have found useful, paid them ¥50 instead of the usual ¥2–3 fee. He adds that the Army usually provided mending services and fixed price goods (that is, not black market prices) for comfort stations in Japan. The women had to prostrate themselves during visits by the orderly officer, though this gesture was a normal one for highly honoured guests. The officer then goes on record as favouring compensation for comfort women at something over service pensions.

Another identified site in Japan, although without remains, is at Yanagimoto in the Nara area. It was associated with a naval airfield built by 3000 Korean labourers, between 1943 and 1944. It consisted of two houses, with twenty Korean women in each. Surviving transport records only record them as munitions. The main source of information about this station is a former Korean airfield employee. When the women were abandoned at the end of the war and locked in, they were rescued by local people. He helped three, who stayed at his home until one died of fever and the other two could be returned to Korea. Their story was included in a history of Koreans in Nara, *Nara Zainichi Chòsenjin Shi*, published by Japanese writer Kawase Shunji (Yun Chung-mo 1992).

The remaining identified site in Japan is at the Kisarazu Navy Air Arsenal, on the east side of Tokyo Bay. The location is called the Six-house Quarter, since it was developed by the establishment of its six comfort stations. The original plan called for fifteen, and in 1942 this number of operators was selected out of sixty applicants. Finally, however, only six Kisarazu houses were built, apart from three others for officers. They were largely staffed by Koreans recruited on the pretence of work in a canning factory at Choshi on the nearby Pacific coast. There were seven women in each house, handling about 100 men a day, the fee being ¥3 an hour and ¥7 a night. Three of the proprietors were women. The Navy held weekly medical checks, and provided all supplies.

In the last two years of the war, most civilian brothels as well as other similar recreation facilities were closed in order to divert all possible labour and resources to the war effort. In 1944 the number of such establishments in Tokyo was reduced from 8500 to about 550. A rather larger number was relocated or converted to serve draft labourers in war industries. Some were also retained as comfort stations for the Armed Forces, as indicated in the field diary of a torpedo boat unit in Kushiro in Hokkaido, where six brothels in the town were designated for Navy use, and the staff instructed on hygiene. At the end of the war the Kisarazu houses continued to function until the entry of the Occupation force, when a United States officer requested the mayor and the head of the Female Entertainers' Union to supply thirty women for the use of Occupation troops. At this stage, however, most women were still terrified of the Occupation troops, and the inmates of the comfort stations fled, leaving only the ordinary waterside prostitutes for the Americans.

The Ryukyu and Bonin Islands

Although the Ryukyu Islands to the south of the Japanese mainland are constitutionally part of Japan proper, there is a strong sense of distinctiveness from the rest of Japan. This results from the Ryukyu's long early history as an active maritime kingdom; its vernacular language, quite unintelligible to other Japanese; its tropical climate; and its distinctive mores. It is sometimes described as a 'quasi-external territory' and the islanders are often not regarded as 'real' Japanese. The Ryukyu Islands are in a strategic position on the southern approach to the Japanese mainland. As such, they had a disproportionate concentration of troops during the war, numbering some 108 500 men. About 500 miles from Japan, the heavily fortified island of Okinawa in the Ryukyu chain was the scene of horrific fighting in April 1945, as the Japanese Army waged a last-ditch battle supported by *kamikaze* pilots and the Navy's Special Attack boat unit. These human torpedoes were the equivalent of the *kamikaze* pilots whose desperate suicide missions in the last phase of the war became the stuff of Japanese wartime legend.

According to Kim Il Myon, the women in the traditional brothel community in the Tsuji quarter of Naha, the capital city on Okinawa, refused to volunteer as comfort women. They claimed to be accustomed to serving only a couple of clients a day, and to lack the stamina for more. They also did not trust the Japanese to pay, in view of their habitual discriminatory attitudes. The Okinawans evaded attempts at draft by a fake form of marriage, or medical certificates of unfitness. Even their proprietors demonstrated the customary islanders' solidarity by releasing them from their debts, or allowing postponed repayment.

The higher class of entertainers, equivalent to the *geisha*, called *zuri*, had never been available for promiscuous sexual service. A Special Services sergeant-major once made a speech to some of them, trying to shame them into providing comfort for the men who, it was said, were there for the sole purpose of defending the island. The islanders remained unimpressed. The authorities did not dare use force, since they could not risk alienating the population in such a strategic area.

A report indicates that some women from the Tsuji quarter agreed to serve the Navy's Special Attack boat unit, possibly because of the special emotions that their suicide missions aroused. Otherwise, comfort stations on the Ryukyu islands were staffed by Koreans, who were kept with the troops to face the all-out American onslaught, even though efforts were made to evacuate some of the local female population to Kyushu, the nearest main Japanese island.

Okinawa is noteworthy in that there are in its military documents a number of references to the construction of comfort stations, or the conversion of existing buildings for this purpose. One neat pair of plans of a house before and after conversion shows the subdivision of six rooms into eleven, giving a vivid visual picture of the cramped quarters often mentioned in other documentary sources.

The remote Bonin Islands are found to the southeast of Japan proper. During the war they had a troop strength of some 17 700 soldiers and officers. Even on these remote islands, there is a mention of a comfort station. They had been settled from the Japanese mainland and were administered direct from Tokyo, so the comfort women were also supplied direct from the Tokyo red light districts of Suzaki and Yoshiwara. The Chichijima Garrison Headquarters Field Diary records two messages received from Eastern Army Headquarters Staff in May 1942, indicating that ten women from each of the two districts, as arranged by their proprietors, were to sail on the fifteenth with ten ancillary staff. It was further requested that the proprietors be given assistance regarding the 'recreation centre'.

Taiwan

The island of Formosa, as Taiwan was then known, was one of Japan's earliest acquisitions. It had been ceded by China in 1895, after the Sino-Japanese War. Assimilationist policies at the beginning of the twentieth century meant that Taiwanese, like Koreans, were classified as Japanese. Also like the Koreans, many Taiwanese were enlisted in the Japanese Army, and were part of the invasion troops. Some proved their worth as interpreters between the Japanese and the southern Chinese in places like Malaya and Singapore, which also had a substantial community of migrants from the same part of China as the Taiwanese Chinese.

Taiwan came to serve as a kind of field headquarters for the planning of invasions of the south. Although there were some 155,300 troops on the island, material on the workings of the comfort system is very limited. What is available relates to the recruitment of women for service elsewhere, rather than to conditions in Taiwan itself. A few sources taken together illustrate the general picture. A couple of these are collections of sketches, still preserved.

One series depicts field hospital life in southern Taiwan from 1944. This was drawn by a former medical orderly, on Army postcards. Ten out of a total of sixty-five portray comfort women. Some carry captions such as 'battle of Amazons and medical orderlies' and depict the weekly inspections, held in a tent, when 200 women were examined in three hours. According to the artist, those found to be suffering from disease were simply dismissed. Most were Koreans, with some Chinese, and their ages ranged from fourteen to eighteen. They were expected to handle up to thirty men a day. Some forty to fifty women were reserved for officers, and were inspected with special care.

Yi Ok Bun

Yi Ok Bun, who was later known as Yi Ki Bun, was an unusual comfort woman in coming from a well-to-do family near Taegu. Her father was not only a landlord but also a legal official in the city. Lured away by two men when she was twelve years old, Ki Bun was taken with a group of girls by warship to Takao (Kaohsiung) in Taiwan. Given her young age, she was made to do the cleaning and other chores in what appeared to be a comfort station. Some of the women wore Japanese costumes and red lipstick. Not long afterwards, she escaped, and made her way to a police station to get help. Enquiries at her home address elicited, however, the reply that her identity could not be traced. It transpired that her mother had taken fright on seeing the Japanese policeman who had gone to make enquiries about her, and then denied any knowledge of Ki Bun. When word got back to Takao, Ki Bun was then taken in by the Japanese officer, Fujimoto, who had tried to help her establish her identity. In exchange for board and lodging, she had to look

after his children as well as do the household chores. She stayed in
the Fujimoto household for five years, until the bombing of Taiwan began. Then Fujimoto sent his family back to Japan. Ki Bun
was reclaimed by the Army, and taken to a comfort station serving
a hilltop unit. At eighteen, she was the youngest of the forty Korean women there, the oldest being twenty-four. In the comfort
station she was renamed Haruko, the name the Fujimotos had
called her.

Ki Bun was only required at weekends at the comfort station
which was housed in a school near the foothills outside Takao.
During the week, she spent her time at the Army unit, where her
job was to cut grass to burn as smoke-screens to obscure bombing
targets in the area. The comfort station itself was managed by a
married couple, the man wearing a military uniform without rank
insignia. The couple collected the clients' tickets as they entered
and cashed them weekly at the Army unit office. The women
were, however, never paid, receiving only food and clothing. They
had to handle twenty to thirty men a day, sometimes more. They
were never allowed to leave the comfort station by themselves,
and any who tried to escape were severely beaten by the manager.

Ki Bun was among a privileged group generally reserved for officers. Their visits were more infrequent and leisurely. They generally treated her better, granting favours she asked and sometimes
taking her to the theatre. This was due partly to her better knowledge of Japanese, acquired from her years in school, which perhaps
also contributed to her survival, fatal illnesses often occurring
among the other women. She relates that those infected with venereal disease were neglected and untreated. Some of her contacts
were the *kamikaze* pilots, and she recalls joining in singing songs
about them, and playing records. Some of these pilots were Korean,
and were most interested in talking about their homeland. Others
were Taiwanese servicemen. She gathered that there were about
7000 comfort women in Taiwan.

On hearing the Emperor's surrender broadcast in August 1945,
the proprietor-couple abandoned the women. Ki Bun herself soon
left, disguised as a Chinese. She had learned enough of the local
language to obtain casual work singing and dancing in bars. She did
not, however, stay too long in one place, to avoid detection. Once
at a bar she was given a circular in Hangul, the Korean phonetic
script, summoning all Koreans in the area to a meeting to consider
safety measures, since many had been attacked and killed by Taiwanese. Something like 1000 attended the meeting at a hilltop
shrine. All the speakers could only suggest, however, that they
should co-operate in devising means to return to Korea. The meet-

ing developed into something like a festive occasion, until dispersed by violent Taiwanese.

Ki Bun continued to work in bars, moving to Taipei and Changhua, in the company of two other women. One was a Korean called Tokiko, and the other was a Chinese. When trouble threatened, they would hide. One day, on tracing the length of a tunnel they had found, they emerged at the sea. As luck would have it, they encountered a cargo ship flying the traditional Korean flag, eventually adopted by South Korea. The ship was taking home Korean prisoners captured on Okinawa. Ki Bun and Tokiko were taken aboard. On the four-day voyage, Ki Bun won a gold ring in a singing contest.

When she arrived back in Korea, she found her father dead and her mother living with her brother. She had changed so much in ten years that she could only convince them of her identity by showing them a mole on her neck. Her friend Tokiko married, but was unable to have children. Ki Bun decided not to marry because, although she told her family she had been doing factory work, she felt she could not lie to a husband in this way.

She first worked in a market in Pusan, then ran a small cafe, until her health failed. She has become one of the women plaintiffs in the Tokyo lawsuit begun in 1991.

All corners of the Empire

Like the Koreans, Taiwanese comfort women also ended up in distant places. Seventy-three were reportedly sent to Sarawak in Borneo, and 253 to Rabaul. One unnamed comfort woman from Taiwan, at the International Public Hearing in Tokyo in December 1992, gave a reasonably detailed account of her experience as a comfort woman on Timor. She had been a nurse, and along with ten other girls had accepted what they thought was a nursing job. 'During the first week, a military surgeon came to examine whether the girls were virgins. All of us were. Then the commander, a very fat man, about forty years old, raped us one by one.' After being deflowered, she was then made to serve the other soldiers in the afternoons. The girls were assigned by a lottery of tickets given out to the men, who were then taken to a Navy comfort station to look for the girls who matched the drawn numbers.

The Pacific islands

The Caroline and Marshall Islands were a strategic inheritance from World War I, when Japan had fought on the side of the British against Germany. The Japanese had a League of Nations mandate to administer these islands, but not to fortify them. When they were fortified, they were an excellent defence against American attack on the Philippines, or even an advance on Japan itself. Except for Guam and some marginal islands which were quickly captured at the outset of the war, Micronesia, as the little island groups are known as a whole, had been administered by the Navy. They were subsequently fortified by it as part of its political contest with the Army, in the long-term controversy over whether to give priority to continental or maritime expansionism. Although the Navy was outwitted during the earlier years of conflict in China, it came to the fore after Pearl Harbour. Both its forces and comfort stations multiplied. The troop strength on the islands was then some 140,000.

Truk in the Carolines group was the principal naval base, holding about 300 comfort women, augmented by those rejected by the Marshall Islands. It also served as a transit centre for those bound further south. There were separate comfort stations for Army and Navy, with the latter having different facilities for officers and ratings. The Navy houses were usually staffed from Yokosuka, the oldest of Japan's modern naval stations, situated in Tokyo Bay. The clientele was distinctive. It consisted largely of young airmen hastily trained in large numbers as the war crisis developed at a faster pace than strategic planning had anticipated. These youngsters, on arrival, were encouraged by their seniors to use the comfort facilities, on the basis that sex would build up their morale.

Some of the more dedicated were reported as less than enthusiastic at such an aid to their patriotism. Most, however, welcomed it, since in many cases it was their first sexual experience. For their part, the women were taken aback by the men's innocence and gentleness, in contrast with the more usual hardened customer. As the number of fatal missions increased the women came to refer to the men, sadly, as 'one-way dragonflies'. They would sometimes make paper tablets to commemorate them, a different kind of tribute from that paid at the Yasukuni shrine to the war dead. There was a branch shrine on Truk. At the main Buddhist temple, memorial prayers were offered.

The women's other clients were the usual throng that would flood in whenever ships docked. The women could gauge the progress of the war from the steady diminution of airmen among their clients, despite official bulletins claiming unbroken victories. Their only consolation, ultimately in most cases a hollow one, was the financial generosity of men who doubted that they had long to live to spend their money. Even if they did live, there was little to buy on these scattered islands.

On Tinian Island there were sixty Japanese comfort women, housed in three-mat-sized rooms, in three barrack buildings. Here they had every Sunday off. Officers were rostered on Tuesdays, Thursdays and Saturdays, and men on Mondays, Wednesdays and Fridays. Within each shift it was the custom to draw lots to determine the order of service. The women also attended officers' parties at night. They had all been engaged on the standard one-year contract, but were killed with the rest of the garrison at the end of the Pacific War.

In the Mariana Islands, which included heavily fortified Saipan, comfort facilities were mainly supplied by a ship. In late 1942 it collected 150 women, partly from the Tamanoi red light district in Tokyo, and partly from Nagoya. The women were distributed at the rate of twenty per island-garrison. A survivor describes the comfort station on one of these outposts as consisting of beds made from split palms, covered only with thin mattresses and lit by candles, under palm leaf thatch. On such a crude bed repeated sexual service was hard on the back. One young woman is remembered as bearing this cheerfully enough because she hoped to save enough money to start a small cafe back home in Tokyo. After two years she sailed home, only to go down, like so many others, in a submarine attack.

Not all the far-flung Japanese Armed Forces resorted to sex as a break from the stress of campaigning, or as a last fling before the expected end. One commander in the Marshall Islands, on receiving an enquiry about his unit's requirements for comfort women, retorted: 'Send us ships and men, not women!' (The women assigned for the Marshall Islands were then assigned to Truk in the Carolines.) The Marshall Islands were a frontline area from the beginning, as were comparable areas such as the Aleutian Islands, Iwojima and the eastern New Guinea mainland. Kim Il Myon found no reference to comfort stations there, and nor have these places been mentioned in any subsequent data.

With regard to the comfort system in the South Seas, Kim Il Myon makes some useful observations on common features, as contrasted with other occupied areas. There was a greater role proportionately for Naval and Air Forces. This meant the growth of the distinct naval comfort system, in which facilities for officers and other ranks were kept strictly separate.

Another feature is the far greater danger of death and defeat in these areas, as the Allied counter-offensive mounted. This contrasted with the wearisome but stable war of attrition in China. In the Pacific theatre, where Japanese Forces faced their first decisive defeats, their psychological unpreparedness led on occasion to particularly frenzied behaviour. There is a theory that all species experience an intensification of the reproductive urge when threatened with mass destruction or extinction, and that such an instinct would tend to combine with a conscious urge to grasp any last opportunities for solace. So there were scenes on the southern fronts where men sought their last earthly joys in comfort stations where the stars shone through holes in bomb-battered roofs. Doomed men persisted even while tropical rains drenched their backs.

In this theatre, Korean comfort women, though still the largest ethnic group overall, were less used. This was partly because the services of local women of many nationalities were available, and also because of an increasing tendency for Japanese women and brothel keepers to volunteer for service in the newly-opened areas. Custom in the home country was drying up because of the large military call-up of the male population, and conditions of wartime austerity, such as shortages of goods, and restrictions on spending made necessary by compulsory loans or the purchase of war bonds. Women were required in war industries at home, but those in the business of supplying sexual service were encouraged to move to the south.

A case history illustrating this movement is by Shirota Suzuko, also known as Mihara Yoshie. She was the first Japanese comfort woman to come to public notice, through a broadcast made in 1986. Although secrecy surrounding the comfort system in Japan was nowhere near as strong as in Korea, publications on the subject had originated from third persons, preserving individual anonymity. Shirota decided to make a public protest at the lack of compensation or treatment for the disease she had contracted in Navy service, particularly as she had not long to live. She wanted to expose the iniquities of the system while she could.

Shirota Suzuko

In 1937, at the age of seventeen, Shirota had accepted a contract to serve as a prostitute in return for a loan of ¥2500 to repay her family's debts. She was then employed at a naval comfort station at Makung in Taiwan. She recalls her disgust at the overwhelming rush of clients whenever a ship docked, and how she wished for an opportunity for freedom. This came when an infatuated Okinawan seaman agreed to redeem her, on promise of marriage. This is a recurrent theme through centuries of Japanese prostitution and *geisha*dom. In traditional East Asian society there was little opportunity for romantic attachment through ordinary arranged marriage, this being more likely to occur in a professional context. In such cases, the man's passion would overrule the customary concern with the woman's chastity.

Shirota's motive, however, was purely release from her situation. She ran away to Tokyo. The Okinawan was somehow able to trace her and sue for repayment, so she was obliged to return to prostitution. She joined the southward movement, in this case to Palau in Micronesia as part of 'naval special personnel'. The comfort women were transported to various units by truck to service the men. In addition, they were called on to perform military duties in emergencies. Perhaps because she had caught syphilis, Shirota was not employed in giving sexual services, but in handling the books and tickets. In her area the women survived the widespread Micronesian threat of combat death or massacre. At the end of the war, she was repatriated by a United States transport ship.

She recalls that, although fighting men were conventionally represented as dying for the Emperor as expressed in the '*banzai* charge' in his name, in reality they spoke of dying to save their mothers from suffering at enemy hands.

In later life Shirota lived on a dairy farm colony, called the Women's Village, established by the Reverend Fukatsu at Kanita on the eastern Pacific coast. Her broadcast earned an encouragement prize from the Broadcast Culture Foundation. With other

contributions added it led to the erection of a memorial stone inscribed 'For the Military Comfort Women', overlooking the sea at
Kanita.

Rabaul

From Micronesia it was an easy descent to Rabaul on the island of
New Britain, the strategic centre of Australian mandated territory.
This became one of the largest Japanese Naval and Army bases. It
was renamed Nankaishi (City of the South Seas), and served as the
focus of campaigns in the Solomon Islands and New Guinea, which
led to the first turning point of the war. This was the action in Guadalcanal in the Solomons, when outnumbered Japanese troops
fought a savage battle for possession of the tiny island, only to be
eventually defeated by the Americans.

Rabaul itself held out to the end. With over 100,000 troops, and
well-fortified, it was not worth the cost of destruction. Once cut off
from their fellows, the garrison became self-supporting. Largely of
peasant stock, they were able to cultivate enough sweet potatoes,
tapioca and hill rice to survive. They made soap from coconut oil
and toothpaste from coral powder. The main shortage was tobacco.

Comfort stations had naturally been provided on a scale more or
less commensurate with that of the base. Most sources, including
Kim Il Myon, indicate that the Japanese avoided the local women,
not so much from any racist aversion—something that will always
dissipate with time and familiarity—but because of the prevalence of
skin disease, pussing cuts, scratches and the smell of coconut oil used
as a mosquito repellent. Film-maker Sekiguchi Noriko, while making the documentary film *Daughters of War*, found local people who
attested to forced sex by Japanese, under threat of harm to family
members.

Comfort stations were set up soon after the landing. The Navy's
first two stations occupied former Australian residences on the hill-
side outside the town, while the Army erected three prefabricated
huts, each containing ten rooms of three-mat size, some distance to
the east. The first contingent was of fourteen Koreans. Not only
were the women brought in 'as quickly as the ammunition', but they

even preceded the arrival of the wireless interception unit—a crucial piece of equipment for remote Rabaul.

In the beginning at least, the women were in such short supply that the pressure on their services was intense. 'Much worse than in China,' a survivor is quoted as telling Senda Kako. She goes on to describe how, instead of a lunch break, she was hastily given rice balls to eat between clients. The immediate pressure on her stomach would then force the food up her throat, and she would have to re-swallow it. Sometimes the men were so rushed they confused her anus with her vagina.

With Rabaul's tropical climate, an additional reason for sexual services was to ward off the combination of listlessness and mental unbalance described by English-speaking troops as 'going troppo'. This was especially crucial in the case of the Air Force, who believed sexual deprivation made pilots accident-prone. Men here were instructed to use comfort services as a duty rather than as a recreation.

Newly-arriving comfort women were regularly examined by a medical officer before being allowed to work. Dr Aso, who had examined the women in the Shanghai comfort station, was stationed in Rabaul with an anti-aircraft battalion. One medical officer in Rabaul found a virgin among a batch of women brought from Japan by a civilian operator, who had told her that she would be working as a typist. When he learned the situation, the medical officer severely reprimanded the operator, and had the girl repatriated to Japan.

There is another account of a large number of women, also recruited as typists, collectively protesting and returning to Japan. Their ship, however, was sunk on the way. There are a number of accounts of such deaths in transit. On one occasion a ship carrying comfort women from Rabaul to the fateful island of Guadalcanal was sunk by a submarine off Bougainville, with a few fortunate comfort women being able to swim ashore. Two survived the war. On another occasion a submarine carrying 200 comfort women back to Japan was sunk by a mine. Only three survived.

An account is given by a young, newly-graduated medical officer of his first sexual experience, in Rabaul. Although specialising in gynaecology, his knowledge of sex had been purely theoretical, 'not so much from lack of inclination, but from self-respect and the feeling that to resort to prostitutes was to reduce himself to their level'. Life in the jungle, which often seems to reinforce instinctive drives and attenuate the effects of civilisation, finally led him to visit a comfort station. On the first occasion he retreated, repelled by the smell of body odour and the general dinginess. On the second occasion he persisted, and was assigned a Korean girl. She knew very little Japanese, but he by then felt this was an advantage: a pure carnal outlet was all he desired. Afterwards she lit cigarettes for both of them, and despite his having had no taste for it before, 'smoking now seemed like incense'. On the same occasion he lost both his virginity and became addicted to tobacco. While still with the woman, he began to feel some post-coital depression. This he dispelled by a repeat.

As enemy air attacks became overwhelming, the enjoyment of sexual service became more hazardous. There are accounts of men persisting in comfort stations even as air raids began, until officers dragged them and the women to shelters. Even there the activity might continue with no privacy whatever. A Korean survivor recalls with surprise her complete lack of shyness in such a case. Finally, the commanders decided that in preparation for a suicidal last stand, all women should be evacuated as an encumbrance. Nurses were returned to Japan, and the comfort women, after a last orgy, were removed to Truk Island in the Caroline group, and Saipan in the Mariana group. Few there would have survived the terrible pounding by the Americans in 1944. After their departure, homosexuality reportedly prevailed in Rabaul, with some men resorting to local women for the first time.

Other accounts of Rabaul appeared in later investigations. One recalls incidents of duelling between officers in attempts to monopolise a woman's services, as well as a case of murder- suicide involving a Japanese woman. Those Koreans who were treated as paramilitary were fed as well as officers and though they worked hard, were relieved every two to three months, while this was possible. While interviewing for her film *Senso* [war] *Daughters* 1990, Sekiguchi Noriko was given a detailed account of a comfort station at the Cosmopolitan Hotel. This had elaborate regulations, and photographs of the women to facilitate selection. Visits in principle were for thirty minutes. Eighty per cent of the women there were Korean. The rest were Japanese and were reserved for the officers.

Another account states that the men did not handle money but were issued with 'thirty-minute tickets'. A bell was rung five minutes before expiry. The informant sometimes sold his ticket to a neighbouring client for ¥5, so giving the other an hour. Apparently the unit cashed the tickets later.

A United States report on 'Amenities' contains some brief reports on Rabaul collected from prisoners captured in adjacent areas. One states that there were about twenty brothels in and around Rabaul, the inmates all being Japanese women. The brothels were mainly patronised by the officers who were charged ¥5; men charged ¥1 in theory could in practice rarely gain admittance. As this informant was a private, he may not have had much direct knowledge of the inmates. Another speaks of two brothels, holding about 100 Koreans and Japanese. Another speaks of a ratio of only one woman to 2000 troops, so that only officers were accommodated. Finally, one captured in February 1944 states that all prostitutes had already been evacuated, so on this count the functioning of comfort stations in Rabaul would have occupied about two full years.

One of the three original plaintiffs in the Tokyo lawsuit, described as 'Plaintiff A', was in Rabaul (see Chapter 7) but this woman was not evacuated because, with about ten others, she escaped during bombing. She survived in the jungle until the end of the war by growing potatoes. The comfort station where she was taken after a spell of hospital duties was housed in a church building. There were about twenty women there, of seven nationalities, including some described as black. There is a brief mention elsewhere of Indonesian comfort women in the New Guinea area. Their photographs were displayed in front of the station.

The Philippines

This group of islands on the edge of Southeast Asia was a Spanish colony for three centuries, and then an American one following American victory over Spain in the war of 1898. When the Pacific War broke out, the Americans were training the Filipino Army and preparing the people for independence. There was thus less anticolonial feeling for the Japanese to exploit, and the islands saw some stiff resistance from Filipino and American troops in 1942. There were nearly half a million Japanese troops involved in the Philippines Theatre, and even after occupation, guerrilla resistance continued to trouble them.

Indigenous prostitution seems always to have flourished here, encouraged by centuries of Hispanic cultural influence. Hispanic society, even more than other Latin societies, resembles the East Asian pattern of close supervision of respectable women, coupled with institutional prostitution. It also tends to be characterised by extreme differences in wealth distribution. Poverty is a big factor in pushing women into prostitution. Despite the availability of local prostitutes, the Japanese, always wary of the danger of espionage, especially when there was an active guerrilla resistance, appeared to have imported their comfort women. There is, however, now evidence that there was *ad hoc* rape and seizure of local women for comfort stations, along the lines of Madam X's experience in Malaya.

In March 1992, when some Japanese documentation of comfort practices relating to the Philippines appeared, women's groups demanded an official inquiry of the Corazon Aquino government. The Presidential Commission on Human Rights entrusted this to a scholar, who reported that he could find no evidence of large-scale forced prostitution. He had largely relied for sources on the wartime Leftist guerrilla movement.

When in July 1992 the Japanese government published the findings of its major investigation into the comfort women issue, this stimulated the Task Force on Filipina Comfort Women. Along with other women's groups, they followed up clues in the Japanese report. They identified the site of the pair of comfort stations mentioned in the *kempeitai* records for Iloilo, on the island of Panay. The records contained a map of the area indicating where the comfort women were allowed to stroll between eight and ten each morning. Any other movement outside the comfort station required special permission.

Other regulations followed the same lines as elsewhere. The two comfort stations were called the No. 1 Comfort Station and the Asia Hall, with the latter being the more upmarket establishment. It charged ¥6 an hour for officers, compared with ¥3 in No. 1 Comfort Station. For the lower orders, NCOs and the paramilitary, who were given only 30 minutes, Asia Hall charged ¥2.50 against ¥1.50, in the misleadingly named No. 1. For the humble private the charges respectively were ¥1.50 and ¥1. Because it was an Army rather than a Navy establishment, the lowly private enjoyed the same girls and the same bed as the officers. Only the time of day was less prestigious.

Were the Iloilo comfort girls healthy? The seal of approval was given by the Iloilo Sanatorium, which in May 1942 found one woman infected with vaginitis. All the others (except one who was menstruating), were declared fit for work. Who were the Iloilo comfort women? Although the names had been blacked out, it proved possible later to restore some of them: healthy Carmen and Gracia and infected Margareta. Unlike the Koreans and Chinese, these women had not been given Japanese names, because the Japanese found Hispanic or indigenous names easy to pronounce and remember.

The women's groups' investigators found aged residents who could remember the situation of the time—how truckloads of women were brought to what they know as the Paris Hotel. Korean and Taiwanese women are mentioned. Although no women who served in the comfort stations could be found, and there are vague references to their having been killed, fifteen women were found on Panay who had been forced into sexual servitude in other circumstances. Among the few whose names are given, Tomasa Salinog recalls being seized from her home in 1942 at the age of thirteen.

Tomasa Salinog

Tomasa Salinog was at home asleep when two soldiers entered her house. In her own words: 'They wanted to take me so my father fought them. My father was struck with a sword by Captain Hiruka. I ran to where he lay and embraced him only to find out that his head was already severed from his body. I cried hysterically, but the Japanese mercilessly dragged me out of our house. They brought me to a house which was near the garrison. It was a two-storey house with three rooms above and below. Each room had its own bathroom. There were already many women in the house but I was not able to count how many there were.'

This certainly sounds like a comfort station, but since she was a very young girl, and given the traumatic way she was taken, it is hardly surprising that she doesn't say much about her daily routine. 'I cannot remember for how long I was inside the mess house because I felt that I was already losing my mind. I'd always remember my father and then I'd cry. What hurt me most was that I was only thirteen when I was raped, and it was done repeatedly. I was still not having my menstrual period at that time. I only started having my period when I was already in the mess house'. For a time she was kept in a house where she had to service four men a day, as well as do laundry. Later she escaped, but was captured by an officer who made her his mistress and maidservant for the rest of the war, occasionally sharing her with other men.

The other cases in Panay and most of those recently emerging in the rest of the Philippines are of a comparable character. They amount to *ad hoc* rape or confinement, on the initiative of individuals or groups, rather than forming part of an official comfort system.

One victim decided to take the lead in initiating lawsuits. In October 1992, she delivered to the Japanese Embassy a letter addressed to Prime Minister Miyazawa demanding an apology, compensation and the cessation of the dispatch of Japanese troops overseas. This plaintiff, Maria Rosa Luna Henson, had been seized on the street in Angeles City at the age of fourteen and then confined and raped by twelve to twenty men a day. She was later held, with six other women, in a rice mill for several months. In early 1944, they were freed by guerrillas. There are several surviving witnesses. She later married and told her husband, but not her children, about her experiences.

Another woman had a more tragic life. Gertrudes Balisalisa had been married to an engineer who was drafted for bridge construction by the Japanese. She was taken to a commanding officer's quarters to become his mistress and housemaid. At the same time she was shared with several other men daily. She was forbidden to speak to the other women being held at the same base, of whom at least one was shot trying to escape. She was beaten if she refused service and is lame as a result. As a final blow, she was later disowned by her husband, who was afraid she might be diseased.

A report from Baguio bears more directly on an official comfort system. This comes from Cecile Okubo Afable, editor and writer for the *Baguio Midland Courier*. As her middle name indicates, her father was Japanese, and would have been part of a long-standing Japanese community. The Japanese Army arrived when she was twenty-five and seized her home, after executing her father, whom she describes as a pacifist. One of the attractions of this home was its grand piano, which the commanding officer used to play at parties held there. It was also used as a comfort station, there being about 100 comfort women in the area. She names three whom she knew, one being a Japanese married to an American serviceman. She has no knowledge of their fate, only having heard accounts of some escaping and some being killed to preserve secrecy.

Another aspect of the military system is illustrated by an application to the Cebu military administration for official recognition of a number of businesses to operate under the Panay Business Control Association. One operator was to combine the management of a bar, a cinema, a hotel and a comfort station, described as mainly catering for servicemen and paramilitary, but with limited service for Japanese civilians. Finances were to be supervised by the Control Association—a common practice, especially in wartime.

The material collected by Kim Il Myon on the Philippines is limited. One source mentions two men being shot for rape, which was not unusual as a disciplinary measure. Shirley F. Huie in her account of internment life in Java mentions cases of men accused of rape being shot out of hand. Others occur in China. Perhaps the authorities in such cases especially resented such acts, since comfort facilities had been provided as an alternative outlet.

A former paymaster officer put in charge of comfort women in Manila recalls that the Forces began by using available Filipinas. They soon supplemented them with women from Korea and Japan, the latter coming largely from the island of Amakusa, the source of prostitutes for the southern regions for many generations. This officer admits having sampled women widely among Chinese, Koreans, Spanish, Russians and Indonesians. In the end, however, he preferred the psychological intimacy to be had with a Japanese. Another source mentions visiting students resorting to prostitution when stranded by the war. Fees by ethnicity are given as ¥3.50 a night for Koreans, ¥5.50 for Japanese, ¥11 for Hispanics and ¥13 for Americans—the latter two based on rarity value.

The 12,000 survivors from the disaster at Guadalcanal were brought to Manila. They had suffered so much from starvation that for some time they had no interest in sex. One is quoted as preferring a sweet potato to a woman. When they finally recovered their interest, they felt reassured for the first time that they were still alive. A later account describes a multinational comfort station in Manila, where several women were always available in the lobby for selection. It bore a sign reading: 'Military Designated Comfort Station Number . . .' Payment was in military scrip, but the women preferred soap or the like. In Davao, there was a long-established Japanese community reminiscent of those of the Japanese towns, but the women were mainly of local origin.

Singapore and Malaya

Singapore was a jewel in the crown of the pre-war British Empire. It was a supposedly invulnerable naval base on which the British government had lavished some sixty million pounds not long before war broke out. It was regarded as one of the four big naval bases in the world, the other three being Pearl Harbour, Gibraltar and Malta.

With its mighty naval base at the southern tip of the Malayan Peninsula, the British hoped to protect their valuable tin and rubber resources in Malaya. So it was a shock to both the British and the Japanese when Malaya and Singapore fell in a lightning campaign of just over two months, to a force previously thought inferior. The seasoned 25th Army under General Yamashita Tomoyuki had two divisions of nearly 40,000 men, while the British had had twice that number. The first bombs fell on 8 December 1941, and by 15 February 1942, the British had surrendered.

Singapore became Shonan (*sho* meaning 'brilliant', from the Emperor's reign title *showa*, and *nan* meaning 'south'). It was dominated by entrepreneurial intervention direct from Japan, much like Manchuria in the 1930s following its annexation. There was a great civilian influx, both of *zaibatsu*-linked 'national policy companies' designed to exploit the region's strategic resources, and of parasitic fortune-hunters. The latter met the needs of the business executive class as well as the Armed Forces' senior officers, who had over-riding authority and who were naturally courted for favours. These would be negotiated in the course of lavish entertainments. For senior officers they presented the opportunity not only for current enrichment but also for building a foundation for a future life of prosperity.

The higher-level entertainment scene in Singapore was dominated by an organisation called the Yamato Brigade, Yamato being an ancient and emotionally-charged name for Japan. Upon landing, this brigade 'hijacked the management of the most attractive hotels, restaurants and cafes in Singapore, like an army, capturing a castle every morning and a fortress every evening . . . an onslaught no less dashing than General Yamashita's conquest of Malaya' (Kim Il Myon 1976).

Kim Il Myon enlarges on the luxurious lifestyle led by officers. They took over the elaborate mansions and hotels of former colonial rulers, together with what was in them. They sometimes used the services of the colonials' women, as well as indigenous women, who were described as being 'liberated from white exploitation'. As an example, Kim quotes an entry from the diary of an officer killed in Burma:

16 April. Arrived safely in Singapore at half past nine. On landing, stayed at a grand hotel confiscated from the British. A British girl under confinement in the hotel came to the bathroom, washed my back and relieved my physical needs after half a month of life at sea. In the afternoon summoned a French prostitute and had her serve my drinks and stay the night.

There are recollections by older local residents of soldiers queuing outside military brothels. None other than Singapore's former Prime Minister Lee Kuan Yew remembers these lines of Japanese soldiers. In mid-1992 Lee was in Japan when the comfort women issue was gaining prominence. He recollected that the general feeling among townspeople, himself included, was one of relief that such provision was made to obviate rape. On learning more of the background of the system, however, he supported compensation for its victims, as well as hoping that any future dispatch of Japanese troops overseas would not lead to any repetition of such practices.

Oral history recollections of the Japanese occupation period by older Singaporeans make references to Japanese brothels. One was in Cairnhill in the now-fancy Orchard Road area. Another was somewhere in the Geylang area, which before the war had a street notorious for its population of prostitutes. One Singaporean in his seventies recalled the comfort station in Geylang as located in a row of terrace houses which had a passageway knocked through the internal partitioning walls, to connect the different houses.

A more general picture comes from a Korean prison guard who had left home and drifted, before volunteering for paramilitary service to avoid being drafted for more unpleasant duties. His prison camp had a comfort station with mixed Chinese, Malay and ethnic Indian staff. There were also twenty or so brothels in the city, housed in deserted Chinese mansions, with staff of about 300 Koreans and 100 Japanese. He finally returned home by ship with many of them, including a woman from his home town.

One Japanese ex-serviceman writing to the press of his wartime experiences recalls how as a young innocent sailor of eighteen, he was taken by older crew members to visit a comfort station in Singapore. He was utterly repelled by the sight of masses of condoms being dried for re-use in the space under the building. 'I was overcome by a sense of wanting to spit at the ugliness of the sex instinct.' Recalling how on board ship superior officers in the absence of women sought a substitute in young sailors, he describes his 'disillusionment with our superiors to whom we entrusted our very lives'. The obvious threat to discipline from such homosexuality would help to explain why the Navy appears to have been the pioneer in setting up comfort stations. The Japanese sailor apparently never recovered from these experiences, since he concludes by expressing a 'sense of the emptiness of the sex instinct, to be borne as a burden for all future ages, from past to present, whether in East or West'.

Among the Defence Studies Library documents is a routine order of mid-1942 prohibiting troops from seeking 'special comfort' from local premises not established by the Forces. As the major port in the region, Singapore would already have had extensive organised prostitution. Another soldier expresses displeasure at troops riding in military vehicles or rickshaws with local women. Troops breaking beer bottles or glasses in restaurants or comfort stations were ordered to compensate proprietors. One officers' comfort station, Masago, was ordered closed for two days as a penalty for neglecting supervision of its female staff.

In the light of information which has since become available, it is remarkable that no material on Malaya was found before 1992, either by Kim Il Myon, or among the numerous documents produced in the Japanese government's report of July 1992. Soon afterwards, however, independent investigators unearthed military documents which gave details on the Malayan situation. Among these are entries in the field diary of a unit which in March 1942 was stationed in Malacca. They record the drawing-up of comfort station regulations, and rosters for unit days off to visit them. They even include the number of men in parties doing so. In April 1942, the unit was in Kuala Pilah where, as in other areas, search and destroy missions against real or imagined Chinese resistance elements alternated with visits to the comfort station. Here it was staffed by twenty-three Chinese comfort women brought from Kuala Lumpur. The diary indicates that regulations were to conform to those for the Seremban garrison, which also survive. Visits to brothels other than approved comfort stations were prohibited, and tickets had to be bought in advance. In Kuala Pilah, no eating or drinking in the town was allowed except at the comfort station, which also served as a canteen. Hygiene reports for the Malaya military administration record the distribution of condoms for certain months in 1943: in July, 1000 for Negri Sembilan, 10,000 for Perak; in August, 5000 for Malacca, 10,000 for Selangor and 30,000 for Penang; in September, 5000 for administrative staff and 1500 for civilian businesses.

Figures from 25th Army Headquarters for Japanese nationals resident in Singapore, Malaya and Sumatra in August 1942 include 195 comfort women. Available evidence indicates that the great majority in Malaya were ethnic Chinese, recruited locally. Singapore and Malaya's substantial Chinese population was implacably anti-Japanese, which led to retribution when the Japanese Forces took over. Although there may have been fear of espionage, abducting local Chinese women into sexual service could also have been seen as appropriate punishment for the anti-Japanese activities of their men. Chinese community leaders had to meet certain Japanese demands at the start of the Occupation, among them a war 'contribution' of $50 million in Straits dollars, plus supplying 'comfort' for the troops. Nothing is known about this cryptic demand for 'comfort', since the demand for such a large sum of money dominated discussion and the efforts of the community then and after the war.

Asahi journalist Matsui Yayori, who has had a long-standing interest in Southeast Asia, heard from a former Army interpreter an account of the establishment of the first comfort stations in Malaya, immediately after invasion (Yun Chung-ok 1992). He had been sent to Bangkok to obtain women from the red light district there. His first efforts revealed only two who were not infected with venereal disease. So he employed these in the first comfort station, which was on the Thai side of the Malayan border. Subsequent recruitment concentrated on the local Chinese. The seizure of Madam X for work in a Kuala Lumpur comfort station was probably typical of the way troops found women to staff the comfort stations.

Since the Japanese believed there was no prospect of collaboration from the Chinese community as a whole, they felt free to victimise them. Better relations were seen as feasible with the Malays and ethnic Indians, most of whom tended to support the Japanese-sponsored 'provisional free India government'. Madam X remembers that in her comfort station: 'We had eight Chinese, three Malays who were from Sumatra, two Koreans and one Thai. I never saw any Malays from Malaya; nor were there any Indian comfort girls.' These groups were spared forced drafting into comfort service although, as elsewhere, some women of varied backgrounds adopted this means of survival as economic hardships intensified. Eurasians were much in demand, as elsewhere. According to another informant, there was at least one comfort station staffed by twenty or so Koreans among the seventeen in Kuala Lumpur. A special feature in Malaya was that about fourteen of the earlier generation of expatriate Japanese prostitutes who had settled in the country were employed managing comfort stations.

Local accounts confirm that comfort stations were established in all garrison towns. There were about twenty. In Kuala Lumpur itself, there were between seventeen and twenty-four comfort stations, often using hotels which had served the same purpose for the colonial gentry. The speed with which these businesses opened after the Japanese invasion under opportunistic entrepreneurs has invited suspicion that the subversive network developed by the Japanese to prepare for their arrival had also provided for this requirement. There was probably also local complicity, even extending to the Chinese community. According to Madam X, soldiers were led to her village in Serdang by a thirty-year-old Chinese. She was taken to the Tai Sun Hotel in Kuala Lumpur: 'The Tai Sun comfort station was run by a Chinese mama-san and her husband. Her name was Choi Chau. Her husband's name was Ah Yong. We never learnt their family names. He looked after the general running of the comfort station while she looked after the girls.' When news of Japanese surrender came, some of the comfort women seized the pair and drowned them.

Burma

This narrow, mountainous, jungle-clad Southeast Asian country is noted in the history of the Pacific War for the Burma Road and the Death Railway. The Burma Road was the back door to China, through which the Nationalist government of General Chiang Kai Shek was kept supplied with war materials by the Western powers. This link with the outside world was a source of irritation for the Japanese, who had found it neither possible to sweep away the Nationalists in their redoubt in Chungking, nor to blockade them effectively. Chiang's ability to keep the Japanese at bay because of his tenuous link with the West via the Burma Road has been cited as one of the reasons for the spread of the Pacific War into Southeast Asia. Supplies landed at Rangoon's docks, were carried up by rail to Lashio, and then by road to Chungking. Capturing Burma and shutting down the Burma Road were the final steps to isolating China.

The infamous Siam—Burma Railway earned the name 'Death Railway' because nearly one-fifth of the 60,000 Allied prisoners-of-war engaged in building it died in the process, as did about one-third of the quarter-million drafted Asian civilian labourers. The railway cut across the mountainous Thai province of Kanchanaburi, over Three Pagodas Pass, into Burma and the town of Thanbyuzayat. The railway allowed supplies to be moved more quickly into Burma, which was a vital war front, through which more than a quarter-million Japanese troops passed.

Asahi journalist Matsui, speaking at a later international conference on comfort women, was able to amplify the remark by a British writer that the first train to travel the Siam—Burma Death railway was a 'prostitute train'. It had been possible since to interview the then-commander of the railway construction unit, who recalled that a comfort station staffed with Korean women had been installed at the Thai terminus at the beginning of construction. The extremely difficult conditions had prevented any movement further forward, until the line was completed in late 1943. Then, to celebrate completion and reward the troops for their efforts, comfort stations were promptly built at each station. A group of six or seven Korean women was taken down the line, stopping one night at each station. There were about sixty men at each, and the number of tickets issued often exceeded the number of men—so some must have made more than one visit. It would, of course, be some time before their next opportunity.

An Australian account also relates that some prisoners, who in some circumstances were paid for their labour as a gesture to international law, were offered the use of comfort women. They declined on the grounds that they would prefer an improved diet.

Burma was not all hard slog—at least not for the officers, and not in the first flush of victory. In its most fashionable summer resort at Maymyo, senior officers would drive up in luxury British cars to a restaurant taken over by an entrepreneur from the Osaka red light district. Here they would sing songs of home to the strings of *geishas'* *samisen*. At a time when women in the Homeland had given up all feminine refinements to lives symbolised by drab wartime attire, these officers were waited on by women dressed and coiffed in the height of fashion. Some of their liquor was locally made but they also had *sake*, whisky and brandy which, like their splendid array of utensils, were brought on ships which would normally be expected to carry only munitions.

Even more elaborately equipped was the officers' club in Rangoon. The occupying division had brought out a complete array of traditional restaurant facilities from its recruitment base in Kurume, Kyushu. The club was fitted with Japanese-style floor matting, bedding, screens, paper sliding walls and furniture. There was a staff of 150, including *geisha*, maidservants, cooks, hairdressers, tailors, launderers and a gynaecologist. The *geisha* also served as officers' mistresses. But for the lower orders, as a war correspondent of the time recalls, even to glimpse these women was 'the most difficult of things'.

Kim Il Myon makes only a brief summary of points gathered from scattered references to Burma. The comfort stations there were distinguished by being virtually an 'anthropological museum', since a good deal of use was made of local women. The proportions of ethnic groups he estimates as ten Koreans to four Burmese to two Chinese and Indians and 0.8 Japanese. Under these circumstances the Japanese were naturally very much the preserve of the most privileged ranks, and generally in a *geisha*-type role.

Burmese comfort women are described as participating with an unusual degree of enthusiasm, because Burma had been particularly restive under British rule. There had been sizeable insurrections in the 1930s, and there was now a widespread welcome for the Japanese promise of liberation from colonialism. This received Japanese recognition in the formation of a client government, the nucleus of the post-war regime.

Senda Kako estimates the total number of comfort women in Burma at about 3200, of whom 2800 were Koreans. Those attached to the notoriously tough Dragon Corps, which straddled the border regions of China and commanded the former Burma Road, were exclusively Korean. As will be described later in the book, many of these women faced a terrible fate in the Japanese Forces' last stand in Burma.

The Wolf Corps, stationed in central to lower Burma, contained a high proportion of Korean volunteers. In 1983, Usuki Keiko, the leading figure in the Association for Clarifying Japan's Postwar Responsibility, was able to interview one of these volunteers, to obtain a good first-hand account of the Burma situation. On one of her frequent visits to Korea, Usuki was shown a five-volume *Chronicle Of A People's Resistance*, containing a vast range of personal accounts of experiences of Japanese rule. Some of these were memoirs by student volunteers. Her attention was particularly drawn to an account by Yi Kyu Dong of a prisoner-of-war camp in Burma.

Yi Kyu Dong

Yi Kyu Dong had been a student at the University of Tokyo, when on 20 January 1944, the date set for enlistment for Korean student volunteers, he volunteered for military service. After six months' training, he became a private in an artillery regiment. Among a total of 5000 troops he was packed into a freighter bound for the south. Conditions were so harsh that at least one Japanese soldier jumped overboard to end his misery. When they reached Moulmein, after disembarking at Singapore, enemy bombing was already heavy. All movement had to be made at night. They sheltered in the jungle by day.

In actions at Bhamo and Meiktila where his duty was to carry ammunition, the Wolf Corps was virtually obliterated, with his unit commanders, from regiment to squad level, being killed in action. Among some remnants who survived largely on boiled potato vines, he reached Thaton in August 1945. He re-grouped with others, his last duty being to compile lists of dead and missing. On learning of Japan's surrender, his feelings were confused. On the one hand, he was cheered by the prospect of Korea's independence. But he had doubts as to how he, as a volunteer for Japan's Armed Forces, would fit into the new order.

After some months in prisoner-of-war camps, those of Korean extraction were separated and concentrated in Singapore, where they were restored to Korean nationality and so could discard their Japanese names. Yi Kyu Dong would no longer be known as Iwamoto Yoshio. They were joined by numbers of former comfort women, some of whom Yi had encountered in his movements around Burma. The Koreans organised a program of preparations for their return home, including Korean language lessons, lectures, plays and a newsletter. The comfort women were almost all illiterate, while even the former students had only a fragmentary knowledge of Korean history and culture. There was also some discussion as to how their volunteering for service should be interpreted, even to themselves. They were aware of the pressures that had pushed them to it, yet recognised that others had succeeded in refusing. In the event, they were welcomed back to 'the bosom of the homeland' without question.

When Usuki Keiko read Yi's memoir, he was employed as a professor at a private university. She was able to interview him and enquire further about his contacts with comfort women. His first encounter with them had been at Moulmein, on his arrival in Burma. An older Japanese soldier named Miyazaki had offered to take him out. Their destination turned out to be a comfort station. As they entered, Miyazaki called out to the women: 'I've brought him!' It then became clear that the women had asked Miyazaki to bring a Korean soldier if there were any in the unit.

The women's name tags were attached to the wall. All were Japanese names. There were five of them, all of whom he thought were under twenty years of age, but made to look older. They welcomed him warmly, and their first question was of his home town. He was from Moppo in Cholla South province, and the woman with the nearest home to that was called Sadako, from Kunsan in Cholla North. Later, at a welcome party organised by another Korean paramilitary so that he could tell them about recent happenings in Korea, it was hinted that he might like some entertainment more appropriate to a comfort station. Sadako took him to her room. He felt no sexual arousal, however, and could only think of her as a fellow-victim of Japanese aggression. They fell into conversation, and she told him how she had worked in a cafe in Kunsan, but that her family had been poor and the hope of obtaining better work had led her here.

After a while there was a call from next door asking whether 'Iwamoto' was finished. He replied that he was. On emerging, he was given ¥30 in military scrip, which he gave in turn to Sadako. As a soldier's pay was ¥20 a month, it seemed that the paramilitary were better off. The implication is, however, that some sort of shady business was the source. On his way back to the unit, Yi wondered whether it was a good or bad thing he had not enjoyed Sadako's services. Perhaps she would have welcomed a countryman as a client. This haunted him—but he never encountered her again. After the war he recalled the experience in a poem called 'A Korean P'.

His next such encounter was at a riverside, where he found a Korean woman doing laundry. He learned she was in an advance party to set up a comfort station. He was invited to visit their quarters that night and did so, accompanied by a Korean officer. There were six or so women, wearing Western-style dresses, in contrast to the Korean costume the women wore at Moulmein. Here they drank around candles, sang Korean songs and exchanged stories. One woman who seemed friendly was from Cholla province, and had had some secondary education, although even primary education was not common among comfort women. The party was broken up by the arrival of a drunken Japanese officer demanding immediate service; it seemed discreet to leave. The women told him they would be open for service next day, and suggested he visit them then. But his unit moved on at dawn.

Yi's third encounter with comfort women was at Toungoo, during the general retreat. He noticed two dishevelled, exhausted women marching, curiously, at the head of a column of men. The only explanation seemed to be that the men were restricting themselves to the pace the women could manage.

In the Singapore camp, despite elation at national liberation, traditional parochial clannishness was much in evidence. Subdivisions according to clan name and locality were observed. Yi belonged to the Kyongju Yi group, which were largely paramilitary, but also contained one student soldier, one volunteer and two comfort women. These groups tended to form a hierarchy in direct ratio to the number of student soldiers, and in inverse ratio to the number of comfort women. Hence the Chinhae Kims ranked lower, having twenty comfort women among them.

It must be noted that in wartime reminiscences, former Korean or Taiwanese servicemen scarcely ever admit to having used the services of comfort women. Today, with the issue so closely linked to patriotic sentiment, as well as moral indignation, it is even less likely they might do so.

The report by the United States psychological warfare team on the staff and proprietors of a comfort station in northern Burma, already mentioned, is among the most detailed sources on the system. The women were captured in August 1944, during the Japanese retreat from Myitkyina near the Chinese border. The proprietor, his wife and sister-in-law had been restaurant keepers in Seoul but, since business had declined under wartime conditions, they applied to Army headquarters in mid-1942 for permission to take comfort women to Burma. This was the common procedure, with the Army making it known that such applications were welcome.

The proprietor concluded contracts with the families of twenty-two women, advancing from ¥300 to ¥1000 according to their personality, looks and ages, which ranged from nineteen to thirty-one. The Army had no part in the financial arrangements, but gave the proprietor a letter addressed to all Army headquarters, requesting assistance with such matters as transport, rations and medical attention.

The proprietor-couple with their staff embarked at Pusan in July 1942, among a contingent of 703 Korean comfort women and ninety Japanese entrepreneurs. Their ship was one of a convoy of seven, passage being free, but meals charged to the proprietor. Another twenty-two women were taken aboard in Taiwan. On arrival in Rangoon the women were allotted in groups to various units, the interviewed group being attached to 114 Infantry Regiment. After various movements, they were stationed in Myitkyina, opening a third comfort station there. Of the earlier two, one held twenty Koreans and the other twenty-one Chinese women who had been obtained in Canton under the same type of contract arrangement. There were no Japanese comfort women further forwards than Maymyo near Mandalay.

Operating arrangements agree closely with Mun Ok Ju's account. The women received half their takings, as well as free (and compulsory) medical attention and food, the former being provided by the Army and the latter by the proprietor with the assistance of Army supply depots. He also sold them clothing and other requisites. When a woman's debt had been repaid, she was legally free to return home. The only member of this group to reach this status was, however, persuaded to stay.

Operating rules were laid down by the 114 Regiment. They followed the same pattern of timetable, charges, ticketing and rank distinctions as already described. At some stage the regimental commander, Colonel Maruyama, reduced the NCOs' charge for a visit from ¥3 to ¥2 and the officers' charge for a midnight to morning stay from ¥20 to ¥10. The comfort station personnel agreed that Maruyama must be 'the most notorious officer in the Japanese Army'. He was massively built, sadistic and coldly egotistical, being known among troops as 'the toad', from his frequent habit of taking refuge in his dugout. He was addicted to striking, not only common soldiers, but even officers, up to the rank of major. He also punched a company commander four times in public, because he had requested increased rations for his men. Even under frontline conditions, he would punish minor departures from the formalities due to rank by five days' solitary confinement.

Even when supplies grew scarce, Maruyama continued to enjoy luxuries, keeping his own fowls for eggs and meat. He spent almost all his spare time in the comfort stations, where he was known as a hard drinker. Indeed, he took more care of the food and welfare of the comfort women than those of the troops. It was rumoured that when he had to remain for even a short time in his dugout, he would take a comfort woman with him. His favourite was Kawahara Sumiko (whose Korean name was Ha Ton Ye). She was among those captured, and denied this, though she agreed the colonel was of a lewd disposition. In the retreat, he was said to have given her a sword belt, as she had no other belt. He had also given the women priority over the wounded in the river-crossing. His own fate was unknown, though suicide was judged an appropriate fate.

Two men from regimental headquarters were usually detailed to the comfort station at Myitkyina, to check visitors' identity. A *kempei* was stationed there to control drunkenness or violence. The daily attendance at the comfort station was ten to fifteen officers, and eighty to ninety other ranks. Among twenty-two women the workload would, then, have been much lighter than the much higher figures sometimes given as general. The women were allowed to refuse clients, especially if they were drunk. Regarding health, during the eighteen months or so in Myitkyina, there were six cases of venereal disease, which were treated by the medical officer at the divisional field hospital. There were also some cases among the troops, attributed to not using condoms, but nothing so serious as to cause difficulties with regimental headquarters.

The evacuation from Myitkyina of the three comfort stations, involving sixty-three women, began at the end of July 1944. The women wore dark green army clothing over their civilian clothes. They crossed the Irrawaddy in ten small boats, the wounded then being floated down the river, as they were not mobile on land. After a few days' trek, the women were caught in a skirmish and scattered. The Chinese women surrendered to Chinese troops, while the Koreans from the other comfort station followed the retreating Japanese. This group decided that the river route was preferable, and remained in a deserted house while the proprietor tried to construct a raft. They were then captured by Kachin troops under a British officer. Of the sixty-three women, four had died on the march, two of whom had been shot when mistaken for Japanese soldiers.

Indonesia

It is unsurprising that the comfort system functioned on a large scale in the Netherlands East Indies. Many Japanese had a good knowledge of the country from previous trade relations, and there was a considerable Japanese settlement, relatively undisturbed throughout much of the war. It is also well known that the draft labour system reached a particularly large scale there. The comfort system, of course, tended to run parallel with this. But the case of comfort women recruited locally in Indonesia is unusual, in that the greater part of the information has come from local investigations.

Kim Il Myon's material is sketchy. In Java, according to his account, comfort stations were recorded in Bandung, Jakarta, Surabaya and Malang. They were all run by private operators. Since the sea lanes to Indonesia were from an early stage more vulnerable to Allied submarine warfare, fewer Koreans were brought in. The large numbers of local Eurasians, however, were much in demand. The forced prostitution of Dutch women is mentioned by Kim, but without any of the later revelations. They are described as being forced to serve Japanese while keeping photographs of their interned husbands at the bedside.

In Sumatra, comfort women were nicknamed '*Jalan* (road) Ps' because they more often followed units on patrol over this extensive, less developed island. Taiwanese were ranked above Koreans in the hierarchy. In Sulawesi, further east, the Navy had civil administrative jurisdiction. The highest-ranking officer at the outset was General Anami, who later became Japan's last wartime War Minister. He committed suicide by traditional *seppuku* (disembowelling) when the Emperor surrendered. In Sulawesi, too, he observed the forms. He opposed the establishment of comfort stations, though was finally persuaded on pragmatic grounds. The main centres were in Menado and the area around Makassar. In the former, the comfort stations were accommodated in former Dutch mansions, with period furniture. The staff were largely local Minahasa women, who were said to resemble Japanese so much that they could not be distinguished from them if wearing Japanese costume.

Some detail on southern Sulawesi is provided in a post-war report from Parepare, dated June 1946. It was submitted to the Japanese Demobilisation Agency by the head of the second batch of staff being demobilised from the Sulawesi Civil Administration. The report uses the term 'prostitution facilities' and states that there were at least twenty-nine of these, in Makassar, Parepare, Bulukumba, Makale, Singkang, Menado and elsewhere. The women 'were allowed to work at their own inclination', and rations were the same as for servicemen. The women received half the takings by regulation, though an operator at Parepare on his own initiative increased this to 90 per cent. Of the total of about 280 women, 111 were Toraja, 67 Javanese, 7 Makassarese, 4 Mandarese, as well as Bugis, Chinese, Karossas, Enrekangese and others—even more of an ethnic mix than in Burma. At the end of the war they were allowed to disperse, retaining their clothes, other belongings and money. A note adds that the report had been compiled from memory, since most of the staff had already left for Japan. As usual, records had been burned.

Recollections of the situation in Surabaya in East Java come from two Japanese women, one of whom was a typist in the Special Operations Unit which handled political relations with the Indonesian community. Having lived in Surabaya since 1935, she was qualified for this kind of duty, and was generally well-informed. On the matter of comfort stations, she notes the common separation between officers' restaurant-clubs, staffed with professional Japanese women, and comfort stations for other ranks, housed in barrack-style buildings and staffed with some Koreans. Fees for the former were ¥2.50, and for the latter ¥1 to ¥1.5. Of the women's takings, 80 per cent was retained for their keep. They handled eight to ten men a day, were given two days off for menstruation and one-and-a-half days off for rest.

The other informant is a former nurse, who remembers the daily routine orders naming which comfort women were menstruating, and which were on duty. Some officers lived out of camp with Indonesian mistresses—an arrangement which figures prominently in Indonesian sources, and formed the theme of a fictionalised treatment in the novel *Kadarwati: The Woman of Five Names*, by Pandir Kelana. The nurse herself rarely left military quarters because of the hostility shown by 'Dutch-related' residents, though not by Indonesians. Like the Burmese, they hoped to use the Japanese Occupation to end colonial rule. When the war ended, the comfort women here pretended to be nurses for the purpose of relations with the Allies.

The newspaper *Kompas* has published a couple of eyewitness stories. One came from a member of the West Kalimantan regional assembly, who had worked for the Japanese in the Riau Archipelago and saw Indonesian women being brought to a 'yellow house' there. Another, who was in Solo, remembered the Fuji Inn and the Chiyoda Inn, which between them employed up to 100 women aged fifteen to seventeen, including Indonesians. They dispersed after the war.

Regional staff of the weekly *Tempo* carried out wide-ranging investigations which produced a variety of data published on 15 July, 25 July and 18 August 1992. As one puts it in words which could apply to the whole system:

> It seems that the fate of the military comfort women varied. For some it was very dark, for others grey, and for some dim.

Methods of recruitment in Indonesia followed the same pattern as in Japan and Korea. Existing prostitutes were sometimes used. Some were enticed by offers of scholarships or work, especially that with a view to the support of parents. But the commonest method was indirect recruitment through local village administrations, like the system of 'official mediation' in Korea. The practice of obtaining a 'signed consent' is often mentioned but most women had no idea of the content of such documents. One informant, named Ngairah, had already been working in Solo as a teenage prostitute for the Dutch, whom she recalls as generous. She could not say the same for the Japanese, who gathered the city's prostitutes, including herself, into a comfort station in the Rose Hotel. Her basic needs were supplied, but she received so little cash that she could not help her family. Nor was she allowed to leave the hotel, probably for reasons of health control. Another informant was a former *Heiho* auxiliary in Rembang (the *Heiho* were paramilitary auxiliaries trained by the Japanese who figured in the Indonesian struggle for independence). He also remembers comfort women in that area as professionals, or at least operating voluntarily. They were housed in the City Hotel and appeared to have adopted the role 'so that they could eat dainties and wear beautiful clothes. As far as I know there was no force. The life of a *geisha* was more secure than for the majority of the population.'

In the May 1993 issue of the Indonesian women's magazine *Kartini*, a Javanese comfort woman told the story of how she and her sister were forcibly taken from their home in Bandung by two Japanese soldiers.

Johana and Rika

It was about a month after the Japanese occupation of Java. Both Johana and her elder sister Rika had stopped work at a thread-making mill and gone into hiding, because their father had heard that Japanese soldiers were looking for young girls. The soldiers were led to them by a procurer, who had been snooping around the house. 'Our father tried to conceal our existence, but to no avail. The soldiers searched from room to room and found us. They forced my parents to give us up: in return they would be paid. Failure to agree with these conditions would have meant instant death for them. Regretfully, with tears falling from their eyes, they handed us over.'

Rika and I were taken to the procurer's house. There were already dozens of pretty young teenage girls there. They were from central Java, Tasik, Garut, Menado and Ambon. I cannot remember all their names, but I can never forget the name of our mamasan, Mami Sukaenah, who later was constantly to force us to drink herbal medicines to prevent us from getting pregnant.

After a month the procurer took them to Jakarta, telling them they were to be given jobs as maids in a Japanese household. This turned out to be a household surrounded by barbed wire and watched closely by armed soldiers night and day. The girls were treated like prisoners. A week passed. Then Johana, Rika and the forty girls were taken by ship to Borneo. There they were put in a camp called Sakura, a high-walled fortress watched closely by Japanese soldiers. 'We were given a room each. Rika and I were in different rooms in the same camp. Each of us was given a Japanese name and each room had the occupant's name on the door. I was called Yoko-chan. We were given some clothing and cosmetics and told to dress up and beautify ourselves.

'One night about 7 p.m. a soldier came to my room. I was forced to entertain him. I resisted at first, and he barked at me. I then squatted down on my haunches to defend myself. He hit me and stripped me naked. Soon I was to be stripped of every shred of pride and dignity as well. The same thing happened to Rika and the other girls . . . We could not resist, nor could we run away, since the camp was so heavily guarded. In the end we had no choice but to accept our fate . . . They should have been ashamed of themselves for robbing us of our youth. We had to service five to ten soldiers a day and would be hit or tortured if we refused.'

One day she was menstruating and could not provide service, whereupon the soldier whom she had denied service took his rifle and hit her on the knees. The injury was so bad that she has been unable to walk normally since, despite repeated treatment.

The girls were exploited by everyone, including the mama-san. 'If a soldier gave us tips then the Japanese mama-san in charge of us took the money away and we were left with nothing. We received just enough food and clothing and had a regular medical check by a doctor once a week.'

The girls were also closely guarded and not allowed outside the camp, where there were a lot of romusha (forced labourers). 'If any romusha was caught talking to any of us, he would be executed immediately.' (She witnessed several of these executions.) Four months later, the girls were moved to a camp in Brunei, where they stayed for a few months before being moved to Singapore, then to Malaya, and then again to Sandakan in Borneo. On the voyage to Sandakan, the ship hit a mine. Johana saw two of her Eurasian friends drown because they could not swim, and had no pieces of wood to cling to, but she eventually reached land, where she found Rika. Those who were injured were taken to hospital for treatment, after which they were made to serve the soldiers again, in company with many other Filipina girls. She and Rika were in this isolated camp in Sandakan for the last three years of the war. Desperation led to a few suicides. One was her friend Inem, who became pregnant and was driven crazy by the thought that she would never know the father. 'One night after serving a soldier she grabbed hold of his gun and shot herself.'

A former Japanese soldier who stayed behind in Indonesia to be naturalised under the name of Nyoman Buleleng, admits having experienced comfort women in Surabaya. 'The Japanese, it seems, realised that, although in a state of war, the troops' biological needs could not be turned off . . . A house for that purpose was automatically set up in every region occupied by the Japanese.' In his area in Surabaya they were usually surrounded by high bamboo walls, and known locally as 'bamboo houses'. Although some were reserved for officers, he attributes their preference for private mistresses to a feeling of embarrassment in visiting comfort stations. The usual pattern of entertainment was a general party in the evening, after which those who required sexual services stayed the night—a more leisurely pattern than the high-pressure service of many reports.

A former comfort woman on Bangka Island recalls how she was recruited under pressure because her parents' farmhouse happened to be situated near a barracks. At twenty she had already been widowed. On learning of this, some Japanese recruiters enticed her with a story of marriage prospects and care for her parents. The chance to escape from her precarious livelihood, with nothing to wear but gunny sack blouses, was an added inducement. In the 'big house', along with around twenty others, her duty was to serve drinks until midnight, then provide sexual service. The practice here was to pay in kind—usually jewellery. One night, however, an officer took her not to a room, but to his own residence. There she led the easier life of a mistress until the war ended. She later re-married.

A harsher pattern of service is described by a former guard at a comfort station in the Wongaye Hotel in Denpasar, Bali. Here the soldiers 'rarely had time to joke, sing or get drunk'. It wasn't possible as so many came, and there were only twenty women. The guard's job was to register the guests' names and units and show them photographs of the women. After selecting one they bought a ticket for Rp300. This gave them only ten minutes of service. He estimates the average daily workload to be ten men. The women retained half the takings—adding up to a very substantial income, considering the guard's own wage of Rp75 a month. But the women could not refuse a guest and 'were afraid of being murdered'. The hotel was open at all hours, with different times for the Army and Navy.

Two *Tempo* reporters tried to follow up clues in the war reminiscences of a former naval officer in the Naval Special Police, the equivalent of the Army's *kempeitai* but without the latter's broad political role. The reminiscences mentioned the establishment of comfort stations on Ambon and at Makassar, in the latter case contracted out to a Chinese businessman called Toh. In the latter city (now Ujungpandang), they found two women who had been in a comfort station there, but only one would discuss it. She had been employed in an office, then as a waitress in the Beangkorop Hotel, where she was raped by an officer. From then on she was both waitress and comfort woman. Next she was confined with other women in another house where they had to service three to five men daily. She was known as Siti 1, as there were several others of the same name. They could eat as much as they wanted and were given clothes, but no money. They had a weekly medical examination at the local hospital.

In northern Sulawesi, two men who had been employed as servants in a comfort station provided eyewitness accounts. Two complexes in Menado and Tomohon were operated by a Japanese officer (presumably retired from active service), and his German wife. In the latter area about 100 girls were recruited from Minahasa villages on the pretence of learning sewing, and lodged in a group of ten houses, which the Japanese had cleared and then fenced off to prevent their escape. The soldiers, who included Koreans and Taiwanese, and even Indonesian *Heiho*, regularly queued for service, from about 3 p.m. to 7 p.m.

Material conditions are described as 'well taken care of'. They included ample food and clothing as well as medical attention. 'They remained attractive and strangely were never sick.' A wage was paid. In spite of these favourable aspects, the women were often heard screaming, and the locality in Menado came to be called Mahakeret, which has that meaning in the local language. Two women are known to have escaped, but were recaptured in their home village.

One comfort woman discovered in Indonesia, Keng Sie Lei, was of Malayan Chinese origin. She had been married, but after her father had been arrested by the *kempeitai*, who were carrying out intensive purges of her community, she accepted a seemingly friendly officer's offer of work in Indonesia. She boarded a ship for Java with nine other girls. But the ship did not stop in Java. Instead more women embarked. Some of them were married. They were carried to Morotai in the Halmaheras. There, on being given rooms in a hostel, they were told for the first time that their duty would be servicing soldiers on leave.

In such a remote place they could only accept their fate. Privates who were charged Rp200 a ticket were rostered from 1 p.m. until 3 p.m., NCOs at Rp350 a ticket, from 3 p.m. to 5 p.m., while officers paid 'thousands' to stay from 8 p.m. to morning. Each woman serviced five to ten men daily. They were paid according to the tickets received and some are credited with the extraordinary monthly income of Rp60 000. They were given holidays and allowed to visit the market. They were also provided with condoms and weekly medical checks, with treatment given as required. After ten months, the Allied advance forced a retreat to northern Sulawesi, where the group was dispersed among villages until the war ended. The Malayans were too ashamed to return home, and Keng Sie Lei remarried in Java. On her husband's death she became a Buddhist nun and was interviewed in her convent. She had no intention of demanding compensation.

There are other cases of women becoming mistresses to Japanese. One, from Solo, Java, whose mother had died early and whose father in the Dutch Army was missing, obtained work as a waitress in a Japanese restaurant in Cepu. A young soldier who had drawn her attention by generous tipping, seduced her in the bathroom, doubtless of the spacious style favoured in Japanese public premises. Soon afterwards they lived together for some time, but he was transferred away before their baby girl was born. Although she resumed restaurant work, no other Japanese disturbed her, since she was regarded as belonging to her first lover. He never returned, so she remarried. Her daughter also raised a family and the two now have only one request of the Japanese government—to meet the ex-lover and father if he is still alive. Otherwise they hope to learn where his grave is.

Another woman had been recruited to work in a jute factory in the Kudus area by a village administrator, on Japanese instructions. Although only twelve years of age, she was soon moved to the home of the Japanese deputy head of the factory, supposedly to supervise three tailors accommodated there. But she was also required to become the deputy head's mistress. This practice of obtaining mistresses from factory staff was common. She was paid Rp200 a month, with extras up to Rp100. She was also given gifts of cloth, which enabled not only her but her family to be reasonably well clothed, even if only in jute garments.

An informant from Tanah Toraja in Sulawesi told interviewers he knew of Torajan women marrying Japanese, but not of any becoming comfort women. In the light of other evidence, this suggests the limitations of popular local knowledge of the subject: comfort stations were not exactly publicised by the Japanese. Not only the station, but often the whole street or area, as with Cairnhill in Singapore, was sealed off, with entry restricted to the Japanese military.

One case the informant knew of was that of a girl, then aged eighteen, who was forced to marry a Japanese under threat to her and her father's lives. But the Japanese treated her very well and on being forced to return to Japan at the end of the war, left her money, clothing and food which lasted a year. Prevented from joining him in Japan, she remarried. The child she had born to him was able to visit his father in Japan, and received financial support until his death in 1982.

Similar cases of a form of marriage seem to have been numerous in Sulawesi, though are not reported elsewhere.

As elsewhere, the licensing and supervision of comfort stations were in the hands of the logistics division, with collaboration by the civil administration and some participation by the *kempeitai*. At the beginning of the Japanese Occupation, the existing pool of professional prostitutes seems to have been adequate. The women were not only of local origin but included some Dutch. The Dutch population was not only very much larger than the European populations in other Asian colonies, but included a much wider range of occupations, among which prostitutes were well represented. The Japanese always required comfort women to sign declarations of willingness, in various combinations of Japanese, Dutch and Malay, irrespective of the actual degree of consent or even whether the signatories understood what they were signing. Many signed voluntarily, but lived to regret this. One record describes the typical pattern as 'to begin freely but end up imprisoned'.

As the original comfort stations staffed more or less by volunteers became depleted by women being removed to become private mistresses, or else kept out of action by venereal disease, the Japanese authorised operators to undertake more intensive recruitment. This increasingly involved Dutch women. It was a year or two before most of the large numbers of these, often with children, could be interned, and those living in poor circumstances outside the camps were highly vulnerable to enticement or pressure. Some, about to be interned, were offered a choice between internment and prostitution. Some who had already experienced the horrors of the camps were prepared to consider prostitution as an alternative.

Shirley F. Huie reports that conditions in civilian internment camps were certainly no better than those suffered by prisoners-of-war, the overall death rate in both cases being well over one-third. In the words of one informant: 'Some girls went willingly with Japanese men when volunteers were called for. They had their own reasons for doing this.' Another, after recording a later case of forced abduction, adds: 'There are others who went voluntarily because they couldn't stand the restrictions and the camp life any more.'

Even when some pretext, such as factory work, was used the internees soon became aware of what was implied:

> When only young attractive girls were approached, it was obvious that the so-called factory was in fact a brothel. One hundred volunteers were found and their duty was to entertain soldiers returning from battle in the South Pacific and in need of R and R. In my experience girls were never forced to go with them. They always gave you the opportunity of refusing.

Two notorious operators who were early given access to the camps, as well as preying on women living outside, were the proprietors of the Sakura (Cherry Blossom) Club, established in June 1943 by order of the Resident (civil administrator) of Jakarta. The Theresa Club was established for high officers. A Dutch observer mentions seeing children waiting at the entrance of the Theresa Club for their mothers to finish work. He adds that, in formal terms, there was no compulsion in these cases.

The administration of the camps themselves was in the hands of the Japanese Home Ministry until 7 November 1943, when responsibility was transferred to the War Ministry, probably with a view to possible Allied landings in Indonesia. But the Army did not effectively take over until 1 April 1944, and all cases of forced prostitution of Dutch women in Java occurred during this transitional period. Paradoxically, the Army takeover ended this practice in Sumatra as well, under circumstances already described.

Reports of pressure on women in camps in Sumatra refer to Aceh, Brastagi, Padang and Palembang, the last involving Australian nurses. Refusal seems, however, to have generally been successful in these cases. In the case of Brastagi, two out of eight women are said to have submitted, and in Palembang threats to women's families are mentioned as effective. They would account for a number of cases where outright force was not used.

The experience of Australian nurses at Palembang forms a supplement to accounts of Indonesian cases. The key incident occurred in March 1942 at a camp where thirty-two nurses were being held, along with about 500 other civilian women. They had survived the sinking of the ship *Vyner Brooke*, which had evacuated sixty-five nurses from Singapore. Another twenty-one of the survivors had been massacred by the Japanese on Bangka Island. The sole survivor from Bangka, Vivian Bullwinkel, was among those at Palembang.

According to the nurses, the Japanese cleared out houses near the camp and equipped them with beds to use as an officers' club and brothel. On the afternoon of 28 March, the nurses were told that they would have to entertain the officers. Initially only four were required. But the nurses refused to allow a selection to be made. At the same time an outright refusal to co-operate also seemed inadvisable. As a compromise, and on the principle of 'safety in numbers', all agreed to visit the club, except for the youngest, and three others who were ill.

Before they set out they tried to make themselves as unattractive as possible. Inside the club the starving women took food offered by the officers, also stuffing their pockets for later. They refused alcohol. They were offered lipstick and told they could have anything they wanted in return for sex, but they refused. After about an hour, all but four of the nurses were told to go. Then even these four were allowed to leave.

The group managed to get word through to the local Resident and were never harassed again, either because of his insistence on proper procedure or because other women at the camp were found compliant.

Pressure in the camps was more persistent and ruthless in Java. The three clearest cases of compulsion occurred in Semarang (as recounted earlier), Magelang and Bandung. The Magelang Club was run by a retired Japanese officer with close *kempeitai* involvement. In December 1943 some Japanese, including the Resident, visited nearby Muntilan camp to check on available women. With the help of the Dutch camp administration, he listed fifty. The Dutch camp administrators tried various measures to stop any follow-up by advising mothers to keep daughters hidden, getting other women to enter hospital, and persuading some reputed to have served the Japanese in Surabaya to volunteer. These did so, but when the Japanese reappeared in January they took not only seven volunteers, but seized eight more. The mothers of the abducted girls resisted so vigorously that Indonesian police had to be used to control them. The girls were then taken to the Magelang Club, with two being returned after a couple of days, while eight more volunteers were taken.

In March 1944 eight women in the Tjihapit camp near Bandung were called to the camp office. After being briefly lodged with Chinese nearby, they were taken to the local officers' club, which was already staffed with both Dutch and local women. Six of the eight persisted in refusal, and were returned to the camp after a couple of days. The other two remained. One woman pressured into service in Bandung was the first to publicly identify herself in the Netherlands. She is Keetje Ruizeveld, who gave the newspaper *Volkskrant* an account of how she was recruited. She says she is thankful that, unlike the case of other mothers, her own daughters were not taken. The eldest at twelve was too young. She submitted herself to an atmosphere of intimidation, particularly as some women who resisted disappeared, perhaps being shot.

Life in the comfort station turned out to be more endurable than she expected. The Japanese she encountered were polite, some even juvenile, and the regulations, which were fairly humane as they stood, were kept. Clients, for example, always took a shower before being serviced. But it was hard for girls of sixteen or seventeen, who sometimes became suicidal. The older women tried to cheer them up, but there were still a couple of cases of girls slashing their wrists. Ruizeveld confirms the general pattern of recruitment, beginning with a search for volunteers who might hope for better food or earnings, then the resort to enticement by the offer of hospital or restaurant work, and finally intimidation.

6. The end of a nightmare, the beginning of another

If being a comfort woman during the war was terrible, for many, the end of the hostilities did not bring relief. First there were the dramatic last phases of the war to endure. Those involved with the women acquitted themselves as badly as one would expect. Evidence on the misfortunes of the comfort women in the last phases of war and the transition to peace—which in Korea was so shadowed and brief—is more fragmentary than for any aspect of their story. Reasons are obvious enough: wholesale death and destruction in areas of intense combat; disintegrating organisation and communications; the loss or deliberate destruction of records; and the long and tortuous process of repatriation or resettlement.

One instance suggesting specific official concealment of evidence on the comfort system is contained in a decrypted message from Chief of Staff, First Southern Expeditionary Fleet, dated 18 August 1945 (three days after surrender) reading:

> On 1st August the personnel employed in connection with Japanese Naval comforts at Singapore were appointed civilian employees of 101st hospital. Most of the girls were made auxiliary nurses. Other commands under 1st Southern Expeditionary Fleet are to conform.

A similar message from Makassar in the Celebes to Civil Administration Departments dated 20 August reads: 'Japanese women in all localities are to be attached to local hospitals as nurses. When this message is understood, burn it.'

As this last message refers to all Japanese women (and probably colonial subjects as was customary) it may have had the wider aim of securing for them the greater degree of protection which might apply to nurses under international conventions. The 1 August date in the first message predates the first clear signs that the end of the war was imminent, so other motives could have been applied then, but the extension of the procedure was clearly a reaction to the surrender. Whatever the motives, the effect was to obscure the nature of the comfort system in the immediate post-war phase.

In areas under immediate military threat, conditions of sexual service towards the end were particularly frenzied. One young officer is described in Kim Il Myon's *Tenno no Guntai to Chosenjin Ianfu*, as obsessively driven to visit the comfort station every night. Each night could be his last, and he did not want to die regretting missed opportunities. This behaviour went on until he was deathly pale and impotent, complaining that his 'little boy' no longer obeyed him.

At least the *Kamikaze* Corps had a fairly clear idea when they had to die. They are said to have been provided with free sex during their last week among the living.

They were not the only suicidal troops. Some Japanese units faced with inevitable defeat were inclined to follow the tradition of *gyoku-sai*—either fighting to the death or committing mass suicide as an alternative to surrender. The term means 'broken jewel' and comes from a saying in Chinese history that 'it is better to be a jewel and be broken than a tile and remain whole': an honourable death is better than a dishonourable life. Troops in this state of mind preferred that their women shared in such a death. In the same way, comfort women visiting pillboxes in the forward areas were told to save the last shots in the guns issued to them for suicide.

The starkest accounts of *gyokusai* involving comfort women relate to the northern Burma front and Micronesia. In Lameng, across the China border from Myitkyina, the Japanese had a network of twelve positions linked by underground dugouts and passages, which their team of comfort women traversed to provide their services. Exceptionally for an area so far forward, there were fifteen Japanese women here as well as five Koreans. From the spring of 1944, the force was attacked by vastly superior numbers of Chinese. In response to their hopeless position, the tactic of sending out suicide squads of twenty men at night to inflict what damage they could, was adopted. They were naturally provided with sex first. As the situation became desperate, the comfort women also had to help with nursing, carry ammunition and prepare rations.

The commanding officer considered evacuating the women while the chance remained. He was persuaded by his adjutant, however, that they would prefer to die with the men. Kim Il Myon comments that this could conceivably be true of the Japanese, but hardly of the

Koreans. He relates that one of the Japanese women and a soldier who had been blinded asked the commanding officer to conduct a marriage ceremony for them. She in particular wished to end her role as a prostitute and die as a married woman. The commander agreed, but not having the customary *sake*, they exchanged the wedding cups with water. At the end of more than three months fighting, the soldier had his wife guide him in throwing his last hand-grenade. The woman committed suicide by taking potassium cyanide—the poison of choice in this situation. A couple of accounts agree that the Koreans at Lameng lived to surrender and a photograph has been published of one being interrogated by Allied troops at Lameng.

Their fellows at the nearby siege of T'engyueh were much less fortunate. This was a traditional-style walled city, occupied by the Japanese as a fortress after the flight of the inhabitants. The forces were accompanied by seven Korean comfort women. After fighting ended at Lameng, the Chinese concentrated both land and air attacks on T'engyueh. They penetrated the walls in mid-August. There was savage street fighting. As medical personnel were diverted to combat duties, the comfort women had to act as nurses, though they could do little for the wounded except bring food and remove excreta. As the fighting got closer, they took refuge in a dugout.

Meanwhile the commanding officer was distributing the remaining hand-grenades, with instructions that the last ones were to be used for suicide. The Japanese wounded killed themselves. Those still mobile died fighting the Chinese. Since it was doubtful the Korean comfort women would willingly follow this practice, he decided to have a sergeant throw two hand-grenades into their dugout late at night, while they slept. The narrator of this shameful episode, who was attached to the Myitkyina component of the force, expressed regret that no memorial existed to the sacrificed Korean women—a sentiment that recurs in other contexts.

This episode has often been quoted to imply that such a practice was common. There is little indication of it, however, except in Micronesia in similar circumstances of overwhelming enemy attack, when retreat was impossible. In Truk in the Caroline Islands, intensive bombardment began in February 1944, and soon most of the installations of this largest naval base in Micronesia, including its three comfort stations, had been wiped out. Some comfort station operators in the area who had close relations with the command staff cemented by bribery, had arranged to be evacuated with some of their women as the Allied offensive approached. But about 100 women remained when the all-out attack was launched. They took shelter in a dugout among the breadfruit trees in the hills behind the base.

A United States landing seemed imminent. In view of the losses of Japanese shipping and fuel, this could only mean *gyokusai* for the garrison, following those at Tarawa in the Gilbert Islands, and other Pacific island fortifications further east. It was concluded the women would be an encumbrance and an embarrassment if they were to fall into American hands. It was decided to dispose of them. During a break between air raids at night, an ensign was sent to the women's dugout with two assistants. He was armed with a light machine gun. As he approached the dugout, it was so quiet he began to wonder whether it was occupied. He whistled the national anthem, the *Kimigayo*, to find out. At this a few women emerged; he shot them on the spot. He then continued the slaughter inside:

> He directed sweeping automatic fire at random into the pitch-dark interior of the dugout. Mingling with the ferocious, deafening reverberations of gunfire were bursts of shrill screams, followed by low moans, until the ensign eased the trigger to end his insane shooting rampage. Within the desolate dugout, the literal silence of death hovered like a frozen pall. He used his torch to examine the results. There were about seventy bodies.
>
> Spurts of blood were sticking to the bare earthen walls like geckos; some of the women were clinging to the rough-hewn breadfruit tree supports with their necks snapped; some were heaped up, some were embracing each other, some had fallen like logs, all drenched in blood. (Kim Il Myon 1976)

On Saipan in the Marianas, comfort women joined practically the whole female population in resorting to suicide by drowning in preference to falling into enemy hands. This was probably one of the grimmest episodes of the Pacific War.

On Luzon in the Philippines comparable tragedies occurred, although here there is little sign of the deliberate elimination of Korean comfort women. Some scope for retreat existed, even if under terrible conditions. The Navy evacuated some of its women, but the Army had little means of doing so. The Army retreat from Manila included about 500 women, among them comfort women. Disabled soldiers and others had been killed by nurses or medical orderlies with morphine injections.

In mid-January 1945, the survivors reached the Santa Fe gorge, and halted for a time in palm leaf shelters. By March, food shortages were becoming serious. By May, the approach of United States forces compelled them to move on, under increasing difficulties, as the Wet season began. They had no suitable clothing, and had to wrap themselves in soaking blankets, whether on the move or for sleeping. Some still had items such as watches that could be bartered for food, but cooking was impossible, and they had to attempt to digest everything raw, even rice. They were even forced to live off what they could find in the jungle, where a variety of possibilities existed, some very dubious. Food included parts of palms, pounded with stones, and swamp crabs which sometimes caused fatal diarrhoea. Less dangerous were lizards, though when women caught and chewed them alive they are reported as acquiring a demonic look, with blood streaming from their mouths.

The next stage was to resort to cannibalism. At first people already dead were eaten, but later 'strays' were killed for food. Many who were discovered by Filipino guerrillas were killed, one motive being, according to Yun Chong Mo's well-researched novel *My Mother was a Military Comfort Woman*, 'to fertilise the ground to repay what the Japanese had plundered'. The luckier emaciated survivors, found by United States forces, were eventually repatriated.

One curious stroke of luck befell a comfort station proprietor in the course of the retreat. A local Filipino wished to marry one of his charges. He was able to pose as her guardian and then, as an adoptive member of the bridegroom's household, was supported by him in his own hut until the war ended. He was reputed to have handled 2000 women in the course of his career.

If Korean comfort women had trouble getting off the Philippine islands during the dying days of the war, Filipina comfort women were also in danger.

Juanita Hamot

On my third week inside the Oraka Building, I could sense the Japanese were restless. I heard reports that the Americans were coming to liberate Manila. It was at that time that many Japanese 'used' us. One day, they herded us and forced us to board a truck. We were brought to another garrison which I came to know later as

Fort Santiago. Upon reaching that place, I saw many Japanese soldiers. They began to rape us. At least ten Japanese abused me that afternoon. I could hear explosions and gunfire outside.

After they were all through, we were again brought outside Fort Santiago, and led inside a church right in front of the garrison. I saw many people inside, while Japanese soldiers, heavily armed, were standing by the door. I felt that something was going to happen so I decided to go in the middle of the crowd. I was trying to look for Pining but could not locate her. Suddenly, I heard gunfire and everybody started falling down. Instinctively, I dropped to the floor at the initial outburst of gunfire. The men and women started falling over me and I could feel blood all over me. I could also hear people crying and shouting. I did not move because I was afraid that there were still Japanese soldiers inside the church.

After a while it became very quiet. All I could hear were the voices of those who were wounded. They were asking for help. I saw some of them standing up and the others trying to help those who were wounded. I was crying. All I could see were dead people and blood all over me. I ran out of the church and took refuge behind a wall near the church. I was found by American soldiers who brought me to shelter.

Far more common than the elimination of comfort women was their abandonment, sometimes without explanation. Those who accompanied the troops on the retreat from Myitkyina, as distinct from those captured and questioned by the United States psychological warfare team, joined the Japanese in an attempt to descend the Irrawaddy river on rafts improvised from drums. Only about one-fifth of those involved survived the treacherous currents and the bullets of the enemy. Also in Burma, in April 1945, the headquarters staff in Rangoon retreated to Moulmein near the Thai border, accompanied by the thirty Japanese comfort women from the officers' comfort station. They went without a word to the seventy or so Korean women in the other comfort stations.

The first indication of the change in their situation was a sudden absence of clients. They then encountered two media corps staff, who had come to destroy films stored in a film distribution centre next door, to prevent them falling into British hands. According to one account, some of the women invited them to stay the night, without payment. Other observers mention encounters with these women during the subsequent retreat. One account recalls surprise at the sight of a solitary Korean comfort woman outpacing a body of troops retreating along a railway line, barefoot and carrying a suitcase on her head. Some of them suggested she slow to their pace. But confidently, she vanished ahead into the darkness.

The main barrier on this route was the 200-metre wide Sittang River, where the railway bridge had been destroyed. The only means of crossing was by raft, either on board or clinging on. One observer noted a group of about 100 women, including comfort women, waitresses and others, gathered at the crossing point, wearing military clothing and burdened by packages of military currency. That this would soon become valueless was either not grasped or not contemplated. These poor bundles were often the only reward the women had to show for their long spells of sexual servitude.

Some had carried their money long distances, from Arakan or the Irrawaddy Delta or across the Pegu Yoma, halting to dry out the soaked notes in the sunshine. They may have been all that sustained the women through jungle downpours and incidents of carnage. Many ended their wanderings in the attempt to cross the Sittang. Weakened by hardship and weighed down by their money, many lost their grip on the rafts and were swept away.

From her room in the Tai Sun Hotel near the Pudu Jail in Kuala Lumpur, Madam X, the Malayan Chinese comfort woman, could see the coming of the liberation forces:

> One day I saw Europeans march into the city. We were let out of the comfort stations and told to flee. None of the Japanese or Chinese traitors wanted us around when the Europeans came back. They were frightened we would point the finger at them. However, the girls in our station caught our mama-san and her husband, and drowned them both. I went back to Serdang and found my parents.

She was one of the 'lucky' ones.

Comfort for occupation troops

One incident reported from Manchuria is typical of the post-war fate of many comfort women. A medical officer at the Hsingshu Army hospital had the nurses parade, and told them that 'in order to ensure our safety and to avoid antagonising the Soviet troops, whatever you may be required to do, you should endure it for the sake of returning home alive'.

If even nurses could be required to offer their bodies to Occupation troops, it is obvious that former comfort women would automatically be expected to fulfil this role, given the traditional view of their 'defiled' condition. A few women found alternatives, though evidence of these is scarce. Several are reported to have drowned themselves when their ships came in sight of their homeland, unable to face undoubtedly bleak futures. Those who soldiered on often continued in their previous role, this time with Occupation troops. Pae Pong Gi, for instance, was a Korean comfort woman who continued her role in Okinawa with the American troops. She also worked in fringe occupations, in bars or cabarets. Like many others in the same situation, she trafficked on the black market in goods obtained from troops, switching from one role to another as need dictated.

The narrator of Yun Chong Mo's *My Mother was a Military Comfort Woman* recalls his upbringing in a hot springs resort, a characteristic red light district. His mother had a business there supplying goods to the hostesses, and engaging in minor money-lending. In the book, he notices that she never deals in smuggled Japanese cosmetics or other such items usually in demand in these circles. As a child, he feels that he would prefer his mother to be a glamorous hostess, rather than a hanger-on to them. It is only later that he learns the truth.

In Japan, the authorities were prompt in applying the logic of the comfort system to the American Occupation Forces. In this case, however, the essential concern was preventing rape and disorder among their own population. The operators who served the authorities in this new context are likened by Kim Il Myon to 'gutter rats', able somehow to survive every eventuality, whether victory or defeat.

The main difference in the system was that, if during the war tactics of deception or coercion had been applied mainly to Koreans, they were now turned on Japanese women. In one case the victims were a number of girls drafted into the student mobilisation program. They had taken shelter in the remaining half of their dormitory after their munitions factory in Kawasaki, near Tokyo, had been bombed out. They had no homes left to which they could return. They were approached by four men in two trucks bearing the sign 'New Life Social Service Association, Tourism Section'. The men, who seemed to be demobbed servicemen, offered the girls work in 'patriotic tourism', telling them that they would be well paid, receive the best food available in Japan, and be employed by a philanthropic president interested in charitable projects.

After some debate the thirty women were taken by truck not to a charitable project, but to a United States Army comfort station. Here they were addressed by a man in the role of representative of the Home Ministry. He said they would have to undertake a special voluntary service and to do so with pride, 'in order to relieve anxiety in the Most Honoured Quarter'—a phraseology customarily used to refer to service to the Emperor or the Imperial House. They would, he said, be remembered in history for their sacrifice.

At night, American soldiers claimed from them the same sort of service their Japanese counterparts had. Any girls trying to escape were forced back by Japanese guards. Some Allied troops after the war took the view that it was excusable to rape Japanese women as a reprisal for the rapes committed by Japanese soldiers. In this case, however, given access to an organised brothel, the Americans may not have thought of what they were doing in terms of rape.

There were other documented cases. In another, a unit of about 100 women, mobilised as part of preparations for the 'decisive battle for the Homeland' near Tokyo, were kept at their post until early September 1945. They were then directed by the Public Safety Bureau of the Home Ministry to act as a Women's Special Attack Corps (formal term for the *kamikaze*) and to 'endure the unendurable' (a phrase from the Emperor's Surrender Rescript), in serving as 'a shield for all Japanese womanhood'. They were then distributed among four comfort stations for United States troops in Tokyo.

In another case, at the major naval base at Kure, near Hiroshima, were nine girls belonging to the Women's Youth Corps whose homes had been destroyed by the atomic bomb. They were visited by an official of the 'Public Safety Preservation Association, authorised by the Home Ministry', who told them that their opportunity to render true service had arrived. They could fulfil the pledges they had sealed in blood in joining their Corps during the war. It was only women like them, he continued, who could 'preserve the chastity of Japanese women from the foul hands of the Occupation forces'.

Persuaded by, or resigned to such rhetoric, they were taken by truck to a wooden two-storey house. There they were searched by

Occupation Navy men, covered all the while by firearms. Apparently there were suspicions that they might be carrying knives to defend themselves. Then they were raped 'until they lost consciousness' (Kim Il Myon 1976).

Later they were taken to a more permanent comfort station, where the eloquent official re-appeared. He asked them if they had acquitted themselves well as examples of Japanese womanhood. One at least took her own life.

Situations such as these reflected systematic planning by central authorities. They are examples of the Japanese bent for meticulous organisation and pragmatic adaptation to change, no matter how devastating. Only two days after the surrender on 15 August 1945, a conference was held by bureau heads of the Home and Welfare ministries and the Metropolitan Police Board, with a view to mobilising the licensed prostitution system to meet the needs of Occupation troops. Next day more concrete planning was undertaken by representatives of the police, together with two major prostitution operators and two representatives of the Hypothec Bank of Japan.

Guidelines adopted were first, that all prostitution operators would co-operate under the direction of the Police Board; second, that the police would issue secret directives to facilitate their operations; and third, that the Hypothec Bank would cover at least 70 per cent of required funds. Not long after, at the beginning of September, police and bank representatives attended a meeting of fifty-seven operators in the vast red light district of Asakusa. The police made it clear they would tolerate the employment of gang groups if intimidation were necessary to recruit adequate numbers of comfort women. The bank promised to provide ¥24 million, and the operators formed an organisation with the English name of Recreation and Amusement Association.

Intimidation in recruitment was in fact little needed in conditions of war-caused devastation and economic paralysis. Not only employment, but even rudimentary shelter was hard to come by. By the end of November, 20,000 women had been recruited for comfort stations. Within another two months, many were infected with venereal disease, which proved equally devastating to the American Forces. Infection rates were as high as 68 per cent in one unit.

The problem was that, unlike with Japanese servicemen, the operators had no authority to enforce the use of condoms. Occupation authorities were slow to realise the rapidity of the progress of infection. They had to declare the comfort stations off-limits, and they were closed. At the same time, it was realised that prostitution in some form would continue. As a safeguard, the authorities could merely develop measures like the issue of condoms, education in hygiene, and the installation of prophylactic aid posts, where soldiers exposed to infection could receive early preventive treatment. The women in some brothels were medically checked, as well.

The failed official comfort stations were inevitably replaced by a network of mainly small brothels, within easy reach of camps. They were organised in large part by former comfort station operators returning from overseas, and staffed by the former comfort women, who otherwise would have been even more destitute than the people who had remained at home. Since the currency was in chaos, they welcomed payment such as cigarettes, food or clothing, items which they could either use themselves or sell on the black market.

Given the Occupation-induced boom in prostitution, it is not surprising that the first rebuilding from war devastation occurred in the red light districts, traditionally known in Japan as 'three trade districts': cafes, brothels and *geisha* houses.

In South Korea, the same situation prevailed. There was no attempt at central organisation. For some time the only central authority was in any case the Occupation administration, which abolished licensed prostitution. The Korean War, however, later provided a major stimulus to camp or base prostitution, which has persisted as a social irritant and the focus of women's groups' protests. As with most other matters, little is known about the corresponding situation in North Korea, though its government showed interest in the comfort women issue when it became public after the lawsuit.

A return to 'normal' life

A considerable number of comfort women survived to be repatriated from Southeast Asia. Others settled where they found themselves. When Japanese businessmen and tourists began to return to the region in the late 1950s, and Japanese restaurants were established to cater for them, it was noted from time to time that some waitresses working in them had backgrounds of contact with the Japanese Armed Forces.

One such case of an assimilated Korean comfort woman came to light in Thailand. There were a couple of others in Vietnam. In 1964, the Seoul press reported that notice had been received a year previously from the South Vietnamese authorities of a 44-year-old Korean woman who had died there, leaving property but no heirs. A search was now on for possible heirs in South Korea, said the papers. The woman's property was valued at US$20,000 or more, and included eighteen diamonds, $1835 in United States currency, interests in cafes and farmland, and some moveable property. Numerous claimants appeared in South Korea. None, however, could be validated.

Since this woman had no family in Vietnam to inherit her property, it would appear she had continued in prostitution after the war as many others were to do.

Another case in Vietnam was one of full assimilation. Pae Ok Su had been taken to Burma as a comfort woman. She later reached Saigon, where she was interned. She subsequently married a Vietnamese, and had a number of children. At the end of the Vietnam War in 1975, she and her five children were evacuated by a South Korean ship sent to rescue anti-communist Vietnamese. They reached Korea as Vietnamese refugees. She left her husband and a married daughter in Vietnam. She died in Korea in 1987, at the age of sixty.

There were cases when in the absence of an official program of repatriation, soldiers took the initiative themselves. In Burma, when a group of Japanese comfort women were being abandoned, some men of the lower ranks took pity on them and smuggled them in the hold of a ship. The postal orderly in Hupei reports that at the end of the war some comfort women in his area were robbed by local people, down to their underwear. He and some comrades, however, gave them some of their own, and brought them out to safety. Since it was fortunately mid-summer, less clothing than usual was needed.

A Korean conscript recalls that while he was awaiting repatriation from Shanghai and frequenting Korean bars there, he met groups of ex-comfort women who had been in Hankow. They had facial eruptions, and he learned that they had been under treatment for venereal disease while with the Army. The symptoms had merely been suppressed, however. Most of these women remained in Shanghai.

Most comfort women from China and the more stable areas of Southeast Asia seem to have been repatriated—in some cases grudgingly. A typist from Surabaya relates that, on her repatriation ship, she was shocked at the conditions suffered in the hold by 100 comfort women and their children. Upon protesting, she was told: 'There is no need to treat them as human. They're less than cattle. They should be thankful we've taken them at all.' A later investigator from Taiwan found 253 names of apparently Taiwanese women among listed passengers on a repatriation ship bound for Korea. He conjectured that most would be comfort women, though their subsequent movements are not clear.

One conspicuous gap in repatriation was southern Sakhalin which, though it had been Japanese territory, was seized by the Soviet Union at the end of the war. Korean labour draftees had been abandoned by the Japanese; some were plaintiffs in a lawsuit against the Japanese government. It is true that at war's end there was little time for considered action. The Soviet Union declared war on Japan only in the last week of the war. After the dropping of the atomic bomb on Hiroshima, Russian tanks at once crossed the border from northern Sakhalin. At Shitsuka (now Poronaisk), were several comfort stations staffed entirely with Koreans, about twenty in all. Alarmed by bombing and the enemy approach, they fled to the railway station just as the last train, carrying all the Japanese who could squeeze aboard, was leaving. The women in their panic pursued the train, calling out for it to stop. Some ran ahead of it on the track in an attempt to halt it. But it continued to pick up speed and, with its whistle blowing, continued on towards the women. Several of them were crushed beneath the wheels. An account of this incident was given to the Sakhalin litigants by a Japanese survivor.

The collapse of Japanese defences in Manchuria was equally swift. The much greater area and an efficient rail network facilitated the repatriation of many, if not all, Koreans. This area, especially the south, was distinctive in having a long-established Korean minority better disposed to Korean refugees than local populations elsewhere.

In 1956 a convicted war criminal who had served his sentence in Fushun in Manchuria, was taken on a tour of China before release and repatriation, so he could observe the new regime's efforts for social improvement. These included women's rehabilitation centres, where former comfort women and others who had been similarly used were receiving venereal disease treatment and occupational training. The Maoist regime long continued to claim a unique degree of success in eliminating prostitution through re-education. Any successes they achieved, however, have proved no more permanent than elsewhere.

Those who were able to return from Manchuria to their families for the most part kept silent about their experiences. Some were able to keep up the pretence that during the war they had done what they were recruited to do—be it waitressing or nursing. In a society dominated by patriarchal views of chastity and morality, and a lack of openness about sex, the shame of the whole repugnant experience silenced many women. Many may have felt themselves to blame for their fate. Women in such a position were more likely to want to keep their whole wartime ordeal hushed up rather than demonstrate for compensation. The very fact that female chastity has such a high moral value made loss of virginity even more devastating and psychologically more damaging to the comfort women victims. Their prospects for a respectable marriage and a family were dramatically reduced. Those who did marry often kept their shame secret for decades, enduring their conjugal activities as a torment, and suffering severe mental anguish which could not find release in an open acknowledgement of the wrong done to them. In societies which placed great emphasis on the birth of heirs, many of these women proved sterile, crippled by a variety of diseases, the brutality of their experiences, the drugs they were sometimes forced to consume to abort unwanted pregnancies or to prevent or cure diseases. Sometimes they had been sterilised by the operations done on them to eliminate menstruation, keeping them always available. They had trouble coping with the need to pretend to normalcy, and to stay silent about their wartime suffering.

The pretence by their menfolk that nothing had happened did not make their psychological suffering any easier to bear. Many suffered a variety of physical and emotional problems linked directly to their wartime experiences, making it difficult for them to work effectively afterwards. Lack of compensation generated economic hardship in the many cases where they could not lead economically productive lives, or were forced to continue as they had abandoned during the war. Many were simply abandoned at the bottom of the economic pile. It would be accurate to say that their wartime experiences ruined many comfort women's chances of a stable family life.

For many of the women, then, rape and brutalisation were but a prelude to a life of suffering. The view that a raped woman is a defiled woman dies hard everywhere in Asia.

Gertrudes Balisalisa of the Philippines, for example, was rejected by her family after the war:

When the Americans came there was much fighting . . . I escaped and ran on foot . . . When I went home to Legaspi City, my husband treated me like I have a contagious disease. My relatives also looked down on me. Just like the Japanese he would come to me when he needed me but afterwards I was just like a piece of furniture. My husband stopped my children from calling me 'mother'. He separated my children from me after a few years. I now have no contact with them as they refused to recognise me as their mother.

The idea of rape as defilement instead of injustice also extends beyond Asia. Jan Ruff, who was going through the initial stages of becoming a nun when war broke out, found that her horrific wartime experiences made her 'unacceptable' to the Church as a nun.

Said Madam X, who had been raped and hauled off to a comfort station:

> You might think that I hate the Japanese, but I don't. I just hate all men and I hate sex. It's a terrible thing to say, but I even hate the sight of my son-in-law, who lives in this house. When I got married, my husband kept asking for sex, and I kept making excuses and putting him off. Of course, I had to agree to sex sometimes, but I was never able to get pregnant. We adopted two children. Because I hated sex, my husband found himself a second wife, with whom he had three children. I never dared to tell him of my experiences. When I was sleeping with my husband, I often had nightmares and he would always ask 'What's wrong? What's wrong?' I could never tell him the cause of my nightmares . . . For nearly fifty years I have lived with my terrible secret. Even though what happened to me was no fault of my own, I dread to think what people would say if they knew my story. Imagine what the neighbours would say. It's awful not to be able to talk to anyone. Not even my own husband or children. Sometimes I am deeply depressed and have a long face. No-one knows why.

In Indonesia, Johana who had spent four years as a comfort woman, was extremely fortunate to meet an understanding man who not only accepted her past, but was able to some extent to convince her that all that had happened to her was not her fault. She should not, he said, be ashamed of herself. She managed to give birth to a son, and now has two grandchildren. She is one of the lucky few to find both an understanding husband and a family. But even she says:

> Even though these horrible things happened to me many years ago, I still have deep sorrow and grief inside me. Time does not heal. I hope the Japanese will give us compensation, but when you come to think of it, no money, no matter how much, can ever compensate us for what we went through.

Ito Keiichi, author of *Soldiers' History of the Army*, wrote that he supported the erection of a monument to nurses and 'field comfort women' in the grounds of the Yasukuni shrine, the premier Shinto shrine, where the Japanese heroes of the Pacific War are honoured. The comfort women, he contended, shared everything that frontline soldiers faced. Kim Il Myon, writing in 1975, commented that although he appreciated Ito's respect for the women, they themselves could only regard such a monument as a perpetuation of their shame. From what he knew of many, they would prefer to 'rub out the past with an eraser, if that were possible'.

It is indicative of the 180 degree turn in attitudes that in 1990 the South Korean women's group most active in the comfort women issue was able to propose just such a commemorative monument to the suffering endured by countless, nameless, faceless comfort women. These women suffered an extreme form of the excesses of a still-current male attitude. This regards women as sex objects to be used and discarded, as necessary.

The behaviour of some of the Allied and American Occupation troops towards the comfort women they encountered clearly illustrates this. One informant who was an NCO with the Allied Forces in North Borneo at the end of the war said that there was large-scale rape of Japanese and Taiwanese nurses, as well as comfort women, by Allied soldiers. If a common view was that it was acceptable to rape Japanese women because Japanese men had raped Caucasians, this extended to a denial of the women's human rights. One Australian soldier, who had captured comfort women and taken advantage of them, said his actions were not rape, because the women did not resist. Another Australian said the women he captured 'were too scrawny to screw', rather than that it was not right to do so.

The question must surely be: Are not all women the victims of wars started by men? Does the abuse and victimisation of women have to be on the scale of the comfort system to become worthy of attention?

7. Consciousness-raising and exposure

The names of both the victims and the accused from the only war crimes trials for forced prostitution have been sealed and the archives are not scheduled to be opened until 2025. The trials were held in Dutch Indonesia over interned Dutch women who were made to work as comfort women. Held in 1948 in Batavia, as Jakarta was then known, they received little attention outside Dutch circles until the issue became internationally prominent in 1992, when records held in The Hague were made public.

There were no following trials, for various reasons. First, conditions during the Indonesian war of independence, from 1945 to 1950, made it impossible to detain potential accused or witnesses. On the wider world stage, the Western Allies decided to terminate war trials from 1949 so as to concentrate on their Cold War strategy, with the co-operation of their former enemies. In the words of Winston Churchill:

> Our policy should henceforth be to draw the sponge across the crimes and horrors of the past—hard as that may be—and look, for the sake of all our salvation, towards the future.

Another major factor in bringing the trials to an end was the great variety of circumstances under which Dutch women came to serve in the comfort stations. They followed much the same sequence as in Japan and Korea, beginning with professional prostitutes continuing their existing way of life, moving on to different degrees of deception or pressure and, finally, forcible seizure. One count of various sources suggests that at least fifty-two Dutch women were forced into prostitution. Others suggest up to 100.

After the Japanese surrender, war crimes investigators were able to trace the responsible officers, doctors and operators in Semarang (see Chapter 2). Colonel Okubo, who had first proposed the idea, was questioned at his home in Japan in January 1947. Two days later, he carried out a ritual suicide in a temple. As in many such cases, he left a note claiming sole responsibility for organising the operation.

The three related trials were described by the Japanese as the 'white horse case': that is, white women being used like horses. Among the accused, General Nozaki committed suicide in prison and Major Okada was sentenced to death, protesting his innocence on the grounds that he had had no decision making role. He was judged, however, to have shown special eagerness in rounding up European women. Eight officers were sentenced to between seven and twenty years in prison. An interpreter who knew Dutch was sentenced to two years. The lightest sentence was imposed on a medical officer for the neglect of the women's health, which had led in many cases to venereal disease. Two officers were acquitted. Some of those convicted admitted having deceived the women by offering them work as waitresses.

A Japanese journalist writing for the *Asahi Shimbun,* who witnessed these and other Dutch trials of Japanese war criminals, criticised the proceedings because

> they pronounced the death sentence without allowing a defence; the proceedings were conducted in Dutch; prisoners were only allowed to answer 'yes' or 'no', and if they tried to add explanations they were threatened with immediate execution; medicines were withheld from sick Japanese prisoners; the judge verbally abused defendants and their lawyers.

As in many war crimes trials, the court proceedings essentially became a simple ratification of the findings of earlier investigations. They were in any case something of a legal hybrid, as the various nations involved in war trials all had varied codes and procedures.

The Japanese-South Korean Basic Treaty of 1965

In Korea, more affected than any other country by the comfort system, the comfort women after the war melted into the general population. The issue of rape and forced prostitution never came to trial. Nor was it part of the compensation talks between the male-dominated governments of both countries. Korea had only a brief peace before the chaos of the Korean War descended on it in June 1950, hostilities not ending until July 1953. The result of this fratricidal

war was a divided Korea and a resurgent Japan whose post-war economic recovery was partially caused by the war.

It was not until 1965 that the Japanese-South Korean Basic Treaty
was signed. It gave the South Korean government the right to handle
all matters of compensation for wartime suffering. The long delay
had been caused by South Korea President Syngman's Rhee's refusal to deal realistically with the Japanese. During his presidency
from 1948 to 1960 he refused normal diplomatic contacts, demanding an astronomical compensation sum from Japan without room
for negotiation.

Debate on the comfort women issue and on the validity of demands made by ex-comfort women and associated groups has
hinged on this 1965 treaty. Important developments which led up to
it began with the freezing by the American Occupation administration of Japanese assets in South Korea, first public and then private
ones. In Soviet-controlled North Korea, all Japanese property was
nationalised by the Provisional People's Committee. Such property
in South Korea was only formally assigned to the local authority by
the South Korea-US Agreement of 1958.

Korea was not a party to the 1952 San Francisco Peace Treaty
which ended the war between Japan and the Allies. As a Japanese
colony, it could not be regarded as a sovereign belligerent on either
side—although North Korea claimed to have been in a state of war
with Japan by virtue of its guerrilla activities in China, in collaboration with the Communists. The Peace Treaty did, however, restore
Korean sovereignty, and provide for a legal settlement of claims by
negotiations between Korea and Japan. This was the basis of the
1965 treaty. In earlier phases of negotiations, the Japanese treated
questions as a matter of two-way claims. The American Occupation
administration, however, ruled out Japanese claims, assigning all
frozen Korean property to South Korea.

Claims by South Koreans included debts owed to them, such as
unpaid wages, savings held in Japan, and specified damages. All
these had to be documented. Documentation was, however, prob-
lematic, because of the widespread chaos of the Pacific and Korean
wars. Administrative acts by the Japanese in accordance with then-
current Japanese law were not clearly subject to compensation, since
Japanese sovereignty over Korea had been internationally recognised in the same way as other colonial regimes.

The international situation demanded an earlier settlement than would have been possible with an exhaustive study of evidence for claims. So a political, rather than a strictly legal, solution was agreed upon. Japanese funds provided under the 1965 Basic Treaty were described as an Independence Congratulation Fund. They consisted of US$300 million in grants, US$200 million in soft loans and an undertaking to obtain private credit of the order of US$300 million. The distribution of compensation for outstanding claims able to be demonstrated, became the responsibility of the South Korean government. Japan was absolved from further claims by the terms of the treaty.

It has been argued, however, that the South Korean government had no right to renounce individual claims. These of course included those of the comfort women. The treaty merely amounted to relinquishment of the right of diplomatic protection for its citizens in this respect. The Japanese government agreed to leave this question to the courts.

Another flaw in the treaty was that the South Korean government could only handle claims for Koreans residing in its territory, not those in Japan. Immediately after the conclusion of the San Francisco Peace Treaty, the Japanese Diet had passed a retrospective Law for Assistance to War-Disabled Veterans and War-Bereaved Families, covering the period when Taiwanese and Koreans still had Japanese nationality. This meant that people of such extraction living in Japan could claim assistance by opting for Japanese nationality. Some did so, but for those Koreans who did not, the option was closed by the 1965 Basic Treaty. Naturalisation then became virtually impossible.

Korean right of permanent residence in Japan had been recognised under the 1952 Peace Treaty. This did not save them and others without Japanese nationality from numerous harassments, however. These included compulsory fingerprinting and the carrying of alien registration cards.

Korean litigants such as comfort women and forced draftees now claim the right to compensation arising from the war on the basis that they had Japanese nationality at the time. They cite the case where the United Nations Human Rights Sub-commission upheld the right of Senegalese to French servicemen's pensions, if they had served in the French Army, and had French nationality at the time. Clearly there is ample scope for protracted legal argument.

Comfort women were completely left out of the terms of the 1965

Basic Treaty. With a series of military men at the helm of repressive regimes, and the Korean War to deal with in the 1950s and 1960s, comfort women were not a priority. The fact that many of the Korean women pressed into sexual service by the Japanese came from the poorer lower classes possibly made the issue insignificant to the ruling élite. The traditionally low status of women in Korean and Japanese society, and in practically all territories occupied by the latter, plus the attitude that rape and abuse of women were part of the war experience, may have combined to turn the abuse into a non-issue. It took changing attitudes to women's rights, increasingly vocal women's groups in both Korea and Japan, and women campaigners on both sides of the Sea of Japan in the 1990s to turn the comfort women issue into a greater one over women's rights, and to make it an indictment of sexist attitudes towards women.

An early move: the 1972 draft labour issue

An attempt to activate the issues was made in 1972, with the formation of the Korean Forced Draft Investigation Group. Investigation was mainly into conscript labourers during the Japanese Occupation. Drafted labourers working in Japan had been paid much less than the equivalent Japanese labourers, and even then, something like half their wages had been retained as compulsory savings to be paid only on discharge. And of course, these savings were rarely received, being lost with the collapse of Japan in 1945. Under the 1965 Basic Treaty, some of the Japanese compensation funds received had been distributed to claimants, but the compensation was far from adequate. Others entitled to a share of such compensation, such as comfort women like Mun Ok Ju, who had kept savings in Japanese banks, were not given anything since they had not come forward after the war.

Another issue was the lack of information on the many who had failed to return. Most would have died from the fighting, bombing or illness, either in Japan or the war zones. It was to prove impossible for a long time to get information out of the Japanese Labour and Welfare ministries, where records were ultimately found.

Draft labour included many women who were conscripted for wartime industries as part of the Women's Voluntary Service Corps. The figure universally quoted is that women draftees totalled 200,000, of whom 80,000 were comfort women. (Figures for males were much higher, but there is less agreement on what they were.) The bulk of the Women's Voluntary Service Corps were not comfort women, but because it had been generally assumed in Korea that all female draftees had become comfort women, even those who had not been involved in forced prostitution were reluctant to come forward. The official term, Women's Voluntary Service Corps, is often used as a euphemistic substitute for comfort women.

Some of the earliest 1992 findings by the first-ever South Korean government committee formed to look into forced draft labour came from school registers, recording the recruitment of schoolgirls to the Women's Voluntary Service Corps. A Japanese woman who had been teaching in Korea recalled how she had been requested in 1943 by the principal to select a number of sixth year primary school pupils for work in the Toyama aircraft parts factory. They were to be robust and from poor families. All were assumed to have become comfort women. She was very worried about this possibility. Later investigation, however, confirmed that, except for punitive cases, most girls so taken were actually employed in industry, where their level of education could be better used.

Although the focus of this early investigative work was on draft labour, it served to raise the issue of comfort women. And if they still remained something of a non-issue for the male-dominated South Korean government well into the 1980s, strong feminist pressure came to a head at the 1988 Olympic Games in Seoul.

Feminism and women's groups in South Korea

Early in 1988, with democratisation allowing the newer women's organisations to make vigorous progress, a group led by Professor Yun Chung Ok of Ehwa Women's University was formed within the South Korean Church Women's Alliance. This became the centre of action on the comfort women issue.

Under the influence of feminist thought, the group abandoned the traditional condemnation of prostitution as an offence against chastity—an essentially patriarchal concept. It favoured instead an emphasis on women's sexual freedom and self-determination. Professor Yun and her associates criticise even the sympathetic Kim Il Myon for distinguishing between Japanese comfort women, who were mainly of prostitute background, and 'innocent' Korean draftees. The distinction between 'respectable' and 'disreputable' women is meaningless, they say, if neither has sexual freedom under patriarchy:

> So long as there is no change in the sexual consciousness both of men, who do not realise that they are being controlled by using women's sex, or of women, who have internalised the 'ideal of chastity' imposed upon them, there will be no end to the danger of sex being used again as an expedient means of control.

For many years the main concern of many Korean women's groups had been the prevalence of sex tourism, mainly from Japan, and of prostitution around United States bases. The authorities had tolerated and even co-operated in these activities, apparently seeing them as sources of foreign exchange. One Director of Education in South Korea even described sex tourism as 'patriotic'. In 1972 when South Korean President Park Chung Hee declared martial law, replaced the previous constitution with his 'new order', and banned political activity of any kind, he simultaneously adopted a policy of intensively promoting tourism as a source of foreign exchange to replace that previously acquired through participation of Korean troops in the Vietnam War. Thus the 'sale of men's blood was succeeded by that of women's flesh', as the number of Japanese tourists flocking to South Korea jumped from 96,531 in 1972 to 217,287 in 1973, in just one year of promoting sex tours in 'the Land of the Morning Calm', to use the name for Korea popular in tourist brochures. The Japanese made up the majority of all tourists for the first time, and in 1973 income from tourism reached US$270 million. Foreign exchange earnings at the height of the Vietnam War in 1968 were only, by contrast, US$150 million.

Despite the repressive political climate of the South Korea of the 1970s, the Church Women's Alliance, acting simultaneously with Japanese women's organisations, held demonstrations against sex tourism at airports in both countries. The response of both governments was restrained—particularly as 1975 was International Women's Year. Most of the women's organisations in South Korea remained, however, for some years dominated by the officially sponsored leadership, carried over from Japanese colonial days.

In 1977, on a Japanese radio talk show about sex tours, the dialogue with a travel agent went like this:

Q. Do wives know about sex tours?
A. Five out of ten do not know. Husbands explain them as domestic or

foreign business trips. Those who do know are only concerned with the effect on themselves, which reflects their attitude of despising other Asians.

Q. How many group tours involve prostitution?

A. Eighty per cent go for this purpose, arranged by the agency and regarded as an integral part of evening entertainment. A large proportion of the earnings go to Japanese enterprises.

Q. What of the local women?

A. Prostitution is everywhere. In view of the poverty in Southeast Asia, fees and tips help both the women and the country. Critics reply that if one realises the background economic structure, one would not wish to hire such services.

Q. Is this shameful for Japan?

A. Tourists of all nationalities participate in sex tourism, but as Westerners proceed individually they are not conspicuous. Japanese are because they move in groups, a national characteristic that can't be helped. Critics reply that in any case it gives Japanese the reputation of being 'sex animals', and is a matter of shame.

Q. Have Japanese women any responsibility?

A. Women of the world understand these things and regard it as an expression of masculinity. It is an adjustment made for the sake of conjugal harmony. Critics reply that this shows a lack of understanding of marital and sexual relations, and that in such cases women bear a heavy responsibility.

Sex tours, however, form just part of the exploitation of women in Southeast Asia. There are believed to be tens of thousands of non-Japanese women being exploited in clubs in Japan, sometimes violently. One case that received wide publicity was that of Filipina Maricris Siosin, an entertainer in Fukuoka prefecture, whose body was returned to the Philippines with head injuries, stabbed genitals and covered with other knife wounds. Despite clear evidence of sexual torture and murder, and photographs of her battered and bloodied body notwithstanding, the official Japanese pathology report said she had died from hepatitis. President Corazon Aquino in response to the outcry banned Filipinas under twenty-three from 'entertaining' in Japan. Male Filipino recruiters objected on the grounds that 'the Japanese prefer teenage girls'.

Yun's group came to adopt the view that the comfort women issue, simultaneously shocking from the standpoints of morality, feminism and patriotism, could be used to arouse feelings against current practices. The two issues could be closely linked by portraying sex tourists as 'industrial warriors', today's equivalent of the wartime Japanese soldier, now working all-out at the industrial frontline to contribute to Japan's wealth as an economic great power, while taking comfort from the oppressed women of foreign lands. Sometimes, of course, the very same procurers who had once served the Japanese military continued as sex tour operators.

Yun, the central figure in the South Korean group, had a personal reason for emphasising the comfort women issue. She herself had narrowly escaped the draft of students. In the nick of time, her parents had pulled her out of Ehwa Women's College, the forerunner of the university at which she later taught. Yun's sense of the link between comfort women and post-war Allied base prostitution had been stimulated by Yamatani Tetsuo's 1979 film, *An Old Lady in Okinawa: Testimony of a Military Comfort Woman*, based on the experiences of a Korean comfort woman, Pae Pong Gi. She was the first Korean comfort woman to be publicly identified. Like so many other comfort women Pae, whose story has also appeared in book form, remained in the same role with the American Occupation Forces.

Pae Pong Gi

Pae Pong Gi had been married, before being solicited, at the age of twenty-nine, by a procuress who promised her work in an area where the living was so easy 'if you open your mouth a banana falls into it'. The lure of an easy life was a recurrent theme with obvious appeal to those forced to live under the wartime austerity of Korea and Japan. Pae had reached Okinawa in 1944, with another woman going under the Japanese name of Harue. With four other Koreans, they had been taken to a comfort station on the island of Tokashiki in the Ryukyu chain.

The local Young Women's Association had protested, but had been told that the comfort station was intended for the women's own protection—against their own troops. The subsequent fighting around Okinawa was so intense that only Pae and one other comfort woman survived the war. Afterwards she remained in prostitution for the American troops, as well as Okinawans. When the Ryukyu Islands were returned to Japanese sovereignty, she applied for a residence permit rather than return to Korea. She was latterly cared for by a local Korean residents' association affiliated to North Korea.

Early in 1988, Yun's group began taking concrete steps towards systematic action. It started with a visit to Okinawa with the express purpose of meeting Pae. Following this visit, in April they reported their findings to an international seminar sponsored by the Church Women's Alliance. The subject was 'Women and Tourism Culture'. A month later, they lodged a protest at a television program shown in Los Angeles, *The World at War*. Former Japanese soldiers interviewed in it had claimed that comfort women were entirely volunteers. The men may well have believed this, since an authority like Ito Keiichi states that the troops as a whole had no knowledge of the means of recruitment. To them, comfort stations were no different from the brothels they were familiar with at home. (This of course begs the question of why they did not think to ask the women how they were recruited for the frontline.)

These actions marked a major development of consciousness. The group showed that the comfort women issue could be exposed as an adjunct to campaigns against sex tourism and prostitution at Army bases. Within the Social Committee of the Church Women's Alliance, a Committee for the Study of the Voluntary Service Corps was formed. In Korea, as noted, the term comfort women was not in use, but Voluntary Service Corps was assumed to equate with it.

A big event of 1989 for the activists was a demonstration held by the Alliance of South Korean Women's Organisations against sending an official mission of condolence to attend Emperor Hirohito's funeral. This was held in Seoul's Pagoda Park, scene of the tragic demonstrations for independence in 1919. The manifesto issued highlighted the comfort women issue, and demanded a Japanese apology.

That same year, Yun and two other members of the group undertook some investigative travels for a series of articles. They started with Okinawa. This time Pae refused to see them; she was described by her friends as totally reclusive. She died late in 1991, and a memorial service was held on the same day as the first-ever lawsuit for compensation, brought by a group of forced labour draftees and comfort women, began in a Tokyo court. The authorities refused to release Pae's body to her protectors because they were affiliated to North Korea, while she had come from the South. This was a distinction that had not been made when she was alive.

Yun's party also visited Tokashiki Island to obtain Harue's ashes. She had died during the war. They also called at the house that had been requisitioned as the comfort station. The occupant, a single woman who was the former owner's daughter, remembers both Harue and Pae, who went under the name of Akiko. The daughter explained how she had been impressed by their fair northern complexions, and their physique. She herself, she explained, had not been blessed with marriage 'because so much love had been made in that house that my portion was consumed along with it'.

The investigating party then visited a former comfort woman in Thailand, as well as the sites of the comfort stations in Rabaul which had figured prominently in Japanese war reminiscences—partly because the troops there were among those who lived to tell the tale. Among these was Dr Aso Tetsuo, first encountered in this book in connection with the pioneer Shanghai station.

Rabaul had been a massive base for both Army and Navy operations. Rather than court wasteful losses reducing it, the Allies had left it alone until the surrender. At about the time of Yun's visit, it was the focus of a documentary film by Sekiguchi Noriko, then based in Australia, called *Senso Daughters*. Yun noted that there were some memorials to both Japanese and Australian war dead, but none to the indigenous people who would have also suffered there. She met a man called Burunai, who at the age of eight had worked as a cleaner for the Japanese. He still retained some basic Japanese, and recalled with amusement how soon women were landed after the troops. This confirmed Kim Il Myon's observation about 'comfort women arriving as quickly as the ammunition'. Burunai remembered how comfort stations had stood in a row beside the Naval headquarters and how servicemen visiting Rabaul from outstations had lined up outside them.

No-one to bear witness

The outcome of Yun's investigative 1989 travels was the series of articles, 'In the Footsteps of the Voluntary Service Corps', to highlight the comfort women issue. Yun's efforts were, however, hampered as late as 1990 by a lack of first-hand accounts. The only authentic cases she could discuss in her articles were those of Pae Pong Gi in Okinawa and Yuyuta, a Korean comfort woman who had chosen to settle in Thailand after the war. Yun had to conclude with the hope that she might find other comfort women surviving abroad and bring them home. She recognised that social attitudes would need to change before this would happen. Her activists were determined to strive to achieve this.

Yuyuta, the second comfort woman to come forward, was discovered by the South Korean Embassy in Thailand. Yuyuta, whose Korean name was Noh Su Bok, was married and living in Thailand. She had in fact in 1985 been brought to South Korea by the government on a lecture tour, to talk about her experiences. Although the *Asahi Shimbun,* a Japanese newspaper with a liberal tradition and interested in war issues, had interviewed Yuyuta then, Yun had some difficulty interviewing her. Yuyuta claimed to have forgotten the Korean language. Yun speculates that this could be linked with the repression of bitter memories. Another factor may have been that although Yuyuta had earlier freely discussed her past with the *Asahi Shimbun*'s female journalist, she was more reserved with Koreans, because the Korean media had that time published more about her than she had wished.

At the age of eighteen, Yuyuta had run away to Pusan from an unhappy marriage. An unlucky encounter with the police led to her being seized and sent with a contingent of comfort women to Singapore. Like so many others, she remained in Southeast Asia after the war, working in a restaurant in Thailand and finally marrying there. Also as in other cases, she proved to be sterile. Her husband fathered two sons by a younger woman. The boys were brought up to regard Yuyuta as their mother, and their own mother as their big sister.

Before Pae and Yuyuta came forward, the closest to direct authentic testimony from a comfort woman had been the publication of a memoir in 1982 under the name of 'Yi Nam Nim'. This gave a woman's first-person account of her recruitment under the General Mobilisation Law in 'early 1945'. By then rumour had made it clear what women had to expect after recruitment. But Yi was resigned to what was to come, since by then the only unmarried women to be spared belonged to families which were either wealthy or in local government. She was also comforted by the thought of saving her family further harassment, and by the chance to send some money home, as conscripted labourers were doing.

As she tells it, she was among 100 women sailing from Yosu, the number increasing to 1000 at Pusan. Her story traces their allocation to comfort stations in Rangoon, where the military situation was already hopeless. There is a vivid description of the extreme hardships they suffered, and their ill-treatment. Only twenty of the fifty are described as surviving the war. After six months in internment camps specially prepared for Koreans, she returned to Korea. She married a customer she met in a bar at the port of Inchon, where she was working rather than returning home. He left her when he learned of her past. The media made efforts to trace 'Yi', without success.

An indication of covert interest in Korea in the comfort women issue was the publication in 1982 by Yun Chong Mo of the well-researched novel *My Mother was a Military Comfort Woman*. The inspiration was the sight of a drunken American soldier dragging a girl by the hair in a Seoul street. Rather than focus on the contemporary scene, the author decided to explore the equivalent theme in the Japanese period. In this she was influenced by Senda's work as well as research by a Korean, Im Chong Guk, who is also quoted by Kim Il Myon. Yun Chong Mo also obtained verbal accounts of experiences in the Philippines, where the action is set. The main part of the story concerns a former comfort woman's confessions to her son. He had suspected he was half Japanese, though he turns out to be the son of a wounded Korean soldier whom his mother had saved. This did not stop him from despising her.

Roh's Japan visit and its aftermath

Yun's reports, published in the beginning of 1990, made a considerable impact in South Korea. There was heightened awareness of the comfort women issue. Following up on this, the South Korean Women's and Church Women's Alliances, together with the Seoul District Female Students' Representative Council, took the opportunity offered by the announcement of President Roh Tae Wu's visit to Japan. In May 1990, they issued a joint statement, addressed to him, on 'Women's Stand on the Voluntary Service Corps'. The issue was not taken up by the government, but using Roh's impending visit as a pretext, the South Korean Foreign Ministry requested Japanese co-operation in compiling a list of all wartime labour draftees.

During Roh's visit, the new Japanese Emperor, Akihito, expressed 'intense sorrow' at the wrongs inflicted on Korea. Korean activists, however, do not regard this as atoning for the lack of adequate apology from his late father, under whom the crimes occurred.

Comfort women were not at this stage mentioned as a special category of draftee. The official request for a list, however, again raised the comfort women issue, in the context of many related ones. Such issues included the post-war harassment of Koreans long resident in Japan. There were several lawsuits demanding assistance or compensation for Koreans abandoned on south Sakhalin after the post-war Soviet takeover. There were others asking for compensation for those who had served in the paramilitary forces, or who had been convicted by the Allies of Class B and C war crimes, usually as prison camp guards. As is usual with major Japanese legal cases, these are destined to remain unresolved for quite some time.

The Japanese government agreed to the Korean demand for a list of draftees. A list of 90,804 names was presented by the Labour Ministry. Of these, only about 20,000 tallied with the list of 126,000 compiled by the Korean Forced Draft Investigation Group, later made public. Another 50,000 were added by the Welfare Ministry. One source was a list of 1587 names on microfilm in the National Diet Library, of Occupation General Headquarters documents. These referred to Korean labourers interned in Okinawa on the capture of the island, then transferred to Hawaii pending repatriation. Of these names 153 appeared to be female. This did not, however, lead to the emergence of any conclusive new evidence.

At about the same time, however, a Korean who had belonged to the transferred Hawaii group published a list of 2818 names and addresses. An attempt was made to trace some of them. But few could be found. No women were identified. It was concluded that most of the labourers would have been illiterate, and would have spoken different dialects, so the choice of characters for their names would have been made arbitrarily by whoever recorded them. Another problem is that Korean given names, like Chinese, are not very gender-specific. Instead of relying mainly on an existing stock of names with generally clear gender associations, names can be freely coined out of Chinese characters thought to be auspicious, or following family usage. To make the search more difficult, there are very few Korean surnames, so that distinctions are often made using the name of a district.

The Japanese denial

About a month after Roh's May 1990 visit, the comfort women issue was raised in the Japanese Diet. A Social Democrat Member, Motooka Shoji, addressed Director-General Shimizu Tadao of the Employment Security Office, in the course of a House of Councillors

Budget Committee session, in June. The Employment Security Office was where relevant documentation was likely to be available. Motooka's question was whether comfort women were included in Korean forced drafts. He had fairly strong evidence of official involvement in the control of comfort women, such as the recently published volume of Fuji Shuppan's Key Document Series on the Fifteen Years War, covering war zone reports by military medical officers. These included the report made by Dr Aso on the Shanghai comfort women, as well as the detailed regulations on comfort stations by the Yama #3475 unit. Motooka could also refer to the recently released and published Monthly Reports of the Former Special Higher Police, commonly known as the 'thought police', since it had been formed earlier in the century for the suppression of 'dangerous ideas'.

These Monthly Reports, originally for internal use and classified secret, had been declassified on the post-war abolition of the Special Higher Police. They were later published and provided a rich source of historical data. Some material related directly to the comfort women issue. But the Director-General and other government spokesmen disclaimed any knowledge of these and the other sources. Though promising to investigate them, they were not disposed to regard them as sufficiently valid evidence.

Director-General Shimizu explained to Motooka that draft procedures had been carried out under the terms of the National General Mobilisation Law. From what he had heard from 'senior people', this had not involved comfort women. Then came the following exchange:

> MOTOOKA: Is it a fact that matters like the Naval Operations Patriotic Corps, the Southern Expeditionary National Service Corps, and military comfort women are in the process of being buried in complete obscurity? I insist that they be clarified in the course of investigations. Surely that would be possible if the attempt is made?
> SHIMIZU: From what I understand, including what is said by senior people, the situation is that as regards comfort women, they had just been taken around with the Forces by private operators so, frankly speaking, I do not believe it is possible to obtain any results by investigation as to the true facts of the matter.

Shimizu's words were later to be constantly thrown back in the faces of government officials by activists. After some further inconclusive discussion, on what constituted forced draft, the Chief Cabinet Secretary, Kato Koichi, assured Motooka that the Labour Ministry, in collaboration with others, would carry out an investigation, though this would take some time.

Motooka continued to press the matter on the grounds that a relationship of trust with Korea could not be built without a proper settlement of such outstanding issues from the war, and Japan's previous colonial rule. He noted that the police authorities were not included among the ministries involved in the investigation, even though the publication of the Monthly Reports of the former Special Higher Police had made obvious to all the part played by the police in the labour draft. He asked that the Police Agency be included in the investigation. The Chief Cabinet Secretary assured him that the investigation would cover all possible sources of evidence—though admitting this was the first he had heard of these Monthly Reports.

The Korean women's six demands

It was some months before the South Korean women's groups learned of this June 1990 exchange, through the Diet minutes. It spurred them to come together as the Voluntary Service Corps Study Association. This combined seven affiliates of the Church Women's Alliance with twenty-four affiliates belonging to the Alliance of South Korean Women's Organisations, some regional groups, and some professional. There were also five other groups, including the YWCA and student bodies, totalling thirty-seven. This combined organisation drafted a letter to be sent to the Tokyo government. It established a permanent co-ordinating body to maintain links between all the organisations involved in the comfort women issue. This was named the Voluntary Service Corps Problem Resolution Council, usually known in English as the Korean Comfort Women Problem Resolution Council, sometimes shortened to Council for the Matter of Comfort Women. It was founded on 16 November 1990, with Professor Yun as chair. She was later joined as co-chair by retired Professor Lee Hyo Jae, who subsequently took an active role in approaches to other Asian countries, and to the United Nations Human Rights Sub-commission.

The open letter to the government, addressed to the Japanese Prime Minister Kaifu Toshiki, had six demands:

> We have learned through the Record of Proceedings of the House of Councillors Budget Committee No. 19 the content of replies regarding

military comfort women made in your country's House of Councillor's Budget Committee session on the 6 June last. According to this, upon Mr Motooka Shoji of the Social Democratic Party requesting a government investigation into military comfort women in relation to the forced draft, the Director-General of the Employment Security Office, Mr Shimizu Tadao, who undertook to reply, stated: 'Draft procedures were carried out under the National General Mobilisation Law and there was no relation between military comfort women and procedures set out in terms of that law.'

We consider this reply on behalf of the government to be contrary to historical fact and that it is an irresponsible statement by a government of the aggressor-nation which brought about the war which claimed innumerable victims. We therefore forward this open letter in protest.

The task of uncovering the history of the comfort women has thus far been delayed by such factors as the destruction of evidence by the Japanese Armed Forces, the Japanese government's insincere attitude to war responsibility and social prejudice against 'comfort women'. Nevertheless part of the truth had been established by some people's courageous testimony and by remaining data. Among these is the testimony [an attached note 1] of a mobilisation officer of the former National Labour Service Association who drafted Korean women from Cheju Island and Shimonoseki into the 'Korean Women's Voluntary Service Corps' as comfort women, as directed by the Japanese Forces directly subordinate to Emperor Hirohito.

According to this testimony and accounts by former comfort women, Korean women, either in the name of the Voluntary Service Corps, or being deceived on the pretext of auxiliary duties or even being seized in raids while working in the fields, were compelled to be comfort women in military comfort stations in war zones. If this kind of forced draft was not set out in terms of the Mobilisation Law, is this not evidence that the Japanese Forces concealed these barbarities?

Again, according to the testimony of a former military medical officer [an attached note 2] the Forces controlled the comfort stations in such respects as laying down regulations for them and conducting examinations of venereal disease. Above all, it was Japanese servicemen who used these comfort stations and their guilt must be rigorously pursued.

In view of the above, the government's reply ignores established facts or, if these statements were made in ignorance of these facts, this reveals the government's lack of seriousness in investigating forced drafts.

During the war Japan committed the crime of carrying out such inhuman acts as deceiving or compelling many young Korean women to serve as instruments for managing the sexual appetite of troops. Then after defeat it compounded its crimes by reversing its former slogan of 'Japan and Korea indissoluble' by killing or abandoning Korean comfort women and refusing compensation to the few survivors. In May [1990] the Emperor of Japan expressed 'intense sorrow' regarding the two countries' past relations, displaying some self- criticism, if inadequate. While the Japanese government announced an investigation into 'all people drafted from the Korean peninsula', [. . . it] immediately afterwards still further compounded the crime by denying any connection with military comfort women and refusing to investigate them.

For these reasons, we make the following demands of the Japanese government:

1. That the Japanese government admit the forced draft of Korean women as comfort women;
2. That a public apology be made for this;
3. That all barbarities be fully disclosed;
4. That a memorial be raised for the victims;
5. That the survivors or their bereaved families be compensated;
6. That these facts be continuously related in historical education so that such misdeeds are not repeated.

By these means can Japan be absolved of its guilt and become a democratic state endowed with true morality. We women of South Korea intend to watch closely the practical steps taken by the Japanese government. We would appreciate your sincere reply by the end of November. [Notes 1 and 2 refer to Yoshida Seiji (1983) and Dr Aso, p. 142 above.]

Copies of the letter, dated 17 October 1990, and signed by thirty-seven organisations, were delivered to the Japanese Embassy in Seoul and to the South Korean government, though at this stage the latter displayed little sign of official interest in the issue. Later that same month an opportunity arose to deliver a copy direct to the Japanese Foreign Ministry in Tokyo. Three of Yun's associates had gone to Okinawa to attend a joint memorial service for victims of the Pacific War. On their way back, they called into Tokyo, where an actively sympathetic Diet-woman, Shimizu Sumiko, also a Social Democrat member of the House of Councillors, organised an informal discussion on the comfort women issue in the meeting rooms of the House. She also arranged for the demands to be delivered to the Ministry.

Following the meeting with Yun's colleagues, Diet-woman Shimizu Sumiko followed up Motooka's initiative. A representative of the Labour Ministry replied that investigations both in his Ministry and the Welfare Ministry had found no evidence on the matter. On her summarising the contents of the South Korean combined organisations' open letter submitted to the Foreign Ministry, the Ministry spokesman replied that since it was a domestic matter rather than a diplomatic one in the context of the wartime General Mobilisation Law, the letter had been referred by his Ministry to the appropriate quarters.

Undiscouraged by this buck passing, in April 1991, Motooka again raised the subject in the Budget Committee session. Prime

Minister Kaifu Toshiki was present. He admitted having seen the letter. He certainly should have been aware of the situation, since the women's groups in Seoul had demonstrated in the Pagoda Park in Seoul on the occasion of his January visit. But he stated that he was not in possession of enough concrete information to reply. Discussion was then taken over by the Head of the Asia Bureau of the Foreign Ministry. He read out the women's six points, and indicated that the Japanese Embassy in Seoul would convey a response direct to the women's groups.

A representative of the Labour Ministry then detailed the procedures specified under the National General Mobilisation Law for recruitment into the Women's Voluntary Service Corps. To the Japanese this meant only draft into war industries, he said. In many cases this was an accurate description. The representative denied that it was related in any way to comfort women, maintaining that evidence was lacking.

Meanwhile the Korean Council on the Matter of Comfort Women had sent two reminders. It threatened to broaden the campaign to involve women's organisations worldwide, in the absence of a satisfactory reply.

In early April 1991, the Japanese Embassy in Seoul conveyed a verbal response to representatives of the Council. On the six demands, the Japanese reply was that there was no evidence of the forced draft of Korean women. So no public apology, disclosures or memorial were forthcoming. All claims of compensation between Japan and South Korea, it went on, had been conclusively settled by the 1965 Basic Treaty. Further, textbooks would 'continue' to reflect Japan's regret for aggression against the rest of Asia. (It may be noted that there has been frequent controversy, both within and outside Japan, regarding textbook coverage of Japan's wartime role. A check on references to comfort women in Japanese textbooks found one that mentioned the topic—briefly.)

The Japanese embassy in Seoul was prepared to distribute copies of this reply to the media—but the South Korean government did not allow it. Even as late as 1991, it is clear that the Seoul government still doubted whether promoting the issue was expedient.

Reaction, action and breakthrough

The Council on the Matter of Comfort Women reacted to the Japanese reply with a campaign to publicise the issue and the Japanese reply. It held a lecture meeting, combined with a display of related poems and pictures. These activities strengthened organisational ties in Korea, as well as between Korean and Japanese groups. The display included Dr Aso's photographs of the Shanghai comfort station, and its set of regulations.

The lecture meeting was attended by 200 people, which some later described as satisfactory, and others as less so. Speaking at it, Professor Yun pointed out that conditions were often worse at comfort stations than the regulations suggested. While most allocated thirty minutes to each client, she quoted Shirota Suzuko as becoming disgusted at having to serve much larger numbers in Japan, as well as being carried around from unit to unit by truck. Other women, she said, had been forced into auxiliary combat duty. Although Shirota had been repatriated, she had received no treatment or compensation for her health problems.

Professor Yun also referred to the failure of North Korea to participate in the issue as a major drawback. She described the division of Korea as the source of the whole range of problems facing its people, from the general and political to the individual level. She quoted a Japanese public figure who had stated that he viewed the possible unification of Korea as a threat to Japan. She hoped, however, to enlist the aid of Japanese of conscience and of similarly-placed Korean males. These had actually not so far shown much inclination to be involved in the comfort women issue.

She also thought it worth mentioning that some of the Voluntary Service Corps had not become comfort women. One case she quoted was of a woman ending up in a spinning mill in Taegu. She emphasised, however, that a distinction should not be made on moral grounds, because either type of service was subject to compulsion. The women themselves had no choice.

Following the meeting, another open letter, reiterating the six demands, was sent to Japanese Prime Minister Kaifu. A petition was also sent to the South Korean Parliament, requesting government support for the realisation of the six demands. There was no marked government reaction.

Not long after the lecture meeting, in May 1991, Yun attended a symposium in Japan, 'Peace in Asia and the Role of Women'. This was sponsored by Japanese women's groups and Korean groups affiliated to North and South Korea. The symposium played an important role in raising awareness, and in furthering co-operation between Japanese and Korean women's groups. Public awareness was further raised by the screening in the second half of 1991 of a film on comfort women called *Song of Arirang*. It is named after a Korean folk song, long a national symbol which constantly appears, in a wide variety of contexts. The film was made by Korean Pak Su Nam, and based on interviews in Okinawa and Korea, mainly with ex-servicemen. Only Pae Pong Gi appears to represent comfort women.

The efforts of the women's groups reached a turning point on 14 August 1991. Then Kim Hak Sun announced her willingness to testify publicly about her experiences as a comfort woman, raising the issue to the level of formal legal action. Such action then seemed the most promising avenue, following the earlier lawsuits on cases of abandonment on Sakhalin, and compensation for Koreans convicted of war crimes arising from service with the Japanese Armed Forces.

Hak Sun's decision was spurred by anger at the Japanese government's denials of responsibility. Her action was facilitated by her lack of immediate family to suffer shame or after-effects. The immediate occasion was presented by her acquaintance with an atomic bomb victim being helped by the women's organisations. (The case of Korean victims of the atomic bomb attack had been one where the Japanese had agreed to special measures after President Roh's 1990 visit. A foundation had been formed to assist them, with funds to amount to ¥4 billion over some years.)

Kim Hak Sun

Kim Hak Sun's experience as a comfort woman had not been as long, nor her experiences as varied as many others. Nevertheless, it presented good grounds for apology and compensation. She was born in Manchuria, where her parents fled after the abortive Korean uprising in 1919. On her father's death her mother returned to Korea and re-married. Hak Sun was unhappy with her stepfather and often ran away. At fourteen, she was placed in a training school in Pyongyang for *kisaeng*, the traditional Korean entertainers similar to the Japanese *geisha*. She studied instrumental music, singing, calligraphy and etiquette. Her fees were met by her adoption by a master of *kisaeng*, who had done the same for several other girls.

She graduated at seventeen, but since she was not old enough to practise for another two years, her foster father took her and another girl to Beijing in 1939, in the hope of finding better business than at home. They were like so many others: 'trade follows the flag'. Accounts vary as to the stage and procedure whereby the girls came under Japanese Army control, though their travel to China must already have been subject to Army approval. In any event, the girls were separated from their foster father, and taken by Army truck on an overnight trip to a deserted Chinese house. There they were stripped and raped. After this 'breaking in', they were placed with three other Korean girls in the charge of an older Korean-speaking woman. She gave them Japanese names, Hak Sun becoming Aiko. The original location of their comfort station is rendered as Tiehbichen, but they regularly followed the troops' movements, close to the frontline.

The women were not paid, only clothed and fed rather poorly. Hak Sun not only had to provide sexual service, but also song and dance, especially before action was expected. As in other reported cases, the women were forced to watch Chinese 'infiltrators' being beheaded—a procedure perhaps also designed to frighten them. She developed a consumptive ailment, but obtained no relief. Then she was rescued by a roving Korean, a dealer in gold and silver coin—a profitable pursuit amid the chaos of available currency. The dealer called at the camp on an off-day and spirited her away to his pawnshop in Shanghai's French concession. There they were married. By the end of the war, they had a son and daughter.

Hak Sun's memories include listening to Kim Koo, head of the 'Korean provisional government' addressing Korean residents on his hopes for their future. Later they followed him home, where he was to be assassinated by Korean President Syngman Rhee's henchmen. Hak Sun was herself interned for a time with others of North Korean origin.

Her husband sustained his family by becoming an army supplier. Relations with him became unhappy. When he was drunk, he would reproach her for her comfort woman past, and remind her that without him she would be long dead. He finally died after the Korean War in a building accident. Her daughter also died, of cholera. She did not consider re-marriage, fearing more contempt, but lived by peddling in various parts of the country. Her last family responsibility ceased when her son drowned at ten in a swimming mishap.

Hak Sun has always maintained that her main purpose is not financial compensation, but the exposure of the truth so long concealed. She had even contemplated suicide in the Emperor's presence as a means of achieving this. The women's groups in both Korea and Japan, with sympathetic legal advice, prepared a lawsuit as the practical alternative.

Not long after Hak Sun agreed to go public, two other former comfort women were found who were prepared to join her in her legal action, though not under their true names. They are referred to as Plaintiff A and B. They claim not to have been paid for their services, though virtually all later cases, as well as regulations, mention payment. Plaintiff A had been taken to Rabaul after being offered a spinning mill job in Japan. Plaintiff B had been taken to Shanghai after what seemed a tempting advance payment of ¥30.

Plaintiff A and Plaintiff B

Plaintiff A uses the pseudonym Lee Jin Hee. A draft order, later popularly known as a 'virgin delivery order', reached her family farm some time about 1942, when there was still little awareness of the comfort system. Hoping to find more congenial work, Jin Hee evaded the draft and ran away to Pusan on her first train ride. There she learned of an even greater novelty—the first lift to be installed in a department store. While viewing it in the store she was approached by a Japanese and a Korean man. They promised her work in a spinning mill where she could make enough money to buy her own sewing machine. She would have been an obvious mark: a naïve country girl away from home.

She was taken by ship to Shimonoseki and thence to Hiroshima, where the cherries were in blossom. There she was transferred to another ship, which took on board over 100 men, but only three women. She vainly tried to avoid boarding the ship, then experienced a miserable voyage of seasickness and regret. The other two women, who were two years older, were Chinese and Korean. Their destination was Rabaul. There they were immediately taken to a field hospital and left with a medical officer. For about ten days they did laundry, including washing bandages.

They were then taken to a church which was partitioned into rooms. In front of them were displayed photographs of women of 'seven nationalities', about twenty in all, including Koreans, Chinese and 'black people'. It was Sunday and the church was filled with soldiers. She was shown around the place and then ordered to join the comfort women in their duties. She resisted, but was beaten until she complied. The times allowed for each client varied but sometimes a convoy of five trucks would disgorge their occupants at once, and impatient queues would form. Anyone who exceeded the time allotted was kicked out, apparently literally.

As the bombing intensified, the women spent long periods sheltering in caves. Finally ten of them seized their chance to escape to the jungle. There they survived on sweet potatoes—the local staple food. Thus they missed the general evacuation of women from Rabaul. For a long time they did not even know of the end of the war. They were eventually found and returned home about April 1946.

By then chronically sick, Jin Hee never returned to her family. She got a job as a housemaid in Seoul, where she was able to earn money to pay for medical treatment. She could not contemplate marriage.

She now says she is tempted to resort to some desperate act, which even if it cost her her life, would be worthwhile if it brought a proper apology from the Japanese government. Meanwhile, she has 'no more tears to shed'.

Plaintiff D, the daughter of very poor casual labourers, had had no schooling at all. When she was eighteen, she was standing outside her home when two men, one perhaps Japanese, told her they knew a place in Shanghai where she could make money. They then offered her ¥30 to ¥40 on the spot, an overwhelming amount, given her poverty. She was thrilled at being able to give her family some relief. She at once handed the money to her mother, and was hurried away by the men.

She found herself among fifteen girls, all of whom were wearing the usual Korean costume. They were assembled at a nearby inn, then taken on a long train via Beijing. They finally alighted at a country station in the Shanghai area. Their two recruiters then handed them over to two *kempei,* who took them on a two-hour journey by military truck to an Army unit.

The girls were housed in tents some distance apart, her tent being described as 'Number One'. She was given the Japanese name Kaneko. The tents were a couple of metres square, with flooring of woven reeds. Bedding consisted only of two blankets. The girls were issued with Army clothing.

Kaneko did not realise the purpose of their presence up until sexual service was demanded by a Private First Class. He beat her into compliance. With no chance of escape, she remained there for four years. Clients would begin coming from 8 a.m., lower ranks in the day and officers at night, sometimes to stay.

Tent accommodation was unusual for comfort stations. It was particularly hard in the rainy climate of the region, with its quite severe winters. When it was wet, the soldiers would wear coats even inside the tents. During winter the women had to combat the cold by hugging hot-water bags wrapped in towels. The tents were also hard to clean. There were two meals a day, at 10 a.m. and 4 p.m. in the mess hall. The women ate in groups of four and, in accordance with military practice, were not allowed to talk during the meal. Their cook did not belong to the Army but was locally hired. They never got enough to eat.

Kaneko saw an average of between ten and fifteen men daily—and sometimes many more on weekends. The officers used condoms, but other ranks rarely did. A venereal disease check was conducted each week by a medical officer, and preventive injections of salvarsan were given. Either owing to this or to her youthful robustness, Kaneko did not develop any symptoms of venereal disease during her whole time there, though the effects appeared later.

Three years later, she was injured in an incident with a Second Lieutenant Miyazaki. He had come drunk to her tent expecting service. Occupied with another man, she could not at once attend to him. He violently abused her as an 'animal' and an 'idiot', shouting that all of them deserved to die. He then slashed at her with a sword, and kicked her in the pit of the stomach. Her hip-bone was injured by the sword thrust, and she still moves awkwardly. She also carries a scar on her abdomen.

There was no redress from such violence. The women were supervised by an aged Japanese couple whom they called 'mother' and 'father'. Kaneko only remembers being given one kimono to wear. When the war ended, the news was announced outside the tents. Kaneko boarded one of two waiting trucks, which took her back to Korea. She found her parents dead, and pretended to her surviving brother that she had been working for an acquaintance.

At the age of twenty-five she married a farmer, but was unable to have children. At the age of fifty she married again, and still lives with her eighty-year-old husband on meagre welfare. She wants anonymity, because she 'cannot bear' to tell him her story.

To co-ordinate steps for legal action in Japan, a group was formed called the Compatriot Women's Network for the Military Comfort Women Problem. At the same time, a fund raising group was also initiated, headed by Takahashi Kikue of the Japan Christian Women's Moral Reform Society. Besides Hak Sun, the lawsuit was to take up the claims of Plaintiffs A and B, eleven ex-soldiers including five represented by their bereaved families, and twenty-one paramilitary, including eleven represented by their bereaved families. The compensation claim was set at ¥20 million each—a 'notional amount' regarded as a minimum. The suit was regarded as a class action on behalf of all those coming under the represented categories.

When Hak Sun became the first Korean comfort woman to declare herself, in the hope of attracting more such declarations, a Volunteer Service Corps Report Line was set up in Seoul, and another later in Pusan. Results, however, were slow and the first reports were either anonymous or pseudonymous. To accelerate the pace, another letter was addressed to the South Korean Parliament, as well as to the Prime Minister's office, the Home and Foreign Ministries and the Presidential Secretariat, demanding the establishment of a Voluntary Service Corps Fact Finding and Resolution Committee.

8. The politics of sex

In 1945, some two-and-a-half million Japanese troops surrendered to the Allies. Almost all, and indeed some of their women, would have known about the comfort system. There were comfort women right on the edge of battlefields. Licensed prostitution was also conducted fairly openly in Japan. Yet by 1962 when Senda Kako started his research on comfort women, collective amnesia appeared to have set in. It took him quite a while to uncover enough information for his book, *Military Comfort Women,* published in 1973.

According to one Japanese academic, it became a 'hidden' bestseller. Copies disappeared from shelves, but few would admit to owning a copy, or even having read one. Senda's book had appeared just a year after the Japanese Women's Association had begun to openly oppose sex tourism, the year that, with Korean women's groups, they had demonstrated against sex tours at Korean and Japanese airports.

The collective amnesia was not peculiar to the Japanese. Korean comfort women were also keen to expunge their abasement from memory. The last thing many wanted was Kim Il Myon's seminal publication on their sufferings. Although a Korean, Kim's book *The Emperor's Forces and Korean Comfort Women* appeared in Japanese, to become part of the literature of the 'Japanese of conscience'. In Korea, the book initially made little impact. Nevertheless it went through numerous reprints, a sign that knowledge about comfort women was spreading.

Not long after, in 1979, came Yamatani's film on Pae Pong Gi. Pae's experience made the link between the sexual activities of the Japanese Armed Forces and that of the American Occupation Force as two sides of the same coin—the exploitation of women. This impressed the growing feminist movements in both Korea and Japan.

The growth of consciousness in Japan took another leap forward in 1982. A woman freelance journalist, Usuki Keiko, later to become the leading figure in the Association for Clarifying Japan's Postwar Responsibility, spent most of that year in South Korea, learning the language, building up contacts, and studying the comfort women issue. The political situation in South Korea in the early 1980s did not encourage activism of any kind. The contacts Usuki made, however, were to prove useful by the end of the decade. Yun Chung Mo's *My Mother was a Military Comfort Woman* was also published in 1982. Then in 1983 came Yoshida Seiji's landmark book, *My War Crimes: The Forced Draft of Koreans,* a singularly stark account of his activities during the war.

Given the official Japanese reluctance to accept responsibility for the comfort system and its forced draft of women, the memoirs of Yoshida are very important. They remain the only independent and semi-official account of the recruitment process, aside from the evidence of the comfort women themselves. During the war Yoshida had been with the National Labour Service Association whose task was to co-ordinate draft labour throughout the country and work with the police force. He was the Mobilisation Department Head in Shimonoseki, less than a day away from the Korean port of Pusan. His main duty was to control the flow of conscript labour to essential industries, on the order of the Army and Navy headquarters in western Japan. The mines in the region were particularly important. At the time and for a long time afterwards, he said he regarded his raids as an inevitable part of war. Later, after his retirement in the late 1970s, he came to reflect on them with increasing horror. As he puts it, this was not due to any sudden change of heart, but to an accumulation of circumstances.

He had been approached by journalists to write articles on his war experiences. On some being published, he was persuaded by a publishing company to write a book-length memoir. Lacking documentary support, except for some diary material, he contacted over forty former colleagues in the hope of exchanging and checking recollections. Most refused, and some even stopped sending him New Year cards. He was, however, able to obtain some help in the Shimonoseki area, and his book was published. Its contents drew widespread attention, leading to television interviews and public lectures. It made an impact in South Korea, too, and, in 1985, he was invited to lecture at Seoul University. He was prevented from doing so by the South Korean government, with its customary fear of agitation. The occasion for the proposed lecture had been the visit to Korea by Yuyuta, the Korean comfort woman. Yuyuta had been visited in Thailand, interviewed and written about by journalist Matsui Yayori of *Asahi Shimbun* in 1983, the same year that Yoshida's book was published.

Yoshida also developed links with Korean residents in Japan. Through them, he learned more about the prevalent discrimination against them: how, for example, schoolchildren had to use Japanese names to avoid being bullied. He also learned of the fingerprinting requirement for all foreign nationals, a measure aimed mainly at the Koreans. He came to feel partly responsible for their situation. By exposing the historical reasons for their presence in Japan, he hoped their lot might be improved.

Despite Yoshida's continued strenuous activities to expose the forced draft, he has been studiously ignored by the Japanese authorities—even after the official fact finding inquiry following the institution of the 1991 lawsuit, and the exposure of damning surviving documentation in various official archives. Yoshida complains more about public apathy than any attempt at suppression. However, Right-wing extremists who have always denied that there were any Japanese wartime atrocities, also took exception to his book, and threatened him.

His main critic is an historian, Professor Hata Ikuhiko, of a university originally founded to provide training for the colonial service. He claims that investigations in southern Korea have failed to substantiate Yoshida's accounts.

The next significant stage in raising consciousness in Japan was in 1986. Then the Japanese comfort woman, Shirota Suzuko, described her experiences in a radio interview. As usual in the Japanese cases, Shirota had contracted to work off a loan to her family. Although much of what she said was similar to what was already known at the time, the interest in her came from the fact she was Japanese, and corroborated what the Koreans had earlier been saying.

After this, the issue could hardly have developed further in Japan without some input from Korea. This became feasible after 1987 as the military regime's grip weakened, giving way to more democratic forces and the formation of the group under Professor Yun Chung Ok, which was, as seen, to become the main motivator to action on the comfort women issue. A professor of English at Ehwa Women's University, Yun also spoke perfect Japanese. She was the ideal liaison person to work with what she calls 'Japanese of conscience'.

The number of groups interested in the comfort women issue then multiplied, both in South Korea and in Japan. Organisational support from Korean residents in Japan began with the foundation in Tokyo of the Association for the Study of the Military Comfort Women Problem in early December 1990. This was followed a few months later by the corresponding body in the Kyoto-Osaka area, the Association for the Study of the Korean Military Comfort Women Problem. Strong co-operation was received from the Japanese-organised Association for Clarifying Japan's Postwar Responsibility, which had already been co-operating on war claims with the Korean Association of Bereaved Families of Pacific War Victims. Usuki Keiko, of the Association for Clarifying Japan's Postwar Responsibility, who had built up her networks of South Korean contacts in 1982, became an effective liaison person. She has also published her own findings in the 1992 *Contemporary Comfort Women,* which covers both wartime prostitution and that at United States bases in Korea and sex tourism in Manila along with other women's issues. At its heart is the awareness that the comfort women issue is not just about Japanese exploitation of women during wartime, but about male exploitation of women in general.

The Japanese Premier visits South Korea

South Korean President Roh's visit to Japan, Professor Yun's publications, and debate in the Japanese Diet on comfort women in 1990, culminated in Japanese Prime Minister Miyazawa Kiichi's state visit to South Korea on 16 January 1992. And two other developments had served to put the comfort women issue at the cutting edge of Japan—Korean relations. On 6 December 1991, three Korean comfort women took Tokyo to court in a highly-publicised legal action which was widely reported around the world. Stimulated by this development, Professor Yoshimi Yoshiaki went to work in the Self Defence Agency Library and soon produced the smoking gun: irrefutable documentary evidence that the Japanese military was behind the running of comfort stations. These damning documents, published by the mass circulation *Asahi* newspaper on 11 January 1992, forced the Japanese government within hours to admit that, despite all its past denials and talk of private operators, the Army had been deeply involved. By 12 January 1992, the whole world knew for the first time the true meaning of comfort women.

Coming only five days before Miyazawa's visit to Korea, it was inevitable that the issue would overshadow the talks. The visit proved a major stimulus to the debate both in Japan and South Korea. As one conservative member of his party regretfully put it: 'The comfort women had emerged like a vengeful ghost from the past at Mr Miyazawa's pillow.' Such phenomena have traditionally been countered, in both Japan and Korea, by Buddhist masses or shamanistic exorcisms but, as a Korean woman commentator put it:

> It is not exorcists now who can relieve the rancour of women who were made into comfort women. It will be the ideal of women's liberation and the awakening of civic consciousness that will achieve this.

Before his departure for Seoul, Miyazawa was interviewed by South Korean media. He expressed his regret and apologies in terms so strong that an attempt at an English equivalent sounds too exaggerated to be convincing.

During his visit, he repeated this apology to the South Korean President at the South Korean National Assembly. He was, however, condemned by activists for not concurrently promising compensation, which he still maintained was ruled out by the 1965 treaty. But he and his spokesmen accepted the right of the litigants to legal recourse. He added that the issue involved a 'wound to the spirit' which merited some 'visible redress'. The possibility of some measure 'in lieu of compensation' would be considered after receiving the report of fact finding committees being set up, one each in South Korea and Japan.

At the same time, the North Korean authorities also issued a statement to the effect that this issue had also affected their people. It had to be settled as part of the normalisation of relations with Japan, it said, something that was in the process of tortuous negotiation. North Korea had, of course, not been part of the 1965 Basic Treaty.

While Miyazawa expressed profuse apologies in the National Assembly, it was besieged by demonstrators from various interested groups, including the Bereaved Families Association. One of its members, an old man who had come to demand the return of his conscript brother's ashes, died during the demonstration, allegedly after being struck by police. This incident highlighted in dramatic fashion Japan's irresponsible attitude to Korean draftees. It had not even confirmed deaths, which would at least have given the bereaved families the comfort of funeral or memorial services, in the knowledge of the time and place of death.

At the same time as action towards redress increased, some elements in South Korea were trying to defuse tension. The leadership of the South Korea-Japan Society, representing interests identifying with co-operation between the countries, issued a statement expressing satisfaction with Miyazawa's apology:

> The comfort women problem is one that must be cleared up at some stage and it is beneficial both in the medium and long term that the Prime Minister has come and apologised at a time when it has reached a peak.

The leader of the Democratic Liberal Party, Kim Jong Pil, said of the 1965 Basic Treaty, which is of course central to the issue of legal compensation:

> At the time Japan did not have much to spare, while South Korea was hard-pressed even to survive. This is a problem that makes the heart ache but at the present time the past situation should be appreciated and not treated emotionally.

The lawsuit begins

The year 1991 had ended on a high note for the activists, with the first-ever lawsuit by Korean comfort women. Kim Hak Sun's suit with two other anonymous comfort women was later joined by Mun Ok Ju (see Introduction) and five others (see Kim Hak Sun and Plaintiffs A and B in the previous chapter). In addition, it carried the claims of thirty-three ex-military and paramilitary plaintiffs. The case, formally described as the Asia-Pacific War Korean Victims Compensation Claim Case, opened on 6 December 1991, practically coinciding with the fiftieth anniversary of the 7 December 1941 attack on Pearl Harbour. The first day consisted mainly of formalities, including submission of the plaint consisting of 143 typed pages.

Argument would follow in later sessions at intervals of months, since Japanese legal procedure follows the 'Continental system'. Major cases in Japan often take a very long time to be resolved. One conspicuous example is the suit against the Education Ministry's powers to screen the content of textbooks. This ended in failure in 1993, after a thirty-year struggle. The suit by Korean draftees abandoned on Sakhalin, which was handled by the chief counsel in the comfort women case, Takagi Ken'ichi, ran from 1979 to 1989, when it was suspended because improved relations between the Soviet Union and South Korea made repatriation to the South possible. It was resumed, however, in 1990, with emphasis on compensation, in view of the difficulties the repatriates faced in South Korea.

The first part of the comfort women's case is entitled Causes of Claims. It begins with an account of the development of Japan's colonial policies in Korea, culminating in the military and paramilitary drafts, and the comfort women system. It quotes various authorities and sources. The second part consists of the case histories of the plaintiffs, several of which, as noted, have already appeared in this book. The third part, entitled Reasons for Claims, presents the legal arguments. The basis of the suit is the charge of crimes against humanity. This has become part of international customary law as a result of the Nuremberg war crime judgments. Such a charge is unaffected by the question of conformity to local law. In fact, local law is expected in principle to conform to international law. The concept of 'crime against humanity' does not refer to individuals but to classes of individuals, such as political, racial or religious groups and, in recent times, to those based on gender differentiation. In the suit, offences are taken as against Koreans as such, because the plaintiffs were treated differently from Japanese nationals in such respects as arbitrary coercion and abandonment. In the case of comfort women, sexual discrimination is also involved, suggesting the high value placed on chastity in Korean society. Since these offences amount to crimes, they can also become grounds for civil action.

The case for restitution arises from Japan's acceptance of the Potsdam Declaration, demanding unconditional surrender. This embodies the Cairo Declaration, which demands, among other things, Korea's deliverance from its 'condition of enslavement'. It implies a general principle of restitution, including the repatriation of Koreans in Japan's service overseas, and restoration of their rights. Until compensation for Japan's war crimes is made, a state of 'enslavement' can be regarded as persisting.

In addition to formal obligations such as repatriation and financial settlement, there is also the principle of the obligation of trust. This is defined as an attendant provision implied in all social arrangements, whereby 'the parties concerned are obligated to a concern for each other's security'. There is a further principle of obligation of reason, whereby the principle of natural justice may be applied to remedy defects in formal law.

The fourth part states the amount claimed as not less than ¥20 million per person, though it notes that the full extent of loss suffered is incalculable. The last part is a summing up. It quotes the preamble to the Constitution, dedicated to the elimination from the world of despotism, servitude, oppression and intolerance. It is noted that the plaintiffs are representative of the large number of others in the same situation. The apologies made by the Emperor and Prime Minister Kaifu on the occasion of President Roh's 1990 visit are quoted as evidence of Japan's responsibility.

The first hearing was on 1 June 1992. An indicator of public interest was the balloting to allocate the thirty-seven public seats from the 187 who showed up for the hearing. The same thing was to happen in later sessions.

Kaneda Kimiko

Kaneda Kimiko came from a poor rural family. Her father had been a clerk with a rice mill, but when she was ten years old he decided to become a minister and entered a theological college in Seoul. He entrusted her to the care of another minister. When her father graduated and took up pastoral duties, the family was reunited. From about 1937, when she was sixteen, her father came under suspicion, and had to spend much of his time in hiding. There was no general policy of persecuting Christians but in some circles Christianity was a focus of resistance to Japanisation, while links were maintained with Christian missions in countries opposed to Japan's policies.

The family was scattered, and Kimiko became a housemaid with a missionary couple. In 1938, two girlfriends suggested looking for work in a factory. They had been approached by a Japanese agent living in a nearby Japanese quarter who had of course assured them that the factory work would be lucrative, and that many people were after it. Next day the three were taken by three policemen to the home of a Japanese near the main west gate of Seoul, where some ten girls were already assembled.

The next morning two Japanese soldiers took Kimiko's group and two others on a train for Tientsin. By the time they arrived at 11 a.m. the next day, the girls were uneasy but helpless. They were then taken by truck with five men on a two-hour journey to an Army unit. There were thirty to forty Korean women wearing either simple tops with slacks or Chinese costume. Some of them spoke to the newcomers in Korean to the effect that they 'would face worse hardships than death but had no choice but to obey orders'. They were at once rebuked for using Korean.

The following morning, with twenty other women, they were returned to Tientsin in horse-drawn carts, for another train journey of four hours, to a provincial centre called Tehsien. They reached their destination only after yet another three hours by horse-cart. They were assembled in the medical aid room of the Kaneyama Force and addressed by a junior officer. He began: 'I suppose you had a definite purpose in mind to come all this way.' At this the women interrupted with: 'We were tricked by talk of factory work! Let us go home!' But he countered with: 'What are you complaining about? The soldiers are fighting for your sake. If you show some patience, good days will come.'

After that, he put them into rooms about two metres square. Kimiko was given Room Number Eight. There were something like forty to fifty rooms, not all of which were taken up by the twenty or so women who had come with her. She and the others were expected to service twenty to thirty men a day, but she felt painful after only three. One woman was taken away by a drunken soldier and shot. On her third day, Kimiko herself was stabbed with a bayonet for resisting. She still bears the scar.

For about twenty days she was confined to her room recovering from this attack. Then she was taken back with four other women via Tehsien to Beijing. She was then assigned to another unit, five hours away by horse-drawn cart. In this comfort station she was allotted Room Number Three. By now she realised that submission was her only means of survival. To make life a little more endurable, she took up opium smoking at the instigation of Chinese military employees. She smoked opium blended with tobacco and found that it relieved her fear and distress. She was located for over a year in this place, Shihchiachuang.

She was then repeatedly moved, spending roughly a year each in a number of places in northern China. She spent six years in all as a comfort woman. Sometimes she had to do laundry, cleaning and nursing during the day, then service twenty or more men at night. There was the usual system of ticketing, queuing, issue of condoms and weekly medical examinations. Meals were the same as for the troops. She does not mention payment, but the mention of tickets suggests that the usual system of fees applied. After all, she could afford opium.

She was given an injection of salvarsan on one occasion for an

ear swelling, which indicates it was attributed to venereal disease.
She finally suffered a prolapse of the uterus in 1944 and was fortunate enough to find sympathy from a Korean officer in charge of
the Yanagi unit, who obtained *kempeitai* permission for her to return to Korea for opium detoxification and a hysterectomy. She
was then twenty-four.

Kimiko's family could not be traced, but her church links made
it easier for her to integrate with less stigma than other women.
She could never marry, and her health had been so poor that she
needed tranquilisers to sleep. Although in modest employment,
she would like before long to retire to a nursing home, if the means
could be found.

The first comfort woman to testify was Kaneda Kimiko. She used
her former Japanese name to avoid discrimination at her place of
work. In a photograph taken with other plaintiffs, she wears head-
gear that obscures her face. Chief counsel Takagi emphasised the importance of the case as a focus of world attention. He drew attention
in particular to its effects on relations with Asian countries. He criticised Prime Minister Miyazawa's statement in Korea that he was
'awaiting the court's ruling', on the grounds that, as head of the Japanese government, he was a party to the case, not a neutral. Since he
had uttered this apology, his representatives in court should adopt
the same attitude. The facts of the case should be treated as established and attention concentrated on the issue of compensation. This
was to be treated as a restitution in the context of justice and morality. It was also urgent because, if not settled during the lifetime of the
plaintiffs, all opportunity of reconciliation with Korea would be lost.

The court was also addressed by counsel Fukushima Mizuho, who
was specifically concerned with the comfort women. She pointed out
that the very fact that some of the plaintiffs were preserving their
anonymity was an indication of the importance of chastity in Korean society, as well as of the mental suffering these women had endured and were continuing to endure. She outlined the known facts
of military control and transport of comfort women. She introduced
factors of deception, coercion and final abandonment. The infringe-
ment of the women's rights continued, she said, while they remained
uncompensated.

The next session was held on 14 September. Mun Ok Ju (see Introduction) testified. The government representatives, in the light of the official reports of 6 July (see Chapter 9), now admitted government responsibility in the supervision and hygiene control of comfort stations. But they would go no further, claiming that data had not been found which confirmed the case histories given by the plaintiffs. Counsel Takagi replied that the identification of Mun's savings account was good evidence for her case history, and urged continued investigation to uncover a wider range of data.

The third session of the lawsuit was on 7 December. Yi Ki Bun was mid-way through her formal statement when she blurted out emotionally:

> Can you imagine how I survived in Taiwan? I lived by copying beggars, smearing my face and body all over with mud and ripping my clothes. This was the way I got money by getting sympathy . . . When I returned home I couldn't bear to hear mothers calling their children. I couldn't stand it, realising I didn't have children and couldn't have any. Can you understand my misery?

Hers was a particularly poignant plea for understanding. Korean mothers are referred to by their children's names, as So and So's mother rather than as Mrs or Madam So and So.

At the first June hearing, the nine plaintiffs had been accompanied to Japan by five other former comfort women who, although not required for the lawsuit, offered to give evidence for the official investigation then going on. Their offer was rejected by the investigating committee. This exclusion of live testimony was later explained away as respect for privacy—a dubious pretext in view of the women's willingness to be cross-examined and the importance of their testimony to the case.

After each session, a report of what transpired in court was made to interested groups. At one of these a message was received from another sympathetic Diet-woman, Takemura Yasuko, in her capacity as representative of the Special Committee on the Forced Draft Problem. This had been co-ordinating action in the Diet. Soon after the June court session, twenty-five Social Democrat Diet Members submitted a petition to Chief Cabinet Secretary Kato. They made five points which covered the same ground as the Korean women's six-point demand of October 1990. Kato continued to maintain publicly that no evidence could be found to link government agencies to comfort women. Then, in a first sign of positive interest from the

Seoul government, the South Korean Foreign Ministry sent a request to Kato asking him to conduct a clarification of the historical facts.

The South Korean parliamentary committee on Foreign Affairs also called Professor Yun and her colleagues to testify on their six-point petition. The lawsuit, slowly as it would move, was setting other wheels in motion. The Council on the Matter of Comfort Women decided to keep up the momentum by holding demonstrations every Wednesday in front of the Japanese Embassy in Seoul. This practice has been faithfully observed since.

The most dramatic, immediate and unexpected result of the launch of the lawsuit, however, was the surfacing of original wartime Defence Agency documents. The Japanese authorities had long held these did not exist. In the absence of official documents on the comfort system, their stance had been that it was run by private operators and that the women were volunteers. These new documents demonstrated the extent of direct Japanese military involvement with comfort facilities.

Early in January 1992, Professor Yoshimi Yoshiaki of Chuo University, hearing of the lawsuit, recalled the original wartime documents relating to comfort women in the Library of the National Institute for Defence Studies attached to the Defence Agency. Japan has not had separate Ministries of Defence since the war, such bodies being restricted under the new Constitution. Professor Yoshimi promptly retrieved five of these documents. His speed showed up the official unwillingness to find relevant documents. The general character of Yoshimi's documents may be indicated by the following extracts:

1. A notice from the War Ministry dated 4 March 1938 to the North China Expeditionary Forces: 'As the recruitment of comfort women has been entrusted to unsuitable agents, who used the Army's name but engaged in abductions which brought police investigations, the Expeditionary Force is to exercise great care in selecting agents and maintain close co ordination with civil and military police [*kempeitai*] to preserve the dignity of the Forces.'

2. A circular from North China Headquarters to units under its command dated 27 June 1938: 'Illegal acts including rape are antagonising the population so that they co-operate with Communist guerrillas. To remedy this situation, discipline is to be strengthened and sexual comfort quickly provided.' (There is a good deal of grim detail on the 'illegal acts'.)

3. A 2nd Army situation report referring to the Hankow area garrison,

dated 10 December 1938: 'To avoid a repetition of previous disorder [regarded as referring mainly to the Rape of Nanking a year earlier] garrison troops are allowed to leave barracks only in organised parties or to visit comfort stations, which have been established from 25 November, a ticket system being used to avoid congestion or unseemliness.'

4. A routine report for mid-April 1939 to the War Ministry by the 21st Army, based in Canton. It contains a table covering 854 comfort women under Army control in its area, broken down by unit and locality, with the percentages affected by disease. It adds that there were another 150 under private management brought by units from their home localities, as well as some local women in forward areas. It adds that comfort stations had declined with the increase in other types of locally managed facilities.

5. A general circular, dated 18 June 1942, to overseas areas, regulating the supervision of comfort stations and the inspection of returning troops for the purpose of preventing venereal disease.

The next day, 11 January, the *Asahi Shimbun* published key extracts from these 'non-existent' documents. The afternoon edition carried the admission from government sources that:

The deep involvement by the Forces of the time cannot be denied . . . The truth of the matter is rapidly being revealed by the efforts of scholars and citizen groups. The facts will continue to be investigated through both official and private channels.

In the same breath, this admission claimed that there was no evidence of 'direct drafting'. Government spokesmen had ignored an announcement by the South Korean Embassy in Washington a few days earlier that United States Forces' wartime reports indicated Japanese Forces had control of Korean comfort women.

Over the weeks following publication of Professor Yoshimi's documents, scores of similar ones were discovered and reported. These included some wartime American studies, stimulating lively debate in the media which both added to the data available and proved revealing as to the variety of attitudes to the comfort women. Professor Yoshimi published the complete text of his documents in the magazine *Sekai* in March 1992, with references to earlier anecdotal accounts to demonstrate their agreement with the 'new' sources.

On 20 January 1992, the Comfort Women Problem Resolution Council demanded that the South Korean government provide urgent livelihood support for the affected victims. It also demanded they erect a memorial to them in the Independence Commemoration

Hall. They addressed the following statement to the Japanese government:

> We opposed the visit to South Korea by Prime Minister Miyazawa, who did not comply with our six demands regarding the investigation of the Voluntary Service Corps problem and compensation. However, having visited South Korea, he has left, still avoiding the issue of substantive compensation, merely reiterating specious expressions of deceitful apology. We sternly admonish Japan that such an attitude, unchanged from the past, desecrates our nation in its demand for the liquidation of colonialism, and the souls of those who have been sacrificed, so constituting an anachronism. We declare again that we cannot accept an apology unaccompanied by the disclosure of all the barbarities and the willingness to pay compensation. We demand:
>
> 1. We resent the fact that Japan compulsorily mobilised pupils as young as twelve years of age in the Voluntary Labour Service Corps, utilising the educational administration and then exploited the Korean victims as slave labour. We strongly demand that the Japanese government disclose the facts of manpower mobilisation and despoliation, including the Voluntary Labour Service Corps during the war and take appropriate measures such as proper payment for labour.
> 2. Since the Japanese government has for the first time formally admitted the crimes committed by the state, compensation must be made by the state. The claim that state compensation for the Voluntary Service Corps was settled by the 1965 Treaty, in which compensation for war victims such as the Corps was not even mentioned, would be difficult to accept even in terms of ordinary common sense. Furthermore, it does not accord with reason to claim that compensation for crimes which could not be 'established' at the time was resolved by the 'collective compromise' clause. Today, with clear evidence demonstrating the fact of Japanese government involvement, as well as testimony by survivors which is emerging by the day, the deceitful South Korea-Japan Claims Agreement of 1965 must naturally be revised and supplemented.
> 3. At the same time, early and appropriate compensation must be made to victims, as well as the bereaved families of victims. In this connection, we strongly protest against evasions which seek to shift the question to the level of charity with reference to a 'relief fund' by the Japanese government. We define compensation as the right of victims and the duty of the Japanese government. We declare at the same time that if the Japanese government utilises the legal system to perpetuate smooth verbal manipulation in the matter of individual compensation, we will not overlook this in silence.
> 4. We attach importance to Prime Minister Miyazawa's utterance that 'we will convey history accurately to the following generations so that the mistakes of this generation will not be repeated' and we will closely observe how faithfully this is put into practice. As regards Chief Cabi-

net Secretary Kato's demand for an end to anti-Japanese education, we declare that truly friendly relations between South Korea and Japan will only be possible when the truth of history is correctly taught and studied.

We vow to continue the struggle until the above demands are fully accomplished and once more demand that the Japanese government demonstrate the will for an early solution.

Following the first appearance of official documents in January 1992, the issue was further pursued in the Diet. In a House of Representatives Budget Committee session in February 1992, the matter was raised by Social Democratic Member Ito Hideko, who had further personally investigated the Defence Studies Library, and obtained fifty-six new documents. She expressed appreciation of Prime Minister Miyazawa's apology to South Korea but, at the same time, her regret for the lack of compensation to give it substance. She then recalled a government statement on the renunciation of claims under the Japanese-Soviet Joint Declaration, to the effect that this constituted a waiver of state claims and of the right of diplomatic protection for individual cases, but not of individual claims on either state or individuals. She went on to ask whether the same applied to the Basic Treaty with South Korea as it affected comfort women.

The head of the Economic Co-operation Bureau of the Foreign Ministry replied in some detail on the coverage of the 1965 treaty, as well as on an internal law passed at the same time, terminating South Korean property rights with a statutory basis. The conclusion was arrived at that there was no bar to action in a Japanese court by individual claimants.

Ito recalled that the Prime Minister had also spoken of waiting on due legal process during his Korean visit. She also pointed out that at the time of the conclusion of the Basic Treaty, the Japanese government had held the view that comfort women had 'just been taken around by private operators'. Miyazawa's apology amounted to a recognition that new facts had since emerged. These raised the question of moral and political responsibility for Japan as the offending party. She described the apology as having had a negative character in that it was based on 'inability to deny military involvement'. She asked the Prime Minister whether he was aware of the fifty-six documents recently discovered, which revealed many aspects not covered in the original five, and whether they had influenced his appreciation of the facts.

Miyazawa referred her to Chief Cabinet Secretary Kato, who was co-ordinating government investigations. He told her that their unremitting efforts were also uncovering new data, and referred her again to the head of his Foreign Affairs section. He stated that the new data confirmed the previous admission that the Armed Forces had been involved in the recruitment of comfort women and the operation of comfort stations.

Diet-woman Ito contended that this did not adequately recognise the significance of the new documents. She drew attention to two key examples, copies of which she had distributed beforehand. One contained the regulations for the comfort station serving the Nakayama garrison in the Canton area. This specified that the adjutant was responsible for supervision, the paymaster for financial matters and the medical officer for hygiene. It set out fees, hours of service and rank differentiation, in great detail. The other was the exchange of telegrams between Taiwan and the War Ministry regarding the Southern Theatre Army headquarters' request for the transport of 'native' comfort women and three proprietors to Borneo. She asked the Prime Minister for his reaction to these.

Miyazawa replied that, although he had not had such detailed information at the time of his visit to Korea, they bore out his basic recognition of military involvement. Diet-woman Ito then asked Foreign Minister Watanabe Michio whether his views had developed since an earlier television appearance when he had expressed uncertainty about the extent of active military intervention. He replied that military involvement had to be recognised in the light of new evidence. Similar discussion kept the issue before the Diet over the year, pending the government's promised release of its findings by July 1992.

Media and public attention

The activist groups were not prepared to wait around until July. Starting on 28 March 1992, members of the South Korean Church Women's Alliance, together with the former comfort women Sim Mi Ja and Hwang Kum Ju, held public meetings in Fukuoka, Tokyo, and Kashiwa, with its identified comfort station. Soon afterwards Mun Ok Ju and members of the Council for the Matter of Comfort Women were invited to visit Fukuoka by citizens' groups. Mun Ok Ju later visited Japan again to pursue the matter of the savings due to her from her time as a comfort woman. This led to the formation of a body called the Association to Demand the Payment of Mun Ok Ju's Military Postal Deposit.

In April 1992, a public hearing was organised in Seoul at the Christian Association Hall by the Council, with the Assembly of Attorneys for a Democratic Society. Its conclusions broadly focused on the need to treat the comfort women issue as a crime against humanity, with no time limit, and to reinterpret the 1965 Basic Treaty. Since the treaty did not mention the issues of comfort women and draftees' deposit money, the agreement should not rule out the possibility of compensation, particularly as the Japanese government had only recently admitted official involvement. While it was acknowledged that it would be more effective if the South Korean government were to take legal proceedings against the Japanese government, in view of its lukewarm attitude, individuals should be encouraged to take action: 'It is not just the problem of our government but is related to the national pride of each of us as individuals.' Another recommendation was to promote co-operation with Southeast Asian war victims. An open letter to the Seoul government was adopted, demanding that it institute compensation claims against the Japanese government and that it provide means of livelihood for draft victims of the Japanese Occupation.

The Seoul government set up Victim Report Centres in all municipal offices for a four-month period, to extend up to the deadline for its own investigation, which was scheduled to be completed in July 1992. Kim Hak Sun was named Woman of the Year by the Alliance of South Korean Women's Organisations during the International Women's Day celebrations. The co-spokeswoman of the Council, Professor Lee Hyo Jae, held a press conference on her submission of the issue to the United Nations Sub-commission on Human Rights and her plans for joint action with women's organisations in other Asian countries.

Regular media reports of the continuing activities of interest groups also kept public attention on the issue. Kim Hak Sun and representatives of the Council for the Matter of Comfort Women took part in several public meetings after attending the opening court session in Tokyo. After their court appearance, Kim Hak Sun and her party had a brief break at the Hakone hot springs. She was in good spirits and demonstrated that she still retained skills from her early *kisaeng* training in music and song.

Several meetings were held both in the Osaka region and in Tokyo. In Kobe there was a demonstration by Right-wing extremists, described as frightening but not discouraging. The principal meeting was organised in Tokyo by the network at the South Korean-affiliated YWCA, and 450 people attended. Kim Hak Sun gave an account of her wartime experience and stated her opposition to current proposals to send Japanese servicemen overseas on United Nations peace keeping operations. She said she still shuddered at the sight of Japanese servicemen. The issue of sending troops abroad was, of course, a major motivation for Japanese Left-wing support of the comfort women's action. The women could form a strong emotional barrier against Japanese rearmament or the revival of militaristic tendencies. In common with the foreign victims of Japanese militarism, the Japanese Left remained conscious of its own suppression. It argued that its cost would be better spent in compensation for war victims, to obtain international trust.

There was extensive debate in Japan. The case presented what the Chief Counsel for the litigants, Takagi Ken'ichi, described as an unprecedented case of popular initiative overcoming official indolence. A hotline was established in Tokyo by four co-operating organisations: the Association for the Study of the Military Comfort Women Problem, the Association for Clarifying Japan's Postwar Responsibility, the Resident Korean Women's Democratic Association, and the Compatriot Women's Network for the Military Comfort Women Problem. Hotlines in the Osaka-Kyoto area were run by the local Association for the Study of the Korean Military Comfort Women Problem. The Tokyo line received 240 significant calls. In nearby Urawa, there were twenty-four. Two others, in Kyoto and Osaka, received ninety-six and sixty-one respectively. A noticeable difference between the eastern and western regions was that supporters of compensation outnumbered opponents in the eastern region, while the reverse occurred in the west. Some of the callers agreed to follow-up interviews, which were to prove informative and useful.

Another sampling of public opinion was a street survey in the Ginza, Tokyo's best-known retail and entertainment quarter. It was found that concern was widespread among women and older people generally. One woman who had been in Taiwan during the war had wished, at the age of sixteen, to volunteer to become an Army typist, but had been given a friendly warning not to do so, 'or she would end up as a human sacrifice'. This had been her introduction to the subject of comfort women. A seventeen-year-old boy said he had learned of the problem through a drama in which a favourite actress had appeared, but had found it hard to believe.

More detailed debate occurred in letters and interviews with the press, particularly in the *Asahi Shimbun,* a newspaper with a long tradition of liberalism going back to the foundation of the party movement in the nineteenth century. It played a prominent part in the historic constitutionalist movement of 1913. Between the wars, it was repeatedly targeted by Right-wing extremists, in particular coming under threat in the 1936 coup attempt. There were even hints of defiance during the phase of totalitarian control. Under the new Constitution it used its freedom to maintain a consistent posture of intelligent criticism of the political-bureaucratic establishment. On the day after the publication of Professor Yoshimi's finds in the Defence Agency Library, it ran an editorial on the comfort women issue, entitled 'Let us not avert our gaze from history':

> The government has maintained an attitude of denial of involvement by either the Armed Forces or the government but it was really so widely known that installations of this kind were established by policy of the Japanese Forces that in this sense the recent data are not a matter of great surprise. No one ever wishes to recall shameful experiences. But, even if it was under the exceptional circumstances of war, it was our country of barely half a century ago that hunted out great numbers of people from Korea, then under its colonial control, forcing men into labour and military service and women into the role of providing sexual comfort for the troops. We must continue to bear the burden of these facts. We cannot avert our gaze from history . . .
>
> Self-criticism and apology can only be accepted as sincere when accompanied by positive redress . . . However particular claims may be handled, the first requirement for the government is to expedite a thorough, fact-finding investigation into the forced draft and comfort women problems. This must not be limited to a perfunctory gathering of data by notification through public offices but by an enterprising investigation, enlisting the co-operation of relevant organisations, researchers and foreign governments.

The editorial recalled the recent cases of the United States and Canada compensating citizens of Japanese descent for their internment during the war, following thorough investigation. These could serve as models for Japan. They concluded that internment was the result of 'racial prejudice', war hysteria and 'the negligence of politicians'. In the following months, Japanese government investigations followed the lines which the *Asahi* editorial had cautioned against rather than those it had recommended.

Letters received by the press supported compensation for comfort women, with reasons ranging from social justice to sympathy associated with nostalgic recollections. From an academic aged forty-nine:

> As I listened to these expressions of apology, I could not help inwardly shouting 'How late! Really too late!' Why couldn't such an apology have been made sooner? I reflected on the fate of many Korean women who had passed away during this too long gulf.

From a student aged twenty-three:

> A formal apology has been made. How many such facts must be accumulated for Japanese to realise the speciousness of the current vogue of talking about 'internationalisation'? . . . Don't we need to re-examine why, fifty years after the attack on Pearl Harbour and sixty years after the Sino-Japanese War began, the scars continue to be called in question?

From a veteran of the China front, aged seventy-three:

> It is natural that rancour should penetrate their very marrow as a result of being physically ravaged in their youth. However, it cannot be said that all were drafted by the military. There were also operators who did business by assembling comfort women; some were Koreans and Chinese. There were also women who themselves became comfort women for money . . . They followed units over mountains and rivers. Sometimes they helped transport the Army's ammunition and food, or joined in the fighting like the troops. The troops used to say that they deserved a Distinguished Service Medal Class A. In any case, I think it is appropriate that some kind of compensation should be made to the comfort women whose youth, never to return, was soiled in the battlefield.

A former *kempei* who had been stationed in China recalled the collaboration in corruption between operators and Army officers, who arranged for the supply of building materials for comfort stations at 20 per cent discount. He favoured compensation, adding that former Japanese comfort women should be included in this. Other accounts came from a medical officer who had been based in China. He had not only examined comfort women but enjoyed their services, he said. Then there was a former second-lieutenant who had supervised all comfort stations in his area, and a former *kempei* who described the system for allocating comfort women between areas.

The film-maker Yamatani Tetsuo criticised the more recent documentary *Song of Arirang* for concentrating too exclusively on *han* (rancour). Some comfort women had been deceived, some were compelled, but some were seeking their fortune, like the *karayuki* of the turn of the century. Sexual problems, he said, cannot be disposed of purely in terms of philosophy and morality: there is a physiological dimension too. Instinctive drives can't so easily be neutralised. He understood that, at the same time, the wartime situation in Korea had reached extremes of discrimination, both against Koreans as colonial subjects and against poorer Korean women as opposed to upper class families. Poor women became sexual playthings for the Imperial Forces' troops. 'The Korean comfort women problem is a life-size negative image of the Japanese,' he concluded. He favoured compensation in the form of service pensions.

Japanese right-wing attitudes

Opposition to compensating comfort women ranged from arguments that they had been compensated by payment at the time, to the position that it was much too late to revive such an outdated issue. Some opposed its raising by Japanese activists on the grounds that all countries have shameful secrets it would be unseemly to expose, much like the pudenda of the human body. The influential economic newspaper *Sankei* carried arguments along the lines of it being proper, as in the proverb, to 'keep a lid on something smelly'. In one feature article it was argued that a subject like comfort women was a thing to be spoken of in whispers, not paraded in public or taught in schools: 'The management of troops and sex is a conundrum that causes headaches in any country.' Not all Korean comfort women were forced to comply, as alleged, any more than the women who served the United States Navy in the Amusement House at the Yokosuka base, it alleged. A history of Napoleon's career related that every company in his army had six 'camp followers' attached to provide this service. These explanations were offered not to excuse the Japanese Forces, but 'this is the reality of a country's lower organs and human history'.

One letter expressed concerns that have probably strongly influenced the attitude of the authorities—even though they have not been openly expressed. From a seventy-year-old retiree:

> If a haphazard investigation is made, it will produce new injustices and there will be a limitless torrent of claims for compensation. It will not stop at China and Korea but doubtless claims will be made from far-flung countries in Southeast Asia and the South Pacific. If settlement is made in amounts acceptable to war compensation claimants, the present Japanese

nation would probably have to shoulder a tax burden several times the current level.

He concluded that Japan should reflect on past mistakes and guard against their repetition. Individual compensation for victims was not practicable but Japan should give as much economic aid as possible.

A letter from a sixty-five-year-old Korean businessman living in Japan represents the attitude of those of his countrymen hoping for a mutually beneficial *modus vivendi*. He concluded that Japan deprived Korea of sovereignty and property, but also recalled that Japan invested a great amount in Korea's modernisation, and that the leaders who had established the basis for the South Korean state had benefited from the modern education introduced. The expansionism of the Japanese leadership had brought 'comparable suffering to both peoples'. The comfort women problem was not one that had suddenly arisen. It went back half a century. The fact that only at this stage had the call for apology and compensation been raised exposed the negligence of the South Korean government. These 'unfortunate women', he went on, have little life left to them.

> The South Korean government should now lend them a helping hand . . . No courage or endurance is required to blame an offender, but courage, tolerance and endurance are required to forgive one. As one of their countrymen living in Japan, I believe that the South Korean nation is one that has such endurance. What about it?

A letter from a thirty-five-year-old company employee represented the fairly widespread attitude of preferring simply to bury the past. 'The comfort women problem, although a matter of past events which cannot directly involve us of the post-war generation, is a serious issue in that we and our country are being accused.' After enlarging on the new world situation where so many barriers between peoples are breaking down, he continued:

> The comfort women problem from the past, which seems to have been abruptly thrust upon us by South Korea, with demands for compensation from the national level, imparts a sense among us, as we are putting forth our best efforts for the present and future society, of being subject to 'psychological aggression'. There can be no need to drag the younger generation back into a relationship like that of the past. I constantly hope that, rather than be bound by history, we can devote our effort to the creation of a future history.

This letter's argument was rejected a few days later by a student correspondent, who argued that the true 'psychological aggression' was

Japan's failure to right the wrongs of the past, arising from failure to come to terms with it. On the other hand, the Korean businessman's letter was warmly commended by another writer as pointing the way to a more balanced and hopeful relationship between the two countries.

Other arguments appeared in a criticism of the *Asahi* studies in war history. One writer warned that, although admittedly the Japanese military establishment was responsible for the war, the unrelieved portrayal of the evils committed by the Forces threatened to cause a loss of national confidence among the present generation, their children and grandchildren. Evidence of this had recently emerged during the Gulf War, he went on, when the confusion and irresolution of Japanese policy had brought worldwide ridicule. 'Can a country without national pride have a future?' Then, coming to the comfort women problem:

> Unlike their representation in the *Asahi*, most of the women had been attracted by the hope of financial gain. The same sort of thing happened when the American Forces occupied Japan and requested the Japanese to open cabarets and dance halls for their recreation, whereupon swarms of the 'dianthi of Japan', who until the day before had been working in slacks in war factories, responded to the call. Unhappy reports of this must remain in the *Asahi*'s files. It is time to call a halt to such masochistic exhuming of history.

Not all women have themselves espoused the cause of the comfort women. The more systematic arguments against their cause have come from a small group of women who perhaps feel their sex saves them from charges of male chauvinism. The most prominent is Uesaka Fuyuko, a freelance journalist and critic with South Korean contacts. She had written about the plight of Japanese women in South Korea who had married Koreans, in accordance with earlier assimilationist policies. On the eve of the lawsuit, with the fiftieth anniversary of Pearl Harbour at hand, she had written a piece in the *Mainichi Shimbun* demanding to know how long Japan had to continue to apologise. Even copyright had only a fifty-year life. She rejected the view that Japan was solely responsible for the war, portraying it as the climax of a long series of moves and counter-moves, in which responsibility was widely diffused.

In February 1992, another article by Uesaka Fuyuko appeared in the *Shukan Post* weekly, under the headline: 'As no one will speak out, I venture to write.' She began by asking why there had been no serious debate on the comfort women issue. 'Do not superficial sympathy and facile apologies amount to a slight on these women who were forced to suffer in the past?' After noting the emotional tension created by the images of fighting men with heroic qualities on the one hand, and needing 'comfort' on the other, she listed some of the 'false premises' which she felt had dominated the discussion.

First, the Korean draftees were not subject to racial discrimination, like American citizens of Japanese descent, because Koreans and Japanese were alike Japanese subjects, with the National General Mobilisation Law applying equally to them. Human rights were denied to all under wartime conditions. Second, the 1905 Protectorate Treaty leading to Korea's annexation, concluded in conjunction with the Anglo-Japanese Alliance and the Treaty of Portsmouth, ending the Russo-Japanese War, was not lawless by the standards of the time. No-one condemned the display in Western museums of art treasures looted from the whole world, she said. Standards change with time. Third, Japan did not refuse to consider compensation for Korea. All relations with South Korea were barred during Syngman Rhee's regime. Only after his fall could negotiations proceed, leading to the 1965 settlement.

She went on to question the sudden prominence of the issue, when some years previously writers like Senda Kako had made considerable studies of comfort women with no political repercussions. She speculated that the present stir might be economically motivated, as a way of putting pressure on Japan, or helping improve relations between North and South Korea.

According to Uesaka, a South Korean journalist friend had expressed the view that the stir had been triggered from Japan, rather than Korea. It was like the textbook controversy of some years before, which had originated from Japanese journalists' misunderstanding that a reactionary change in terminology had occurred. Uesaka's own feelings were that the comfort women were being used as pawns in some design to bring about a form of social change. She considered Prime Minister Miyazawa's apologies to be ill-conceived, whether he hoped that they would settle the matter or was simply playing for time. She preferred United States President George Bush's refusal to apologise for the American use of nuclear weapons on Japanese cities, even though she herself had written a book on the victims. She contended that Miyazawa should have had the courage to say 'I am not prepared to apologise at this stage for what the then Japanese Forces judged was a necessary evil to be adopted in war zones to avoid harm to local women'. She does not believe that the present Japanese government, forty-seven years after the country's complete reconstruction, can be made responsible for the deeds of the long-vanished Armed Forces. She does admit, however, the right of individuals to sue for damages and to receive due compensation. She concluded with the warning that ideological involvement could only lead to purposeless confusion.

Following this piece the *Shukan Post* received a flood of letters, of which more than half favoured Uesaka. This conservative position could reflect the nature of its readership, but probably also represents a sizeable body of opinion reacting against what one writer called 'masochistic history'.

Not long afterwards, the *Shukan Post* published a follow-up in the form of a debate between Uesaka and Pak Chung Ja, a former South Korean parliamentarian and head of the South Korean-Japanese Women's Friendship Association, and of the Women's Problems Study Association. The exchange as printed was fairly urbane, but given Uesaka's conservative stance and the emotiveness of the issue, it was also rather heated. Uesaka emphasised as usual the legalistic aspects, such as that the post-war Korean republics were different entities from Korea's previous status as a recognised part of Japan. She also accused the litigants in acting as individuals, of contempt for their own government. She had been impressed by President Roh's statement during his visit to Japan, she said, that Koreans should reflect on the reasons for their failure to resist seizure by Japan. The argument elaborated by Pak was that true friendship between the two countries could only arise from proper compensation and recognition of the past.

The arguments against the comfort women's case have been summarised by the women's groups as falling into the following categories:

- Enormities of all kinds are inevitable in war;
- Comfort women were a 'necessary evil' to maintain order and health;
- Apart from possible coercion, which is asserted and not proved, recruitment was on a contractual basis in accordance with then-legal procedures;
- Compensation was settled by the 1965 Basic Treaty;
- The whole issue is Japanese media hype to gain public interest and sell newspapers;

- The past is past, which most people prefer to forget like a bad dream;
- Why only Koreans? (This, however, can be applied in the positive sense of expanding the scope of the issue.)
- Korean brothel keepers were involved;
- There is no way of determining the total number of women involved;
- The issue is best ignored for the sake of future good relations, since it can only be a source of friction.

In lieu of compensation, an apology payment?

Compromise solutions of some measure 'in lieu of compensation' have also been much debated. Precedents for this are first, the payments of ¥20,000 each paid in 1987 to Taiwanese ex-servicemen incapacitated by war service, and to bereaved families, and second, the fund established for Korean victims of the atomic bombs following President's Roh's visit to Japan in 1990. The problem of comfort women differs from these cases, however, in that there is so little information on the number and identities of possible beneficiaries. Although Chief Cabinet Secretary Kato was not enthusiastic when Diet-woman Takemura raised the matter of a fund immediately after Professor Yoshimi's revelations, a later spokesman spoke favourably of such a fund because 'it is a matter approached from a humanitarian standpoint so that, unlike the case of individual compensation, there is less need for rigorous testimony and it can be considered more readily'.

Suggestions from unofficial quarters have raised the possibilities of private contributions, or diversions from the consumption tax or military pension funds. Professor Yun, however, in an address to an Amnesty International meeting, insisted that only an 'atonement payment' should be considered. She rejected the concept of 'relief'. Comfort woman Sim Mi Ja similarly preferred the idea of an 'apology payment' to 'compensation'. Official spokesmen for some time predicted that a plan would be formulated within the year. Later, during a discussion of possible association with the Red Cross, it was announced that this target could not be reached because new documents continued to surface which required consideration. Some of these involved the former Japanese-occupied territories.

9. The governments speak up

Activists won an important victory when they took the opportunity presented by Miyazawa's 1992 visit to South Korea to press for an official report on comfort women. The resultant setting up of two fact finding committees in Japan and South Korea had disappointing results. The official documents which surfaced appeared to activists to be only a fraction of what was likely to be there, given the national penchant for recording and note keeping.

The Japanese report

The Japanese committee was the first to publish its report, on 6 July 1992, under the title 'Results of Investigation into the Question of "Military Comfort Women" Originating from the Korean Peninsula'. Despite the title, it also included material on comfort women of other nationalities.

The report was the basis of a general statement of apology to all countries concerned, and contributed significantly to the information available on comfort women. The Japanese government also appeared for the first time to be taking the subject seriously. However, it did not escape notice that there were no relevant documents released from the Police Agency or the Labour Ministry, the two agencies most implicated in the forced recruitment of women. Their documents would be crucial to substantiating the charges of deception, intimidation and coercion brought by Kim Hak Sun and the eight other comfort women against the Japanese government.

The government agencies which did participate are as follows:

- the National Police Agency, which had asked for investigations by all prefectural police headquarters in addition to its internal resources;

- the Self-Defence Agency, which had focused on historical materials in the National Institute for Defence Studies as well as the Land, Sea and Air Self-Defence Forces and the Self-Defence College;
- the Foreign Ministry, which focused on material in the Diplomatic Archives Institute and included some from the former Home, Colonial and Greater East Asia Ministries, the latter during the war having taken over diplomatic relations in Japan's sphere of influence;
- the Education Ministry, which had asked for investigations by prefectural educational committees, covering public libraries, as well as privately established ones and university libraries abroad;
- the Welfare Ministry, which focused on material relating to demobilisation and lists of servicemen and paramilitary;
- the Labour Ministry, including related organs and local employment security agencies.

There were 127 documents produced, including those first found by Professor Yoshimi and other individual investigators. Of these, 70 came from the Self-Defence Agency, 52 from the Foreign Ministry, 4 from the Welfare Ministry and 1, actually already published, from the Education Ministry. The areas covered by the documents were:

- establishment of comfort stations (4);
- control of persons recruiting comfort women (4);
- construction and extension of comfort facilities (9);
- management and supervision of comfort stations (35);
- hygiene control of comfort stations and comfort women (24);
- issue of identity cards and the like to persons connected with comfort stations (28);
- general references to comfort stations and comfort women.

The absence of documents on the recruitment of comfort women provoked a torrent of criticism on the shortcomings of the scope of the committee's investigations. Professor Yoshimi, the various women's groups and, a little later, the South Korean government's report on its own investigations, were particularly critical. The lack of police documents, particularly from regional sources, was described as remarkable, since Foreign Ministry documents indicated widespread police activity on such matters as identity cards. The Labour Ministry's failure to produce documents was similarly seen as not good enough. The Justice Ministry was not even involved in the investigation, although it was known to have the full records of all war crimes trials, including the Dutch cases. The Self-Defence Agency Library was known to hold large numbers of personal war diaries not open to the public. Except for a limited thirty-year period for the release of Foreign Ministry documents, public access to official records is only possible on their release to the Public Archives at the departments' own initiative, with national interest and privacy governing considerations.

There was also criticism from the activists of the paucity of interviews with those actually involved. A group of Korean comfort women had offered to give interviews, but their offer was refused. The failure to use data from the phone-ins conducted in three Japanese cities, the exclusion of foreign documents such as the thorough United States Army reports and the microfilm list of Koreans taken from Okinawa to Hawaii, and the failure to search for material which might survive in Korea from the former Government-General or in wartime occupied areas, were also of concern. In a press interview given by Chief Cabinet Secretary Kato, he stated that investigations would continue but that no interviews were contemplated with the women because these involved 'technical difficulties' and the question of privacy. Interview material from South Korea would, however, be taken into consideration. Asked whether Japanese comfort women were included in the general apology, Kato replied that most of the women were of Japanese nationality, which at the time included Koreans and Taiwanese. He added that it was regrettable that women had undertaken such work as a result of poverty, implying that this was the likely explanation for the availability of comfort women, rather than overt coercion on the part of the military. But rather than necessarily implying voluntary prostitution to avoid it, poverty could have led to a willingness to trust deceptive offers of work. As Professor Yoshimi has emphasised, deception and intimidation are included in the broader sense of coercion.

Information on the comfort system itself came mainly from the Self-Defence Agency and Welfare Ministry documents, but the Foreign Ministry documents were valuable in demonstrating much wider official involvement in the comfort system than could be attributed to the arbitrary initiative of the Armed Forces alone. These documents fall into two main categories: first, the issue of identity cards, travel permits and passports relating to the comfort system, and second, reports from consulates in China on the comfort system there. The latter come mainly from the consular police, an institution operated by all the colonial powers in China, including Japan, in accordance with the extra-territorial rights accorded their subjects or citizens under the unequal treaty system.

The Foreign Ministry document that comes closest to saying something about the recruitment process is one that relates to a military document which is listed first among Professor Yoshimi's original five discoveries, and is often quoted for its implications. Originating from the War Ministry, and dated 4 March 1938 when the comfort system was being developed, it is addressed to the Chiefs of Staff of the North China Regional Force and the Central China Expeditionary Force:

> There have been cases where, in recruiting female staff in the Homeland for the establishment of comfort stations in the theatre of operations of the China Incident [the diplomatic terminology current at that time to avoid the implications of a declared state of war] deliberate use has been made of the claim to have the Forces' approval, involving the risk of injuring the dignity of the Forces and inviting misunderstanding among the general public; also, through the intermediary of war correspondents or providers of amenities, uncontrolled recruitment has been carried on, with the risk of causing social problems. As a result of those engaging in recruitment not being suitably selected, there have been cases of recruitment methods amounting to abduction, which have resulted in charges and investigation by police authorities. Great care is therefore needed in future to ensure the proper control of recruitment by the Expeditionary Forces, with the exercise of due care in the selection of persons so engaged, together with close co-ordination with military and civil police in the related areas and consideration to preserving the dignity of the Forces and the avoidance of social problems.

A Foreign Ministry document from the same period and context is dated 23 February 1938 and was addressed by the Director of the Police Bureau of the Home Ministry to all prefectural governors who were in those days appointees of the Ministry with authority over the elected councils. It is entitled 'Procedure For Women Travelling To China'. It begins:

> Recently, with the restoration of order in many areas of China [that is, areas under Japanese control], there has been a marked increase in the number of travellers there, including many women having connections

with the operators of restaurants, cafes, houses of assignation and the like or themselves engaged in such business. In the Homeland there has also been the frequent and widespread appearance of persons engaged in the recruitment or brokering of such women who irresponsibly claim the approval of the military authorities.

The notice concedes that a need exists for such travel by women but continues:

If proper control is lacking in such recruitment of women, this will not only injure the dignity of the Empire and the honour of the Imperial Forces but will have an undesirable effect on the home front, particularly the families of soldiers on active service, while there is no assurance that this will not conflict with the provisions of international treaties on traffic in women.

The following instructions are set out:

1. Tacit approval to be given for the time being to travel for the purpose of prostitution by licensed prostitutes or other women, for practical purposes in prostitution, who are over twenty-one in full years [that is, not the traditional count which adds a year or more] and free from venereal disease. Their identity cards are to be issued as prescribed by Foreign Ministry procedures.
2. The women to be instructed to return upon the expiry of their contracts or when no longer needed.
3. Application to be made in person at police stations.
4. Applicants to have the approval of the senior next of kin at the same address or the head of the household or else explain the lack of any such person to give approval.
5. An investigation to be made of the business contract or any other aspects to ensure that traffic in women or abduction is not involved.
6. Stern action to be taken against persons engaged in such or similar recruitment involving moral issues, who claim to have military approval or contacts or make any other irresponsible claims regarding the Forces.
7. Stern action to be taken against advertising or the falsification or exaggeration of facts, as well as the strict investigation of all persons engaged in such recruitment, refusing recognition to any not holding proper permits or identification issued by diplomatic agencies abroad, or to persons of dubious character.

The international treaties referred to were a series of agreements on the traffic in women for purposes of prostitution, which banned the procurement of females under twenty-one, and that of any woman involving deceit, intimidation or coercion. Japan had signed these treaties in 1925 during its liberal and conciliatory period. The last of them, however, contained a provision that countries with colonies could exclude them from the scope of the treaty, and Japan did so with respect to Korea, Taiwan, the Kwantung-leased territory in southern Manchuria, southern Sakhalin and the mandated territory of Micronesia. This meant that, whatever the degree of protection Japanese women enjoyed under these treaties, there was none for women in the Japanese colonies.

There is a mass of detail in the documents. An example of the practical functioning of the procedures laid down is provided by a query from the Governor of a prefecture in Kyushu, directed to the Foreign Ministry. It stated that a resident of Tsinan had obtained certification from the local Consul-General to return to Japan for the purposes of employing 'hostesses' and, having recruited them, was applying for identity cards for them. The Governor enquired whether it was in order to issue identity cards for comfort stations on the basis of certification either by diplomatic agencies or military authorities. The reply stated that this was in order within the limits stated in the notice of 23 February.

There is evidence that procedures in the Armed Forces were not uniform, with the result that the position of the civil authorities was undermined—a very common situation during this period. One illustration is an exchange of messages between the Foreign Ministry and the Consul-General in Hankow in 1939. The Ministry's enquiry referred to a notice from the Home Ministry. This stated that an Army unit stationed in Hankow had directly recruited fifty comfort women from its home prefecture in Shikoku and, with the support of the local military, applied for travel permits for them, which had been 'informally agreed to as there seemed to be no alternative'. The Ministry enquired whether the Consul-General had approved in advance.

The reply stated that the unit had not contacted the Consul-General and that, from local military headquarters, it was learned the unit had not observed the normal military permit system. Nevertheless, it had been agreed that as the unit had already completed its arrangements, consent would have to be given after the fact. The unit had then requested the Consul-General to supervise the comfort facilities so set up. Another message from the same source during the year mentioned that there were twenty comfort stations, with permits issued either by the Army logistics division, the *kempeitai* or the Consul-General. There had been such a rush to the area of profiteers in this and other fields, that pressure on accommodation and services presented problems. The Ministry was requested to tighten procedures to prevent uncontrolled travel by 'unsound elements'.

In 1940, after the establishment of the client Wang Ching Wei regime, there was an attempt at tightening controls in the interests of social stability. A Ministry circular indicated that identity cards for travel to China would only be issued either to persons holding permits from the War or Navy Ministries, or the consular police for domestic or business purposes. A related directive to the police instructed them that although they had no jurisdiction over paramilitaries or employees of the Forces, they were to guard against false claims to such employment, and to issue certifications to 'special class women' only when replacements were needed to maintain numbers at the same level as of 20 May 1940. These women were defined as including *geisha,* hostesses, waitresses and employees of military comfort stations.

In Nanking and Shanghai matters of this sort are recorded as being handled by a liaison conference of Army, Navy and diplomatic representatives. These agreed in 1938 that in the case of Nanking:

- the consulate would not be concerned with purely servicemen's comfort stations.
- the consular police would supervise the operators of comfort stations which were also used by civilians, while the *kempeitai* would supervise servicemen frequenting them.
- the *kempeitai* could take action regarding them whenever necessary.
- the logistics division could incorporate civilian comfort stations as military comfort stations.
- when military comfort stations were established the military authorities would keep the Consulate-General informed of their business conditions and the personal particulars of the operators in considerable detail.

Various documents from the Foreign Ministry between them provide the following information about comfort stations in these areas of China between 1938 and 1939:

- Shanghai: 7 Navy comfort stations, 300 Army comfort women;
- Hangchow: 4 comfort station operators, 36 hostesses;

- Chiuchiang: 24 comfort stations, 107 Japanese and 143 Korean women;
- Wuhu: 6 comfort stations, 48 Japanese and 22 Korean women;
- Hankow: 20 comfort stations, 398 *geisha,* prostitutes and hostesses [another reference in an officer's memoir states that 11 of the 20 comfort stations were run by Koreans and that 150 of the women working there were Korean];
- Nanchang: 11 comfort stations, 11 Japanese and 100 Korean women;
- Amoy: 1 comfort station; Navy comfort station, 4 female operators and 13 staff.

A Consulate-General report on the occupations of Japanese in its area at the end of 1932 is of special interest in the history of Navy comfort stations. The report indicated that 17 such stations had been established during the year and that 3 had closed, though 17 remained in operation at the end of the year. This indicates that at least three had existed previously, and throws light on General Okamura Yasuji's account, in which he said during 1932 he had followed Naval practice in introducing comfort stations for the Army. This seems to be the earliest recorded use of the official term *kaigun ianjo* (meaning naval comfort station). (The Army's comfort stations are described only as *ianjo,* while women with either force are called *jugun ianfu* in full, *ianfu* for short.)

Monthly reports for 1941 and 1942 from consular offices in Canton, Amoy, Hankow and Swatow give figures for Japanese moving into these areas, broken down by occupation. For the 11 months covered by the reports, the figures for military canteens and comfort stations total 86 for Canton, 39 for Amoy, 8 for Haikow, 4 for Swatow and 22 for Hong Kong.

Regarding travel from Taiwan for work in military canteens and comfort stations in China, documents originating from the former Colonial Ministry contain a large number of monthly returns between 1938 and 1941. These were submitted by provincial governors to the Government-General on the issue of identity cards and passports for China. The figures are broken down among ethnic Japanese, Koreans and Taiwanese, and for destinations in northern China, Shanghai and southern China. Numbers are very small except for the provinces of Taipei and Kaohsiung, and even these rise to over 100 on only two occasions in each province—in late 1938 and early 1939. Japanese are most numerous. After 1939 the numbers fall off markedly, to around 30 or under.

Such a decrease, as well as the general lack of Foreign Ministry material dating from around 1942 would be due to procedural changes, which are poorly documented. One sign of these is a brief exchange between the Taiwan Government-General and the Foreign Ministry in January 1942. The former enquired about the procedure to be followed for travel for the purpose of establishing comfort stations in the southern occupied regions. The Ministry's reply was that such travel only required certification by the Armed Forces. A couple of draft phrases are crossed out, but still legible and these read 'as the issue of passports is inappropriate' and 'by the Forces' ships'.

An early example of the eclipse of civil authorities by the military is the exchange of messages already referred to, between the military authorities in Taiwan and the War Ministry, in March 1942. This regarded the transport of 'native' comfort women southwards, without any reference to civil authorities. The assumption by General Tojo Hideki of the post of Home Minister, as well as War Minister, was the ultimate symbol of militarist domination. The takeover of East Asian diplomacy by the Greater East Asian Ministry in 1943 is referred to in a couple of messages from the military authorities in Saigon and Hanoi enquiring about travel and residence procedures for auxiliaries, including comfort women.

There is very little documentation of this kind relating to Korea. There were few formalities to travel from Korea to Manchukuo, and there are only a couple of returns dated 1942 from the Government-General to the Colonial Ministry on the issue of identity cards for travel to China. They are broken down among ethnic Japanese and Koreans, and for destinations in northern, central and southern China. Under the usual term for licensed prostitutes, the return for the second half of 1941 shows 21 Japanese and 381 Koreans. For the first half of 1942 there were 32 Japanese and 286 Koreans. This would appear to cover the more or less voluntary movement of professional prostitutes, and have no bearing on the great numbers of comfort women obtained by other means.

The South Korean government's report

The South Korean government's report appeared on 31 July 1992, a couple of weeks after the Japanese report. Its title was 'Interim Report of the Fact-Finding Investigation on Military Comfort Women under Japanese Imperialism', in the name of the Working Group on the Voluntary Service Corps Problem. It consisted of a thorough survey of the contents of the Japanese government's report, together with the United States Army reports, and summaries of testimony received through the Victim Report Centres set up to collect information in two Korean cities. These, however, were kept anonymous, and being of the same general character as earlier case histories, did not add a great deal of substance. There was no reference to any other documentation except for school registers recording recruitment to the Voluntary Labour Service Corps. The Education Ministry had 245 records of recruitment for the Corps, one from a high school and the rest from primary schools.

The report began by defining its underlying purpose as the achievement of a better relationship with Japan. This was being hampered by the comfort women issue. It then reviewed the activities of the Working Group which consisted of representatives of seventeen government agencies led by the head of the Foreign Ministry's Asia Bureau. It acknowledged the key role of the women's organisations, but somewhat overplayed the government's interest in the early phase. The group had held monthly as well as special meetings and planned to continue meeting until the end of 1992. Diplomatic missions abroad had been instructed to investigate the presence of comfort women.

The Victim Report Centres functioned from 25 February to 25 June 1992. They revealed a total of 392 cases, 235 on Labour Service, of which 139 victims still survived. There were 155 on comfort women, of whom 74 were still alive. The report stressed the need to distinguish between the two categories and stated that Labour Service women rarely became comfort women. The Japanese had used the blanket term Voluntary Service Corps to 'obscure the anti-civilised nature of their recruitment methods', and the terminology had remained confusing in Korea.

The report then went on to criticise the Japanese report as lacking comprehensive coverage in such areas as methods of setting up comfort stations; their locations and number; recruitment methods; living conditions; and rates and conditions of payment. The South Korean Foreign Ministry had urged continued investigation and a decision on the resolution of the issue. An historical survey followed, using the better-known publications, from the Siberian expedition, the Shanghai situation in 1932 and 1938, the major recruitment drive in Manchuria, and so on, down to Yoshida's account. It traced the main phases of professional prostitution, deception and intimidation, to outright force. The report correctly identified the Armed Forces' logistics division as the organisational basis of the comfort system. The report also contained brief summaries of thirteen representative cases, all anonymous.

South Korean comfort women

- The family was arrested in August 1938 for refusal to deliver brass articles (required for the war effort) and for opposition to the adoption of Japanese names. The victim was persuaded to volunteer for the Labour Service Corps in exchange for her father's release. She was at once transported to a comfort station in Jakarta and on the way, in Canton, forced to undergo an operation for sterilisation. She returned to Korea in 1946.
- When alone at home in 1943, the victim was seized by two unknown men on the pretence of urgent business, and taken by train to Harbin. She had to service twenty men a day and was beaten for refusing service or using Korean.
- In 1940, following police threats to her family's lives, the victim was taken to Osaka. There she had to service five to seven soldiers a day, having one day a month off for a medical examination.
- In 1942 the victim was seized by draft notice, kept in a warehouse, and sexually assaulted three times daily. There was no mention of travel outside Korea.
- In 1938, the victim was carried off by two Japanese soldiers and a Korean while gathering herbs in the mountains with her sister. She was taken via Pusan and Osaka to Hokkaido, where she remained for a year. She was then returned to Osaka and so violently ill-treated that she developed schizophrenia, and was 'abandoned in the mountains by the military'. [This case possibly relates to an account in a publication by Professor Yun and her colleagues of a visit to a reputed former comfort woman in a mental institution in the Kobe region. No clear communication was achieved on that occasion.]
- The victim was recruited on the pretence of a job in a sugar factory, but became a comfort woman on Palau and neighbouring islands from 1937 until liberation.
- The victim was among fifty women offered work in a Pusan factory in 1941 by two Japanese women and a Korean man. Instead she was taken to Japan as a comfort woman for a unit there. She had to service twelve to fifteen men a day and accompanied the unit on extensive movements to Singapore, Nanking and Manchuria. She was never al-

lowed to leave her quarters. Over half of the older women with her died.

- In 1942, when aged sixteen, the victim was seized during a train journey to Mukden by a Japanese Army fellow passenger. She was confined with twenty others including some Chinese, in a comfort station within the barracks grounds.

- In 1944 when the victim was on night duty in a textile factory, a group of Japanese servicemen entered and told the employees they were to become nurses. The more alert women fled, but the remaining fortynine were seized to become comfort women.

The Women's Council reacts

The Comfort Women Problem Resolution Council of South Korea recorded its reaction to the Japanese report in an open letter to Prime Minister Miyazawa, dated 13 October 1992:

> Even among the war crimes committed by Japan, the comfort women issue involves the most inhuman, atrocious national crimes, unparalleled in the world. We have consistently demanded that the concealed truth of the matter be brought to light and that apology and compensation be made to the victims. This is a movement to restore the human rights denied the comfort women. It also aims to correct the distortions in the history of Korean and Japanese relations and to sound an alarm bell to the world so that such war crimes are not repeated.

It described the report as 'no more than an enumeration of data, something extremely insincere which does not mention the concrete content of injuries or the locus of command and responsibility'. The Council had placed the issue on the agenda of the United Nations Sub commission on Human Rights, and, it said, the world was showing strong concern for the establishment of the facts and their legal treatment. Although the Japanese and United States [sic] governments had discarded and concealed evidence, both data and witnesses were appearing in both Koreas, the Philippines and other Asian countries. Regarding proposed compromise solutions:

> We feel deep disquiet and indignation on receiving reports that your government has recently been considering the establishment of a relief fund for former comfort women as 'a measure in lieu of compensation'. It is clear to anyone that such a move by your government arises from a wish to find a hurried monetary solution to its own shameful crimes which have surfaced as a matter of worldwide concern.

We realise that your government takes the position that the question of compensation was settled by the South Korea—Japan agreement of 1965. We repeat, however, that the comfort woman question was not discussed at that time. You and your government must well realise that under the *jus cogens* [enforcing norm, or fundamental law overriding any inconsistent national law or international agreement] individual rights are not extinguished even by agreements between states. We therefore declare that a 'livelihood fund' as a 'measure in lieu of compensation' is a deceitful conception incompatible with reason.

The former comfort women are described as unable to accept such money, for it would only signal renewed humiliation for them. The Council regarded relief measures as properly the duty of the Koreans' own people, and noted a national fund raising movement for former comfort women was being developed. The essential role for Japan is the sincere exposure of the truth. Finally:

In conclusion, we cannot help feeling deep disquiet at your country's efforts to dispatch peace-keeping forces overseas and to become a permanent member of the United Nations Security Council without first clearing up the comfort women issue and wartime and post-war responsibility. We strongly emphasise that if your country truly wishes to make an international contribution commensurate with its economic power, this must begin with a settlement of its past war crimes.

The North Korean report

On 1 September 1992, North Korea issued a report along lines similar to South Korea's. It clearly attempted, however, to outdo the South Koreans in vehemence. It succeeded, in a style appropriate enough to what is virtually the world's last surviving pure Stalinist state. The report is entitled 'An Indictment: The Japanese Government Must Fully Establish the Truth on the "Military Comfort Women" Question and Sincerely Apologise'. The report was prepared by the Committee for Measures on Compensation to Military Comfort Women and Pacific War Victims and headed by O Mun Han, vice-chairman of the Committee for International Cultural Relations. It began:

Recently in Japan there have been exposed the atrocious criminal acts whereby, in the past, the Japanese Armed Forces forcibly drafted the women of Asian countries, particularly Korea, as sex slaves for the 'Imperial Forces', so arousing the anger of the people of the world.

The 'military comfort woman' problem may be described as involving the most cowardly and immoral crimes, never before occurring in human history or military history. The shame and humiliation suffered by women drafted as 'military comfort women' and violated by the 'Imperial Forces' are a matter of such inhumanity that they cannot be witnessed in idleness by anyone who values humanity and morality. The Japanese government authorities nevertheless have as yet made no attempt to reflect sincerely on the past crimes recklessly perpetuated by the former Japanese Armed Forces.

To refuse to utilise the lessons of history is in fact equivalent to repeating past errors. This committee issues this indictment in the interests of joint action by all the progressive peoples of the world, international agencies, national governments and social organisations in order to draw attention to the Japanese government's unjust procedures in refusing to apologise sincerely for the Japanese Forces' past crimes and to ensure that such inhuman evils as the 'military comfort women' problem are not repeated.

The report went on to sketch the story of Li (Yi in southern pronunciation) Kyong Sang whose case had surfaced in the May 1992 normalisation talks with Japan. Yi Kyong Sang's husband had just died, without ever learning of her misfortunes. She was then willing to bear witness against the Japanese government. In 1929, when she was twelve years old, she had been forced with eight others into a comfort station serving a munitions factory. Until she escaped in 1933, she daily serviced seven to ten factory officials and Army guards. The report now added details on how she and two companions escaped from sexual service, by making the guards drunk. These underlings could not afford much liquor, whereas the officers enjoyed a surfeit at the parties they held, waited on by the women. They saved surplus liquor until they had three bottles full, which at standard size would be about 5.5 litres. This proved ample to intoxicate the guards, and the three escaped and split up. Kyong Sang found refuge, married and lived with her husband in China until the war ended.

The historical outline of the report then follows that known from Japanese sources. It comments that 'these crimes exceeded in foulness and barbarity anything that the Nazis committed'. The overall number of comfort women is estimated at 'hundreds of thousands'. The minors, aged twelve or thirteen, and recruited from schools, are regarded as having been subjected to sexual slavery. The accent on horror is still more pervasive and unrelieved than in the earlier studies. The accounts would perhaps command more confidence if they originated from a more open society.

North Korean comfort women

- The victim was sold as a maidservant to a landlord by her poor family, and was so worn out with drudgery that she accepted an offer of work as a 'labourer' in the hope of some improvement. She was carried off to the southern front as a comfort woman.
- The victim was conveyed by her ward chief into the custody of Japanese troops, included among hundreds of girls assembled at Pusan, and transported with them as comfort women to Indonesia. [Accounts of this kind, unlike those from South Korea, emphasise oppression by upper-class Koreans and collaborators with the Japanese.]
- The victim relates that her recruitment as a comfort woman was defined by an officer's order to 'fulfil her duty to the Emperor', with the threat that any who failed to do so would be decapitated.
- A girl who resisted fiercely was executed as an example by having her head and limbs roped to horses and being torn apart—a method of execution historically associated with Genghis Khan's Mongols.
- A woman of about thirty who 'refused to bathe'—presumably to discourage men from going near her—was suspended upside down from a tree, battered by rifles, had her nipples cut off, and was finally shot through the vagina.
- The women were forced to drink water in which had been boiled the head of a Chinese who had been captured and beheaded.

The North Korean report finally attacked the recent acknowledgements of the Japanese government as 'deceitfulness, a challenge to humanity'. 'From the first round of normalisation talks', the North Koreans had demanded investigation, publication and sincere apologies from the Japanese government, but the latter had denied official involvement until the revelation of January 1992, it claimed. Rational Japanese had recognised their governments' promised investigation as an evasion. Writers in the *Asahi* newspaper are quoted to the effect that, 'the state and people must accept war responsibility and the case for compensation to gain acceptance in the post Cold War world, so as not to be isolated in the stream of world history'.

It was recalled that on 5 May 1992 at the seventeenth session of the Working Group on Contemporary Slavery under the United Nations Sub-commission on Human Rights, the representative of the International Educational Development Association had pointed out a basis for compensation under the Convention on Forced Labour, which Japan had signed in 1932. Japan had infringed almost all of its provisions, including forced labour by women, and the drafting of minors, students and men over forty-five.

Japan's report of 6 July had further aroused the anger of the people of the world, the report went on. Japan's role as the chief offender was still not clear, since its report claimed to have no evidence of recruitment by coercion. On the grounds of 'technical difficulty and inequity', it excluded oral testimony such as Yoshida Seiji's. This amounted to an 'anti-international challenge mocking the peoples of the world'. Japanese spokesmen also distorted the facts by describing most comfort women as being of Japanese nationality. This concealed the preponderance of those of Korean origin.

The indictment closes by listing international reactions to the Japanese report. These included statements by the Indonesian government and the Philippine New Progressive Alliance, and media coverage from Nepal, the United States, Italy, Austria and Zaïre:

> We appeal to the sense of justice and conscience of the world to raise still louder the voices of censure of the Japanese government's insincere attitude in the matter of the military comfort women.

North Korea had become involved in the comfort women issue from the time of Miyazawa's visit to the South in January 1992. Then its Ambassador to International Agencies criticised Japan's bias towards South Korea, emphasising that the comfort women question also involved North Korea. It had to be settled for the normalisation of relations with Japan. A Japanese official press conference the next day was made the occasion to state that Japan's apology applied to North Korea as well. At the same time the Japanese regretted the disproportionate concentration on this issue by the South Korean press.

The sixth round of normalisation talks with Japan was held in the North Korean Embassy in Peking. The Japanese ambassador formally extended his country's apology to North Korea. The North Korean Embassy representative declared support for South Korea in pursuing compensation, and South Korean journalists were admitted to the embassy for the first time ever. The issue, therefore, appeared to form part of tentative moves towards unification, then being explored. The North Korean position was that normalisation should include recognition of the evil and illegal nature of colonialism and provide for individuals to be compensated by Japan on the same principle as had applied to the atomic bomb victims.

The Japanese position was that reparations were not applicable because Japan had not been in a state of war with North Korea, contrary to the latter's assertion. Compensation was not applicable in respect of acts carried out in accordance with the law at the time, although property claims could be made as recognised in the San Francisco Peace Treaty. Thus there was no liability for death or injury to draftees conscripted under law, but they could claim unpaid wages or deposits for which they could present evidence. North Korea was, of course, not affected by Japan's 1965 treaty with South Korea, though Japan's policy was to avoid any disadvantage to South Korea by comparison with the North.

The North Korean position was that Japan, as the offender, should be in possession of more evidence than the plaintiffs could produce. Statistics published in 1953 by the Public Safety Research Agency were quoted to show that there were 360,000 Korean servicemen and paramilitary in Japan at the end of the war. Considerable data must be held on them in Japan. On the issue of legality, the International Military Tribunal for the Far East was quoted to the effect that 'it is irrelevant whether or not inhuman acts infringe internal law'. The Japanese concern with permission for Japanese women married in North Korea to return to Japan was regarded as too selective among the many possible issues relating to displaced persons. North Korea regarded its first priority as, not its own economic relief, but the benefit of the whole Korean people, so it 'would not assume the same level as the South Korean administration'.

10. The international dimensions

Japan's economic clout and the fear of blighting economic relations have been strong disincentives for the governments of her former colonial subjects to press the issue of their women's rights. There is no better indicator of the way the wind blows in investment-hungry nations than the steps taken by the People's Republic of China to keep its comfort women out of sight during Emperor Akihito's visit to China in January 1993. Indeed, there is a general ban in China on campaigning on wartime issues. In most of the former Japanese-occupied territories, the comfort women issue is a non-issue.

Some are preoccupied with other issues. The Burmese, for example, have been too embroiled in their own fight for democracy and some semblance of constitutional rule, to want to espouse more causes. Burma did not initially look on the Japanese Army as an occupying force, since there was a strong national antipathy to British colonialism. Although there are many references to the country in accounts by Korean comfort women, there is so far virtually nothing about Burmese ones. However many there may be, and however harsh or unjust their treatment at the hands of the Japanese, the grievances of Burmese comfort women are not likely to interest the military leaders who have since after the war had a stranglehold on the political process.

Singapore and Malaysia

In 1992 Singapore commemorated the fiftieth anniversary of the start of Japanese Occupation with exhibitions, talks and several new publications. Nothing on comfort women surfaced, however. Whatever their numbers in Singapore, it does not seem likely that the grievances of what might crudely be seen as a bunch of dying old women will be allowed to become a bone of contention between the Japanese and Singapore governments. Despite the constant reminders in 1992 to its citizens of hard times under the Japanese Occupation, including massacres of ethnic Chinese, the Singapore government has continued to maintain excellent relations with the Japanese. As with most lobbies, the women's movement cannot be characterised as particularly active in Singapore. The comfort women issue has been put on the agenda of the leading women's organisation, the Association of Women for Action and Research, but it is likely to be some time before something comes out of that.

Malaysia, now made up of the Federated States of Malaya and the territories of Sabah and Sarawak, once part of Borneo, appeared at one time to want to take up the issue. In early 1992, Japanese documents indicated that there had been comfort stations there, despite official denials. During the Occupation, the Japanese had favoured the Malay majority on their principle of 'every man to his proper place'. This gave the appearance of promoting Malay nationalism, and discriminated heavily against the Chinese. But the Japanese did not racially discriminate when it came to pulling people off the streets for work on the Death Railway, other labour projects and, presumably, in comfort stations.

Haji Mustapha Yaacob, the secretary of the international affairs bureau of the youth wing of the Malay ruling party, the United Malay National Organisation, initially announced the party's intention to take up the forced draft issue with the Japanese. Appeals in various newspapers produced only one comfort woman who was willing to be interviewed, on condition of anonymity: Madam X. There is also another identified Malayan Chinese comfort woman, Keng Sie Lie, who was enticed away to Indonesia on the pretext of a job. She has remained in Indonesia since, and is included among the Indonesian cases.

In interesting contrast with the other active countries, the person who appears most concerned with seeing that something is done for the surviving comfort women is a man. However, Haji Mustapha Yaacob does not have the support of his organisation. In April 1993 it was announced that UMNO Youth was going to drop the comfort women issue in the interest of maintaining good relations with the Japanese. Apparently soon after the announcement that it was taking up the cause of Malaysian comfort women, it received a letter from the Japanese, the contents of which have not been revealed.

Whatever was in it, however, succeeded in making UMNO Youth think again.

Taiwan

The 1992 Japanese documents indicating that there were Taiwanese comfort women drew media attention to the issue. Official action was inhibited by the lack of diplomatic relations with Japan since the latter's recognition of the People's Republic of China.

The press also reported in detail developments in Japan and Korea, and discussed material available in archives. Nothing conclusive was found, since women recruited for service with the Japanese Armed Forces were recorded as nurses or nursing aides. Reports of some preferring to stay on the mainland, and of others committing suicide after the war, suggested that comfort women were included among them. Such cases are, however, beyond contemporary investigation.

The head of the Federation of Ex-Servicemen's and Bereaved Families Associations, Liao Mu Ch'uan, who had been in Manila during the war, was quoted as saying he had seen Taiwanese comfort women there. He had contacted three who had been enticed to Manila by deceit. All three were by then living comfortably, and were unwilling to discuss their past. One had a grandson in public office, and two other grandsons who were prominent in the business world.

In Taiwan there has been no parallel to the build-up of concern which has taken place in Korea. Unlike in Korea, there were none of the intense passions towards Japan, partly because the Kuomintang regime had been (if possible) more harsh than Japanese colonialism. In February 1992, the Taipei Women's Rescue Foundation began accepting complaints from victims. In March, the head of the Foundation, Wang Ch'ing Feng, visited Korea and Japan on a fact finding trip, and that same month, the government set up a hotline for calls from victims. The response was limited, however, and all calls were from third parties. The first one of note was from the foster-daughter of a former comfort woman who at seventeen had been taken to the southern area on the pretence of nursing duties. In common with others, the character for 'comfort' was still tattooed on her arm. Of three others who had accompanied her, two still survived, but one had become deranged. The caller's foster-mother was herself much disturbed. The family had opposed any action but the foster-daughter insisted that compensation be sought.

Soon afterwards, the first two direct calls from former comfort women were received. One had been caught in the labour draft, while the other had volunteered to save her family from further difficulties. Neither was willing to be publicly identified. All three were interviewed by the active Japanese Diet-woman Ito Hideko when she visited Taiwan to discuss the issue with the Foreign Minister. She found them interested in taking up the matter of compensation, but on condition that no personal particulars were released. The number of contacts gradually grew. Still no-one was willing to be identified publicly.

Since the Japanese documents indicated that both ethnic and Chinese Taiwanese were drafted into the comfort system, the Taipei Women's Rescue Foundation, which had been incorporated in the government's Team for Measures on Military Comfort Women, again made a public call for information in November 1992. This time it received 66 calls, again mostly third party ones rather than from the victims themselves. After careful investigation of each case, it was concluded that the known number of comfort women in Taiwan was 50, of whom 35 were still alive and willing to be interviewed.

There were 13 cases available for comprehensive study. Only one was willing to be publicly identified, but she was dissuaded by her foster-daughter. All came from a poor background, in most cases working in hotels, bars or cafes, where even in normal times recruitment into prostitution was not uncommon. Three had knowingly been recruited as comfort women, but the others had been enticed by offers of work in clubs or hospitals, attracted by the hope of good earnings and travel. Two had even become nurses before being pressured into becoming comfort women. Seven had entered into contracts for ¥100 to ¥500, and of these, four had completed their contracts and been released.

Six had gone to Hainan, agreeing with the Japanese report; five went to the Philippines; three to China; and one each to Indonesia, Malaya and Ryukyu. They had serviced both Japanese and Taiwanese of all ranks. Seven were in comfort stations directly run by the Forces, while the others were run by Taiwanese or Japanese operators. Medical inspections ranged from weekly to monthly, and none had caught venereal disease. Those becoming pregnant were allowed a month off work before the birth. Abortion was not mentioned. They were generally well treated if compliant, and the Japanese seemed to find them congenial. Most found initial adjustment difficult due to a sense of isolation, shame and fear, though only two mentioned that this was their first sexual experience. Their periods of service ranged from seven months to six years.

After the war, most had married or lived as *de facto* wives, although these relationships were mostly unstable. Some had divorced husbands who drank or gambled excessively. There were several remarriages. Only two women had stable marriages, including one whose husband did not know about his wife's past. The other knew and accepted it. This was probably the case vaguely mentioned in earlier reports, the couple meeting while on military service and later marrying. The woman was, however, unable to have children, so their main interest was in working together. Nine of the women seemed to be sterile and in poor general health. As to the possible total number of Taiwanese comfort women, a pooling of all accounts suggests a minimum of 180 to 250 being forced into service, though many would have died.

Since the war, as in other cases, the women have suffered from a sense of shame and isolation, from their felt need for secrecy about their past. They are described as having become fatalistic, and, except in two cases, as having lost any particular bitterness towards Japan. Most feel that if Korean former comfort women are compensated, they should be compensated, too—particularly those suffering poor health.

For cultural reasons, Chinese women are often loath to speak out or to step forward. The Chinese feel that any scandal within a household must never be leaked to the outside world. Fear of bringing shame to themselves and their families far outweighs the lure of any possible compensation—even though Wang Ch'ing Feng of the Tai pei Women's Rescue Foundation has concluded that 'all the comfort women we interviewed are leading a hard life'. Like most other former comfort women, they are at the bottom of the island's economic pile.

As of April 1993, according to a *Japan Times* report on the lawsuit filed by the Filipina women, a group of Taiwanese comfort women was considering filing a lawsuit. The Taiwanese government has little incentive to take up the issue with the Japanese, since the two governments are economically interdependent. Nor are women's groups particularly active, since most are little more than public relations spokespeople for the government.

The Philippines

The first of the Japanese military documents relating to comfort stations in the Philippines was published in March 1992. It was a medical report, dated 19 March 1942, submitted by a Japanese Army doctor to the *kempeitai*. It included a sketch of the location of a comfort house in Iloilo, on the island of Panay. The response of the Philippine women's organisation, Task Force on Filipina Comfort Women, was immediate. A press statement released on 13 March condemned the sexual abuse of Filipinas and other Asian women. It called on the Philippine government immediately to conduct an investigation and seek justice for the women. They demanded that Japan issue an apology and be prepared to pay compensation to any possible survivors.

This demand prompted a reaction from the Philippine government, then headed by Mrs Corazon Aquino. It challenged the women's Task Force to provide evidence on Filipina comfort women. With the ball in their court the Task Force, under Nelia Sancho Lios, held a rally on 4 May in front of the Japanese Embassy in Manila. They submitted a letter to the Ambassador demanding that the Japanese government conduct an inquiry into the allegation that it had a conscious and systematic role in the forced conscription of Asian women into comfort stations.

The following day, the Philippine government announced it would conduct an investigation through the Presidential Commission on Human Rights. Professor Ricardo Jose of the University of the Philippines was put in charge. He set to work to study the official documents on the Pacific War concerning the Philippines and Japan. Not surprisingly, he found no evidence that there were Filipina comfort women. On 26 June, in a statement based on the report, the government announced that there had been no sex slaves in the Philippines, and that there was no need to seek an apology and compensation from Japan.

Suspecting either a cover-up, gross incompetence or both, the Task Force decided to conduct its own field investigations. It was considerably aided by the appearance of the Japanese government report on 6 July 1992, which put the spotlight on Iloilo in Panay. The elderly residents in the town were interviewed, and a number confirmed the existence of wartime comfort women. According to Nelia Sancho Lios, a former Filipino spy for the Japanese Army confirmed the existence of Army-built comfort houses, and also that a Filipina comfort woman he had known had died a few years before. The investigators identified the site of the two comfort stations mentioned in the *kempeitai* records for Iloilo, which contained a map of the locality indicating where the comfort women were allowed to stroll from 8 a.m. to 10 a.m. each morning. Any other movement outside the station required special permission.

Japan's admission that there were Filipina comfort women completely destroyed the credibility of Professor Jose and the Philippine government's investigation. Yet the government, fearful perhaps of Japanese displeasure, failed to make any demands of Japan on behalf of the Filipinas. This inertia incurred the wrath of Filipina activists. They set up an umbrella organisation to deal with the issue on 13 July, a week after the Japanese report appeared. Called the Task Force for Women Victims of Military Sexual Slavery by Japan, it was made up of seven women's organisations which had previously been actively opposed to sex tourism, the export of Filipina prostitutes to Japan, and the dispatch of Japanese forces overseas. It had had considerable success in investigating sexual coercion during the war, and in preparing legal action. The group set out the following seven demands:

1. That the Japanese government apologise to the Philippine people, especially the comfort women victims and their surviving families.
2. That the Japanese government take responsibility for reparation to comfort women victims and their surviving families.
3. That the Philippine government support the comfort women victims and adopt a clear stand in demanding responsibility for reparation from the Japanese government.
4. That, to prevent a repetition of the same thing, textbooks and history books record the facts of the crimes committed by the former Japanese Armed Forces, namely the violation of women's human rights in the matter of military comfort women.
5. That support be given to the women of South Korea in their application to the United Nations Commission on Human

Rights to investigate and censure the Japanese government for
the violation of human rights.

6. That the Japanese government's assertion that the comfort
women were not compelled be nullified and admission obtained that authority and coercion were employed in the drafting and treatment of comfort women.

7. That procedures for litigation be studied upon identifying surviving Filipina comfort women.

The scope of the group's investigations was described in some detail,
with emphasis on the need to overcome the Philippine government's
reluctance to offend Japan, its biggest source of economic aid. The
task force soon swung into action with a dazzling array of activities,
many of which were directed towards locating comfort women. In a
report she wrote in August 1992, Nelia Sancho Lios reported:

> The first phase of the field investigation project has now started in Iloilo.
> In the coming weeks we will continue to search for survivors in Leyte,
> Antique and Manila. The investigation will look into documents and rec-
> ords of the local government, hospital and town clinic, police/army sta-
> tions, libraries and schools. Townspeople and local historians will also be
> interviewed and testimonies will be gathered. A telephone radio hook-up
> will be used to call on the public to help us find survivors.

This intensive activity produced results. On 18 September 1992,
Maria Rosa Henson, a sixty-five-year-old grandmother of twelve,
told a news conference that she was ending decades of silence to seek
justice. She encouraged other Filipinas forced into prostitution to reveal their experiences:

> Our lives were wasted by the Japanese. We were treated like animals.
> Japan should at least say that it is sorry.

Maria Henson was the first non-Korean comfort woman to go
public—and she was not to be the last. Less than two months later,
Jan Ruff also spoke out, at a UN-organised conference in Tokyo.
The courage of Maria Henson and Jan Ruff has turned a dispute
between Seoul and Tokyo into one with wider ramifications for Asia.

The next stage in the Philippine drama was a massive mobilisation
of public opinion in late September to apply pressure on the newly-
elected President, General Fidel Ramos. The groups wanted a serious and decisive response in support of Filipina comfort women. Finally stung into action, the government set up a Government Task

Force on Comfort Women on 29 September which, among other things, was to lead to formal negotiations with the Japanese government on matters related to the comfort women. Meanwhile a stream of Japanese newspaper reports had listed various cities and islands where comfort stations had been established in the Philippines: Manila, Tacloban in Leyte, Santa Cruz in Laguna, Masbate and Cagayan in Mindanao were only some of them.

Radio stations and other mass media gave publicity to the search for Filipina comfort women. In the months that followed, dozens of Filipinas came forward to tell their stories. Most of these cases fall into the class of *ad hoc* rape and confinement on the initiative of individuals or groups, rather than forming part of the official comfort system. Unfortunately, the oral testimony taken from these women has not been very satisfactory, and even those who were part of the comfort system were not asked appropriate questions. For example, there is no mention in any of the testimonies of payment for comfort services, although we know from Japanese records of the Philippines that, as in other areas, this was regulated. However, while the Filipino accounts reveal little about the institutional aspects of Japanese military prostitution, they leave the reader in no doubt about the use of coercion.

In March 1993, Japanese Premier Miyazawa apologised to the Filipina comfort women and expressed remorse, during Philippine President Fidel Ramos' visit to Japan. On 2 April, Maria Henson and Julia Poras, representing eighteen Filipina comfort women, filed a suit against the Japanese government seeking ¥360 million in compensation. This was only the second lawsuit to be filed by former comfort women.

Indonesia

When the Japanese government report was published in July 1992, together with an apology to the women of Asian countries who had been forced into the comfort system, the Indonesian Foreign Office reacted by demanding a thorough investigation, leading not only to compensation but to the punishment of those responsible. At the same time there was no sign that the Indonesian authorities intended to take any special initiatives of their own. As in the case of Korea, all claims on Japan were regarded as settled by the 1958 reparations agreement. In a press interview, Secretary of State Moerdiono said:

'We want to forget the past.' S. Tasrip Rahardjo, chairman of the
Central Liaison Forum of ex-*Heiho,* spoke of presenting a claim of
US$700 million to Tokyo but no ex-comfort women appeared at
that stage willing to move things forward.

One problem that has emerged in both Indonesia and the Philippines is sifting the real comfort women from those lured by the
thought of compensation. The author personally interviewed several
'comfort women' who told barely plausible stories of rape in the jungle. They appeared to know little about the comfort system, with its
tickets, hours of service and supervisors. One possible reason for the
ease with which the women spoke of sexual crimes is that chastity is
not such a deeply ingrained social moral value. If in Korea and Taiwan, women were reluctant to be photographed, Indonesians and
Filipinas appeared to have fewer inhibitions.

On 16 April 1993, five lawyers from the Human Rights Council of
the Japan Federation of the Bar Association arrived in Jakarta on a
fact finding mission. This connected with the association's plans for
a symposium on war reparations, to be held in Japan in October
1993. The following day they held a meeting with the Jakarta Lawyers Club and the Indonesian Legal Aid Institute. Their spokesman,
Murayama Akira, said:

> We are looking into the comfort women question because we want to
> know the facts. But we don't have any intention to bring the cases to
> court and demand compensation for the victims. The Japan Federation
> of the Bar Association cannot provide legal assistance for compensation.
> You have to contact members of the Bar Association as individuals for
> legal assistance.

This cautious statement notwithstanding, the rumour swiftly swept
Jakarta and beyond that compensation was in the offing. Within a
day streams of ex-comfort women appeared, the first Indonesian
comfort women ever interviewed. Previous attempts in July and August 1992 by the weekly *Tempo* to locate comfort women had only
limited success. Suddenly there were thirteen claimants during the
four-day visit of the Japanese lawyers. Eight of these were either
comfort women or victims of *ad hoc* rape, while the others had been
forced labourers. The wide and often sensational publicity given by
the Indonesian media to the comfort women story has brought forward more than forty women, as of May 1993. However, of this
number, it is obvious that some stories have been made up in the

hope of getting some of the rumoured compensation. Caution and tact are needed to separate out the genuine cases.

Asia Solidarity Conference on comfort women

The comfort women issue was put on the broader international agenda by the Asia Solidarity Conference on the Military Comfort Women Issue, in Seoul, on 11 and 12 August 1992. Jointly sponsored by the Korean Comfort Women Problem Resolution Council and the Asian Women's Theological Education Institute, the conference represented an extension of earlier conferences on action against sex tourism. It drew over 100 representatives from South Korea, Korean residents in Japan, Japanese (including a speaker from Okinawa), and others from the Philippines, Thailand, Taiwan and Hong Kong. A number of comfort women were present. Throughout the proceedings there was special emphasis on opposition to the overseas dispatch of Japanese peace-keeping forces as an issue that gave strong contemporary relevance to the comfort women question.

The conference was opened by Professor Lee Hyo Jae, the cospokesperson of the Council. She was followed by two former comfort women, who recounted their experiences. One was Noh Chong Ja, one of the plaintiffs in the Tokyo lawsuit. The other was Kim Pok Tong, a new figure whose account had a number of features not encountered earlier.

Kim Pok Tong

Kim Pok Tong came from a well-off land-owning family with six daughters. On her father's death, the family lost most of its property, to settle his debts. Her three elder sisters were married off 'to save them from the Japanese Army'. At only sixteen, Pok Tong was thought to be safe. Her mother, who was illiterate, was prevailed on in 1941 to seal a form of approval for her daughter's recruitment to the Voluntary Service Corps by a Korean local official, and a Korean in Japanese uniform. The family was given to understand that Pok Tong would do three years of factory work.

She was taken, with about twenty other girls, similarly recruited, to Taiwan. They were kept idle there for some months, supposedly waiting for an assignment to a factory making military uniforms. Finally they were taken to Canton, where she was forcibly stripped for an examination by an Army medical officer. This both humiliated and bewildered her. She was completely innocent of the facts of life.

Pok Tong was then taken to a comfort station, which occupied most of a multistorey building, the ground floor being occupied by troops. The women were only allowed out afterwards under escort. She was expected to provide service from her second day there. On resisting, she was beaten and denied food, so she yielded. The usual daily total of men was fifteen, rising to fifty or more over weekends. All bought condoms and tickets, which were handed over nightly to the Japanese manager. The women received no money, being told that they would be paid when Japan won the war. Clothes and cosmetics, however, were given on request. Pok Tong was examined weekly and never caught venereal disease, but when signs of injury were discovered she was given time off until the medical officer pronounced her able to return to work.

She was taken along with the troops in the holds of troop ships to Hong Kong, Singapore, Malaya and Java. She was in the habit of changing the Japanese name she used for every change in locality. Her surname was always Kanemura, but her given names were usually Fukuyo or Yoshiko.

When the war ended, Pok Tong was among fifty women from various 'clubs' who were assigned as nursing aides to the 16th Army hospital in Surabaya. (This agrees with the earlier account that comfort women in Surabaya were represented to the Allies as nurses.) There was, of course, a real need for nursing help, and Pok Tong was in fact trained in giving injections by practising on melons, as well as instructed about the use of medicines. While at the hospital she was discovered by her mother's brother-in-law. She had written to her mother from Taiwan, enclosing a recent photograph. Since her brother-in-law was then being drafted for service in the South, the mother asked him to find Pok Tong and bring her home, so whenever he met Korean women he had tried to identify her from the photograph. When he succeeded, he persuaded the hospital authorities to release her to the nearby internment camp, apparently in Surabaya. There was a separate section for women, but they could meet freely. It was administered by Koreans and, as in the Singapore camp mentioned earlier, the Koreans reverted to their original names and wore badges bearing the design of the Korean flag. The women had enough surplus clothes and the like to exchange for extra local food.

After more than a year's internment they were returned to

Pusan aboard a ship with 3000 mixed passengers. Pok Tong found her mother at home, left alone by the departure of the rest of the family for Japan. None of the returning women admitted having been comfort women, claiming to have worked in factories or hospitals. She herself spoke only of hospital work. This was supported by her skill with injections and knowledge of medicines, which proved useful in a rural area with few medical facilities. Finally, however, she felt compelled to reveal her experiences to her mother, because she could not agree to attempts to marry her off.

Gradually, her secret came out. She began running a bar. Some of her wartime friends had remained in prostitution as the only means of survival. She herself eventually married a man whose first marriage had failed. Her husband was a simple man who did not drink, and had before his death been fond of his numerous nieces and nephews. She had been unable to have children: medical treatment had proved ineffective. After her husband's death five years earlier, she had resumed the bar business. Now she was living on her meagre savings.

Other speakers also presented a great amount of information and commentary. Professor Yun gave a breakdown of the twenty-five former comfort women contacted through the Council's phone-in. She concluded by linking up the comfort women issue with the peace keeping operation issue and describing Japanese imperialism as an imitation of Western imperialism, as advocated by Fukuzawa's classic 1885 article 'Abandoning Asia and Joining Europe'. The use of his portrait on the new Japanese ¥10,000 note suggested, she said, that such attitudes still prevailed in the Japanese establishment.

The following two speakers, Chong Jin Song and Yun Mi Hyang, also from South Korea, gave an impressive synopsis of the dynamics of Japanese imperialism up to the war, 'an interaction of national, racial, sexual and class contradictions'. They added a concise summary of the women's groups' activities over recent years. The second speaker eloquently criticised the South Korean government's negative attitude. It had only set up the Victim Report Centres under intense public pressure, and its late July report suffered from the same weaknesses which it attributed to the Japanese report. All it did was supplement overseas material with some very sketchy case histories.

As Professor Yoshimi had noted of the Japanese report, surviving material from the Government-General, and records in local offices, must contain some evidence of recruitment numbers and procedures.

Further, the comfort women's plight had remained concealed because in South Korea:

> politics since liberation had been maintained by prolongation from the Japanese imperialist period and with the one nation divided into two states, the ideology of division, rather than the liquidation of Japanese imperialism, had directed politics to the protection and utilisation of those who were loyal to the imperialist order.

The first Japanese speaker was Suzuki Yuko, a prolific and erudite author of studies in women's history, including two valuable works on the comfort women. She saw the comfort women system as a natural outgrowth of the inferior position of women in Japanese society and a corollary of its expansionist drives. In the first modern family law code of 1871 which superseded the feudal code, both wives and mistresses were classed equally as in a second degree of relationship compared with the children, who were classed as in the first degree. The civil law reforms of the same period had established the licensed prostitution system which later provided the framework for the comfort women's contractual system. The revised family law of 1898, although accepting monogamy, was based on male primogeniture—a system which still applies to the Imperial family.

Suzuki highlighted another use of women by the Japanese. In the hope of securing a long-term hold on Manchuria by rural settlement, and to induce young farmers to migrate to the alien land, the Japanese government promised settlers brides. There were patriotic drives to recruit 'continental brides', 'mass match making' and 'mass marriage'. This led to many of these brides being stranded in Manchuria after the war.

Suzuki gave five reasons for the long dormancy of the comfort women issue. These were: the Japanese government's evasion of post-war responsibility; the Cold War, and Korea's division; Japanese contempt for other Asians; fear of repercussions on the Imperial system; and limitations in the traditional Japanese women's movement, such as in the Japan Christian Women's Moral Reform Society which, although energetically opposed to prostitution since the nineteenth century, had failed to link this issue with the problem of the sexual oppression of women as a whole, and their human rights. Thus prostitution was treated as affecting only a special class of women, while there was general indifference among most Japanese women to the implications of sex tourism.

The next speaker was Takahashi Kikue, a leading figure in the Moral Reform Society. She outlined her relationship with Professor Yun Chung Ok, which went back to a conference on sex tourism in early 1988. She had sent her copies of Senda Kako's publications and arranged for numerous visits and activities in Japan. The Moral Reform Society was affiliated to the International Women's Year Liaison Association, embracing fifty-one organisations, and the Japanese umbrella organisation of sixteen organisations called the Military Comfort Women Problem Action Network, formed earlier in the year. Takahashi reviewed the generally unfavourable public reaction in the media, which she said demonstrated the need for a spiritual reconstruction in Japan, which she saw as 'an economic great power but poor in heart'.

After Takahashi came Diet-woman Shimizu Sumiko, who reviewed the debates in the Diet and the issues surrounding the 1965 Basic Treaty. She had found that, although the treaty had been described as covering both compensation claims and economic aid, only 5 per cent of the grant had gone for compensation, covering the cases of 8000 military and paramilitary war dead. The rest had been devoted to economic aid, so that the matter of savings in military post offices and unpaid wages of labourers remained unsettled. Her group of activists in both houses of the Diet were pressing for a wide range of related measures, such as the passage of war compensation laws to resolve the various lawsuits, testimony by witnesses in the Diet, and the adoption of a resolution of apology. They also advocated that the Prime Minister take direct responsibility for the contents of textbooks. Naturally, the group was continuing to oppose participation in peace keeping operations, and discrimination against Korean residents. Shimizu concluded with her plan to place the comfort women issue on the agenda of the International Women's Conference to be held in China in 1995. This seemed to suggest she did not expect an earlier resolution to the issue.

The last Japanese speaker was the lawyer, Fukushima Mizuho, one of eleven members of the legal team in the Tokyo lawsuit, four of whom were women. She reported that the scheduling of sessions and the time allowed represented favourable treatment by the court relative to customary Japanese practice. This was probably a response to public interest, which remained important. The government's suggestion of a relief fund was pure evasion, she pointed out, and asked that other Asian groups promote investigations in their own areas.

The next group to speak consisted of three Korean residents of Japan. They represented, respectively, the Compatriot Women's Network for the Military Comfort Women Problem, the Osaka-based Association for the Study of the Korean Military Comfort Women Problem and the Resident Korean Women's Democratic Association. The Osaka group's record was particularly impressive, including the nationwide collection of nearly 35,000 signatures in support of the Korean women's six demands; dramatic productions such as the play *We Do Not Forget,* in which, in traditional mode, the ghost of a comfort woman suicide tells her story through a shamanistic medium; and three valuable collections of media and other material on the comfort women issue. The last speaker emphasised that the ultimate solution lay not only in apology and compensation but in proper understanding of history by all Japanese, to enable them to become part of a peaceful Asia.

Taiwan was represented by Chen Mei Ling, executive director of the Taipei Women's Rescue Foundation, and the Philippines by Nelia Sancho Lios of the Asian Women's Human Rights Council and the Philippine Military Comfort Women Project Team. Both gave an account of the information available on comfort women in their countries, and the current lines of action. There were two Thai speakers, the first resident in Hong Kong, from the Asian Migrants Centre there. She spoke in very general terms about comfort women on the Burma Railway, and the questions of sex tourism and peace keeping operations. The other Thai speaker reported on the history of British Army prostitution in India, but otherwise only listed accounts of atrocities in China. Little remains known, then, about comfort women in Thailand. In the absence of delegates from Malaysia, the situation there was discussed by the *Asahi* journalist Matsui Yayori who had early on interviewed Yuyuta, the Korean ex-comfort woman found living in Thailand.

The distinctive experience of Okinawans was examined by Takazato Suzuyo, a city councillor of the capital, Naha. She pointed out that, although Okinawa was territorially part of Japan, it had more in common with the other Asian countries in two respects: namely, its people were regarded by the Japanese as inferior, and it had experienced devastating land warfare. Even today, notices on

Tokyo boarding houses tell Koreans and Ryukyuans they are not wanted. A quarter of Okinawa's then population of 600,000 were killed merely to postpone by a few months the necessity for the Emperor to surrender.

In some cases in smaller Ryukyu islands, as in Micronesia, there were mass suicides of both garrisons and inhabitants in the face of the Allied advance. One such island was Tokashiki, where Pae Pong Gi was a comfort woman.

Over the preceding months, with the support of the Mayor of Naha, investigations of wartime comfort women had intensified, revealing there had been 114 comfort stations to serve the 80,000 troops on Okinawa itself. These had been spread over 31 of the 53 local government units on the island. Staff numbers ranged from 2 or 3 to large centres holding women to serve a wide area. The average number would be between 7 and 10. Although overall figures are unobtainable, it is clear that the women were either Korean or Okinawan, the latter mainly of prostitute background. In at least 47 cases, civilian homes were commandeered, families sometimes being forced to shift to stables or outhouses. Other comfort stations occupied hotels or public buildings, and there were as well specially constructed quarters.

General information of this kind could be gathered from the recollections of the inhabitants but, as elsewhere, former comfort women themselves remain silent. Some older men regretfully remembered how, as schoolboys, they had mocked the 'Korean Ps' or thrown stones at them. Upon Takazato's pointing out that Naha's voluminous city history contained no mention of comfort women or conscripted military porters, it was agreed to incorporate data on these.

On the last day of the conference, in the name of the Asian Solidarity Network on the Forced Military Comfort Women Problem, the following resolution was adopted:

The military comfort women issue involves unprecedented, atrocious criminal acts of organised abduction, mass rape, torture and massacre under Imperial fascism and Japanese militarism. It is an example that starkly demonstrates how militarism combined with patriarchy mercilessly trampled women's sexuality and obliterated their humanity. We therefore consider a solution to the issue important for preventing a recurrence of war and for building peace. Japan shows no sign of reflection on the crimes it committed and is evading its responsibility for post-war settlement. Not only that, but it has recently passed the Peace-Keeping Operation Co-operation Law, opening the way to the dispatch of Self-

Defence Forces overseas. We cannot but be apprehensive about the revival of Japanese militarism.

In order to become a true neighbour to the countries of Asia, Japan must reflect on its past history and adopt a responsible attitude to post-war settlement, including the case of military comfort women.

We have confirmed the need for strong solidarity among all citizens' groups and individuals in the countries of Asia, such as South and North Korea, China, Taiwan, Thailand, the Philippines, Indonesia, Malaysia, as well as Japan who together are striving for a solution to this problem. Today the representatives of the six countries of South Korea, Taiwan, the Philippines, Hong Kong, Thailand and Japan have formed the Asian Solidarity Network on the Forced Military Comfort Women Problem and have adopted the following resolutions:

1. To continue factual investigations on military comfort women throughout Asia who became victims of the Asia-Pacific War.
2. To demand a responsible post-war settlement by Japan in respect of clarification, reparation and compensation regarding military comfort women.
3. To enlist the co-operation of world human rights organisations such as the United Nations for a solution to the military comfort women problem.
4. To urge Asian countries which could not participate in this conference to participate, so strengthening and confirming our solidarity.
5. To promote respect for the human rights of Asian women and world peace.

International Public Hearing on Post-war Compensation by Japan

A still more significant international undertaking, with perhaps the best prospects so far of ultimately exerting a decisive influence on the Japanese government, was the International Public Hearing on Post-war Compensation by Japan. This was held in Tokyo on 9 December 1992. A specialist seminar followed the next day, as a key step in pressing the comfort women issue in the United Nations. Moves at the UN had begun in February 1992, when Professor Lee Hyo Jae of the Council had applied to the Commission on Human Rights for closed hearings on the subject. Support had been obtained from the International Educational Development Inc., a non-government organisation in consultative status with the United Nations. In May, its East Asia representative, Totsuka Etsuro, addressed the Working Group on Contemporary Forms of Slavery, on the need for an appropriate investigation. He cited the comfort women issue as a violation of the Convention on Forced Labour ratified by Japan in 1932.

On 13 May the Working Group submitted to the Sub-commission on the Prevention of Discrimination and the Protection of Minorities, to which it was attached, a recommendation to the Secretary-General that its Special Rapporteur on Human Rights be furnished with information on women forced into prostitution in wartime, and on compensation and restitution for the reported victims. Although, as customary, no nation was named, it was stated in a press interview that Japan's case would be involved. As the lawyer Fukushima Mizuho, of the Tokyo lawsuit, commented:

> As Japan is amenable to external pressure, this could be a breakthrough, though not only for the comfort women issue but for a solution to the question of post-war compensation in all Asian countries which fell victim to Japan's aggressive war.

In the plenary session of the Sub-commission, in August, Professor Lee Hyo Jae, with the backing of the World Council of Churches, requested the passage of a resolution on compensation and a fact finding mission to Asian countries affected by the comfort women issue. The former comfort woman Hwang Kum Ju supported her with a press conference at the UN press centre in Geneva. But early action seemed to be unlikely. The plan was therefore developed of inviting the Special Rapporteur to a hearing in Tokyo where he, together with interested United Nations and non-government organisation representatives, could obtain direct evidence which he could present in his report on 'compensation for the victims of gross violations of human rights' for the Sub-commission, due in August 1993.

The Public Hearing concentrated mainly on comfort women as the 'breakthrough issue'. Some other categories of victims were included, but there was some criticism of a lack of balance. It had also been hoped that more Diet members would attend than the ten who did. But this action succeeded in its main aims of establishing closer contact with the United Nations and gaining a demonstration of wide public concern. About 800 people attended—far more than the hall was designed to accommodate, and 69 organisations were represented. Of these, 18 represented Korean residents in Japan, affiliated to both North and South Korea; 9 were Christian; 8 had legal connections; 8 were anti-war bodies in which Buddhist organisations are usually active, one temple organisation also being recorded; 5 were educational, representing teachers and students; 5 were devoted to compensation issues; 3 were labour organisations; 2 were outcast emancipation bodies; 2 were other women's groups; 1 was an anti-prostitution body advocating the effective enforcement of the legal ban on prostitution, while the others were a variety of *ad hoc* bodies.

Guests with United Nations and non-government organisation connections were:

- Professor Theo Van Boven of the Department of Law, University of Limburg, Special Rapporteur of the Sub-commission on Human Rights concerning restitution, compensation and rehabilitation for victims of gross violation of human rights. He was attending unofficially, but had been contacted by Foreign Ministry representatives and heard their position, which he described as unchanged in denying evidence of coercion of comfort women.

- Professor John P. Humphrey of the Faculty of Law, McGill University, who had helped draft the Universal Declaration of Human Rights and played a leading role in the adoption of the International Covenant on Human Rights.

- Ameur Zemmali, legal advisor to the International Committee of the Red Cross.

- Wong Soon Park, member of the Board of Directors of the Korean Bar Association and Visiting Fellow at the Harvard Law School.

- Karen Parker, attorney-at-law, chief representative to the United Nations of the International Educational Development Inc., and co-author of the 1989 Jaudel-Parker Report to the Commission on Human Rights on substitute prisons in Japan. A world authority on *jus cogens,* here rendered as 'compelling law of human rights', she defined it as 'the generally and intuitively known law, the failure to observe which threatens the existence of civilisation', over-riding international treaties or domestic law, without time limitation and retroactive.

- Totsuka Etsuro, member of the Japan Federation of Bar Associations, East Asian Representative of the International Educational Development Inc., and member of working groups and non-government organisations such as the International League for Human Rights.

The program of the Public Hearing was crowded, running from 2 p.m. until 8 p.m. with a half-hour break. It consisted of half-hour segments, alternating introductions of guests, research reports and testimony of victims. Reports, part verbal and part documentary, were presented by the following:

- Yi Mi Gyong, a director of the Korean Comfort Women's Problem Resolution Council, and Vice-President of the Alliance of South Korean Women's Organisations;
- Lourdes Indai Sajor, co-ordinator of the Task Force on Filipina Comfort Women;
- Ho Sok Til, executive member of the North Korean Committee for Measures on Compensation for Military Comfort Women and Pacific War Victims. (He presented a summary of the North Korean report of 1 September prepared by his committee, adding that 123 former comfort women had been identified as at the end of November, and of these 21 had volunteered to declare themselves publicly);
- Wang Ch'ing Feng, lawyer, of the Taipei Women's Rescue Foundation;
- Professor Yoshimi Yoshiaki, who presented a report including key documents;
- Murayama Akira of the Japan Federation of Bar Associations;
- Kim Yong Hi and Hong Sang Jin of the Japan-based National Liaison Council of Groups Investigating the Forced Draft of Koreans. Kim Yong Hi had visited Pyongyang in September, together with some members of the Social Democratic Party, in the course of a tripartite conference on draftees also attended by South Korean women's representatives. Four former comfort women and six female labour draftees had been interviewed. The former group had been described at the time as uncomfortable with the interview, and as preferring to leave the question of compensation to others; they themselves only insisted on a sincere apology.

Hong presented a comprehensive tabulation of sites associated with forced labour, broken down between the main local government areas and three main categories of work, with a total of 1141 sites. He also summarised a document recently found in the National Archives containing the earliest dated reference to Korean comfort women so far known. Although that term is not actually used, the document, which is a collection of military hygiene reports from September 1932 to December 1933, refers to a health check in northern Japan of 38

Japanese and Korean prostitutes commencing business in April 1933. There are also statistics on venereal disease in the Forces in Manchuria and Shanghai.

The victims testified with trilingual simultaneous interpreting in Japanese, Korean and English.

Comfort woman at the International Public Hearing on Post-war Compensation by Japan

- Kang Sun Ae of South Korea, who had been drafted at the age of fourteen to pick mandarins in the Hiroshima area, was then taken as a comfort woman to Palau.
- Maria Rosa Luna Henson of the Philippines was the first Filipina comfort woman to go public.
- Kim Yong Sil of North Korea was not among those previously named from that country. At the age of thirteen she had been sent by her poverty-stricken family to be cared for by a relative, but had to resort to begging and casual work as a housemaid. Thus she accepted an offer of work from a Japanese in civilian clothing. She was taken with twelve other girls to a roughly-constructed comfort station in the North Hangyong province bordering the Soviet Union, given the Japanese name Eiko, and dressed in Japanese costume. Her deflowering was done by her recruiter, now in officer's uniform, followed by seven others. She had to service twenty to thirty men a day, with occasional visits to mountain units. There were weekly medical checks, when pregnant or diseased women were removed and replaced. For trying to resist, she was subjected to water torture and punched, losing two teeth.

    She escaped while the comfort station was being moved at the end of the war. Afterwards, she never married, and her lack of family enabled her to speak publicly. When she finished testifying, Kim Hak Sun, who was in the audience, mounted the rostrum and embraced her, thus presenting the noteworthy spectacle of North—South solidarity. She was followed by other plaintiffs recently in Tokyo in connection with the lawsuit. Some faced the audience, with a cry of 'it's the fault of you Japanese!'.
- Jan Ruff, whose case has been outlined earlier, held her daughter's hand as she spoke. To quote a press report: 'In a powerfully controlled presentation that she agreed later was in contrast to the more emotionally-charged displays of others, she read out a horrific story in painful, graphic detail.'
- Wan Ai Hua from China presented the greatest such contrast to Jan Ruff. Although the Chinese government had not encouraged action by comfort women, it had allowed arrangements to be made by Chinese

residents of Japan, the Chinese Association for the Promotion of International Friendship, and provincial authorities in her province of Shansi. Offences against women were especially marked in that area, probably because it contained the ill-defined zone of combat with the Communists. Wan began by relating how she had been sold at the age of four and at fifteen was seized by the Japanese and assaulted daily for months. Beatings had ruptured her ear and broken various bones, which had resulted in the reduction of her height from 160 cm to 140 cm. As she exposed marks left by her injuries, she collapsed, shouting 'How I hate the Japanese!'. The curtain was dropped and she was attended to by Professor Humphrey's wife, a medical doctor. She was then taken to hospital. After recovering, she later gave a press interview in which she told how she had been disowned by her relatives as 'defiled', and had never married.

• An anonymous Taiwanese woman told how she had been recruited as a nurse at the age of seventeen and taken as a comfort woman to Timor. She said that she did not wish to give further details, and that she was too old to make any claims. She also asked not to be photographed.

Victims in other categories, who also spoke, included a Korean drafted to the Mitsubishi shipyards in Nagasaki and affected by the atomic attack there, and a survivor of the massacres of Malayan civilians.

A seminar the following day entitled 'War and Human Rights—Legal Analysis of Post-war Settlement' was convened by the Japan Federation of Bar Associations, in a small hall packed with 450 people. Professor Van Boven, leading the discussion, outlined the development of human rights by the United Nations, in such formulations as the Universal Declaration of Human Rights, and the functioning of the Commission on Human Rights. The Commission could receive evidence of abuses from any quarter, and its decisions or views are then put to the relevant state with requests for an effective remedy. The process involved establishing the facts, and meting out justice and compensation to victims, he said. Since the preventive aspect was important, appeals to 'reasons of state', fostering a sense of irresponsibility, were frowned on. If reparation to victims was not possible, similar ends might be achieved by commemorative acts and the full exposure of the facts. There is no statute of limitation, he pointed out.

Professor Humphrey noted that the date, 10 December, was Human Rights Day, the anniversary of the Declaration of Human

Rights being adopted as a resolution of the United Nations General
Assembly. Machinery for realising its ideals had been developed
under the Covenant of Civil and Political Rights, which had been
ratified by Japan, by such means as periodical reports to the Commission on Human Rights. He referred to the *jus cogens* as the 'fundamental law of nations', defined by the cumulative effect of decisions of the International Court of Justice, conventions and usages
accepted as just. It invalidated the waiver of reparations in the 1952
San Francisco Peace Treaty. On the issue at hand, he concluded:

> An apology, you will agree, is equivalent to an admission of guilt. I am
> confident that your government will eventually compensate the victims of
> these crimes. The sooner this is done, the better for Japan's image abroad.
> I say this, Mr Chairman, in a spirit of friendship for Japan.

Professor Humphrey was reported as alleging that Japan was exerting influence on member-states of the Human Rights Commission to
impede action on the comfort women issue, and that international
opinion should be organised to frustrate such moves. Japan was a
rich and powerful country and as such had 'a lot of friends'. The
Japanese Foreign Ministry, however, denied that such pressure on
the Commission was possible.

The organising committee for the Public Hearing was later reor-
ganised on a continuing basis and incorporated as the Preparatory
Association for a Japanese War Responsibility Resource Centre. Its
immediate aim was to co-ordinate research and put pressure on the
Japanese government for a satisfactory resolution of the comfort
women issue. In April it held negotiations for official recognition
with the Cabinet Secretariat's External Affairs Office, while mobilising public support by a campaign for a million signatures. A public
opinion survey, which drew a reply rate of over 70 per cent, indicated
that only 10 per cent opposed compensation, 36 per cent supporting
both it and apology, while 25 per cent supported humanitarian aid in
some form.

The organisation's longer-term aim was to establish a Memorial
Centre for the Engraving on the Mind of Japan's War Responsibility, which would serve both commemorative and educational purposes. Its activities and financial headquarters were set up in Osaka,
and its research headquarters in Tokyo. It consisted of ten departments headed by specialists in each field, Professor Yoshimi heading
that concerned with comfort women.

Legal developments were a lawsuit filed on 2 April 1993 by eighteen Filipina comfort women for ¥20 million each. Another was filed on 5 April by the first identified Korean comfort woman residing in Japan, Song Sin-do. She did not specify compensation, formally demanding only an apology, because she did not wish to be regarded as motivated only by financial gain. She did, however, state that a sincere apology might be expected to be accompanied by some tangible form of redress, but she would leave this to the government's discretion. She had been recruited from Korea in the usual way but, exceptionally, was brought to Japan at the end of the war by a sergeant-major. He deserted her, and later she was married and widowed. Since the unit involved was identified, the women's groups hoped to discover more of the background of this unusual case, but this proved difficult. Evidence of her past is a tattoo of the Japanese name she was given, Kaneko.

In the next session of the Commission on Human Rights, held over February—March 1993, Japan was attacked eleven times by both Korean governments as well as non-government organisations, on the issues of comfort women and forced labour. South Korea used unprecedentedly strong language, stating that its own investigation showed that coercion and violence were used both at the recruitment stage and thereafter. Friendly relations depended on Japan's cleansing itself of its guilty past. North Korea claimed that Japan had seized six million Koreans—over one-quarter of its then-population! The non-government organisations involved were the Dutch Foundation of Japan's Honorary Debts, the Korean Forced Draft Investigation Group, and the Korean Comfort Women Problem Resolution Council. The question of punishment of those responsible was raised for the first time and the proposal for Japan's permanent membership of the Security Council was opposed.

Another non-government organisation, the International Fellowship of Reconciliation, reported that Japan's treaty of protection with Korea in 1905, which prepared the way for annexation, was an example of a treaty invalidated. This was because it had been procured by coercion or threats applied to individuals—in this case the Emperor of Korea and his ministers. This meant that Japan's internal law at the time of the draft was irrelevant to present claims.

The Japanese chief envoy was absent, leaving a female diplomat to deliver the government's reply, to the effect that 'Japan has sincerely dealt with the issue of claims, including the question of compensation, in accordance with multilateral and bilateral treaties, as well as other relevant treaties with concerned countries'. 'Sincere apologies and remorse', she said, had been expressed to comfort women.

During the same period, the Security Council, in approving the establishment of an international court for serious crimes against humanity (with more immediate reference to Bosnia), also mentioned the Dutch military court cases relating to comfort women.

In the session of the Working Group which met in May 1993, the Japanese took the offensive. While repeating that their government was still making 'utmost efforts to research the facts on this issue' and was 'giving serious consideration as to how it might best convey its feelings of compassion to those who suffered', they chiefly argued that recommendations on individual cases were outside the Special Rapporteur's mandate. This was to submit conclusions and recommendations in order to develop general principles and guidelines. Such an approach was clearly aimed at neutralising any recommendations arising out of the Tokyo Public Hearing which might be made by the Rapporteur in his August report to the Sub-commission.

The Japanese delegation still maintained that claims regarding South Korea had been resolved by the Basic Treaty of 1965, and that those regarding North Korea were currently the subject of normalisation talks. Regarding the argument by the International Fellowship of Reconciliation on the 1905 treaty, they pointed out that this was based, not on an official report by the United Nations International Law Commission, but on one made by its Special Rapporteur, and prepared for consideration of the Convention on the Law of Treaties. It had, moreover, only quoted this treaty as an example of treaties 'alleged' to be invalid by way of coercion.

The Working Group was also presented with reports compiled by Karen Parker of the International Education Development Inc. and by a mission from the International Commission of Jurists. Parker's report did not concentrate on the data, which was abundantly available elsewhere, presenting only some samples of victims' testimony from the Public Hearing, 'primarily to honour their courage in coming forward and to present first hand descriptions of the acts so that there is better understanding why they are war crimes and crimes against humanity'. She concentrated on legal analysis, centred on the principles of *jus cogens* and the corollary of *erga omnes* ('flowing to all', i.e. universal applicability of recognised principles and norms). As against Japan's arguments, *jus cogens* voids the use of treaties to deny victims compensation, and equally voids any national law in conflict with it. It also annuls statutory limitations. Nor was the vast scale of potential claims relevant.

The International Education Development Report recommended:

1. full disclosure of all information;
2. full and adequate apologies;
3. full and adequate monetary compensation to all victims.

The United Nations and its several bodies could assist Japan in setting up a compensations claims process and provide guidance on reasonable monetary award levels. Claimants should be allowed to file claims in their own countries, whose governments should take direct action if necessary by seizing local Japanese assets. Other states could co-operate by freezing Japanese assets in their jurisdiction. The United Nations should refrain from any changes to the Security Council or the Charter involving Japan until these violations were fully redressed.

The International Commission of Jurists' Mission was carried out by Ustinia Dolgopol, of Flinders University, Australia and an Indian barrister, Snehal Paranjape from Bombay. From 19 April to 8 May they visited Manila, Tokyo, Seoul and Pyongyang, interviewing over forty victims, three former soldiers, representatives of governments and non-governmental organisations, as well as lawyers and interested academics and journalists. The mission had been asked by the Working Group to consider three questions:

1. whether the women were forced to provide sexual services;
2. the responsibility of the Japanese government;
3. the issue of compensation.

After sketching the historical context and a summary of key documents on comfort stations, the preliminary report presented the contents of testimonies from six Filipinas and eleven Koreans, six from the South and five from the North. Most of these were cases already outlined here and no new features occur in the others.

The three former soldiers had been stationed in China and Manchuria and had been concerned in supervising comfort stations, though not directly in recruitment. One, a former *kempei,* gave some revealing details of the closeness of *kempeitai* controls:

> The Military Police kept an accurate account of the number of times a soldier visited a comfort house. Given the low rate of pay of the soldiers

their suspicions would be raised if a rank and file soldier visited such a house more than once or twice a month as they would not have had the funds to support such frequent visits. Too great a frequency might indicate that a soldier was trafficking in a prohibited substance or was defrauding the local population. Every morning the Korean couple [in charge] provided the Military Police a list of users of each woman and the Military Police would look to see if one particular soldier was visiting the same woman too often [as intimacy might lead to security leaks].

Another pointed out that the comfort system was not highly successful in its aims of preventing venereal disease, rape and other disorders.

The report's preliminary conclusions gave positive replies to the three basic questions, noting that even the contract system amounted to a form of debt slavery, one category long recognised in legislation. Its recommendations were more cautious than Parker's. They suggested that negotiations should basically proceed between Japan and the women's organisations, though adding that the former Allies should give the organisations every support possible. Finally, the Working Group passed a resolution to convey all these and other data to the Sub-commission for its August session.

Japanese coercion admitted

On 4 August, the last day before the Miyazawa cabinet was to be replaced by a coalition including socialist components for the first time since 1948, the government issued a report, supplementary to that of July 1992. For the first time, deception, coercion and official involvement in the recruitment of comfort women was admitted by the Japanese. As evidence, it cited interviews with comfort women in Seoul and field studies in Okinawa, as well as previously excluded sources from the United States and the Korean Comfort Women Problem Resolution Council. The timing of the report prompted some conjecture, but was doubtless largely due to the suddenness of the Liberal Democratic Party's loss of power. Preparation had been proceeding for some months, partly with a view to anticipating the August session of the Sub-commission on Human Rights.

Early in the year the government had proposed interviews with former comfort women, but had been rebuffed by the Problem Resolution Council on the grounds that this was only appropriate after the publication of all existing data in Japan. Interviews should not be conducted by officials, it was said, but by authorised specialists from both Japan and Korea. The incoming South Korean civilian administration, for its part, announced that it would not pursue the issue of compensation but settle for full disclosure of all data.

Interviews were eventually held over three days in late July with sixteen comfort women, with the co-operation of the Association of Bereaved Families of Pacific War Victims. The interviews, although strongly opposed by the Problem Resolution Council, gained legitimacy from the participation of Fukushima Mizuho, the member of the Tokyo case team primarily concerned with comfort women. The report, copies of which had already been sent to interested governments, contained the following new admissions:

> In many cases recruitment was carried out by agents at the request of operators in response to the requirements of military authorities, but with the expansion of the war the need to secure staff increased and under these conditions there were numerous cases of agents using deceptive enticement or recruiting in a manner contrary to the will of those concerned by such means as intimidation, while cases are also found where public officials directly participated in this . . . Besides numerous cases where women were transported to war zones by military ships and vehicles, there were also cases of their being abandoned in war zones during the confusion of flight on defeat.

The release of the report was accompanied by another public apology by Cabinet Chief Secretary Kono Yohei, about to become the leader of the Opposition. The apology was along the lines that 'the government takes this opportunity to offer its deepest apology and sense of self-reproach to all the women for their irreparable mental and physical suffering and injuries', promising that means of compensation would be studied, and the lessons of history squarely faced.

The reaction of the three governments immediately concerned were quite favourable. Both Korean governments, though recognising that much appropriate follow-up was needed, spoke of removing the issue from the future diplomatic agenda, while a presidential spokesman in the Philippines described the report as 'further promoting the existing good relations with Japan'. Citizen groups in these countries, however, as well as in Japan, were less enthusiastic, pointing out the considerable remaining scope for investigation, and of course stressing the issue of compensation.

In other countries, not so formally involved, particularly

Malaysia, Taiwan and Indonesia, citizen or semi-official groups became more vocal in demanding equal treatment for their own nationals. Further afield, the *Times,* in an incisive review of this and related issues, concluded with: 'The coalition which takes over today has promised a new beginning. It could start with compensation for the women whose sufferings Japan has too long hidden under the name of "comfort".'

Chief Counsel Takagi expressed some optimism that the government's acknowledgement of coercion might lead to an early conclusion to the litigation. Since the matter is *sub judice* in relation to the plaintiffs, the regular procedure would be for the government side to concede this point, as had been done in an earlier session regarding the management of comfort stations. Takagi suggested the establishment of a Diet committee to handle the matter. This would normally involve all parties, including the LDP and the Communists.

The change of government certainly introduced factors hard to assess. Socialist influence, as in the past, would presumably favour the plaintiffs, the new Social Democratic Speaker in the Lower House, Doi Takako, having participated in the Diet members' Special Committee on the Forced Draft Problem. The outgoing government's tactics may be variously interpreted but at least seem to have been intended to deprive the new government of an opportunity of presenting the report as its own initiative, or of handling its release differently. Regarding possible future approaches, the proposals made by Diet-woman Shimizu at the Seoul Solidarity Conference in August 1992 would provide a comprehensive basis for the settlement.

The Japanese admission of the use of coercion looks likely to signal, even if remotely, the end of the comfort women as a live issue, while at the same time opening the door to other victims who suffered at Japanese hands to press their cases for compensation.

Conclusion

Many comfort women will forever remain unknown, whether buried in the dust of foreign lands, or still unwilling to stand up and demand the justice that is their due. Then as now rape is not something that is easy to talk about. Seeking justice, then as now, is not something lightly undertaken. Reputations and family honour are involved. Then as now, the rape victim often ends up feeling responsible for what has happened to her. With a high moral value placed on female virginity in Asian societies, rape meant defilement and condemnation to a life of isolation and alienation.

Noh Chong Ja

Noh Chong Ja was the child of a poor farmer. Her only education was four years of night school of the kind held voluntarily by public spirited people. She was seventeen when, one day, she was warned by villagers that 'the Japanese are trying to take girls away'. This was soon followed by a warning from her mother to keep out of sight, because Japanese soldiers were coming. It was decided that she should take refuge with an aunt. She was given her mother's skirt to wear as a hood to obscure her identity on the long walk of some kilometres to the aunt's home. On a bridge, just before she reached her destination, she was seized by the *kempeitai*. Since she knew no Japanese, she tried to protest using gestures. These were ignored, and she was taken, with another girl already seized, to a road about 100 metres away, where three trucks were waiting. It was already evening. There were ten soldiers apart from the *kempei*, and some thirty-eight girls on the trucks. She knew none of the others, although they were from the same area. Above all else she wondered if she would ever again see her fiancé, a clerk in the village office, whom she was to marry in five days' time.

When the convoy reached an unknown railway station, the girls were each given a rice ball and transferred to open rail trucks. After four days and nights of travel they reached Tientsin. Following another rail journey, they were taken by a truck to a frontline force named Wu Tai Shan, after the nearby sacred mountain in Shansi Province. There they were lodged in a hut newly built for the Army, subdivided with plywood partitions into small rooms. Each was numbered, Chong Ja's being Number Seven. Each room opened to the outside, with a curtain at the doorway.

From seven o'clock on the first night, soldiers of the rank of private began entering the rooms. Chong Ja resisted, and was beaten and kicked until her mouth and nose bled. There are still traces of these blows on her buttocks. At 10 o'clock a meal of rice and soybean soup was brought in mess-tins. Later there were more visits by soldiers until three o'clock. At nine o'clock the women were given baths in storage drums. Throughout, they were under the supervision of two Japanese women.

From then on their routine was to rise at six o'clock bugle call and share a meal brought in a wooden pail by soldiers. She says that she was never hungry at this time. Between nine and ten o'clock they bathed. Soldiers began arriving from eleven. Afterwards, the men came later, leaving most of the daytime free. Officers came in the evenings and their visits continued until about three o'clock in the morning. During the course of a day the women would service from thirty to forty men, and had to remain bare from the waist down during the long working day. Saturday was their day off. They received no money, only occasional comfort bags with basic necessities. When the units left or arrived, the women had to bid farewell or welcome them, wearing shoulder bands inscribed Greater Japan Defence Women's Association.

The force was stationed within a city wall some kilometres around. Chong Ja sometimes saw Japanese shooting through holes at approaching Chinese troops. To pass through the city gates, identification marks had to be attached to one's chest, so unauthorised exit was impossible. There was a settlement outside and properly identified tradesmen could frequent the walled area. After about eighteen months, Chong Ja was allowed outside. Koreans were running restaurants, and stalls selling clothes like sweaters and suits had been set up by both Koreans and Chinese.

She came to know a Korean couple who were trading in clothing between this area and Tientsin. They had been so impoverished in

Korea that they had tried to improve their lot elsewhere. They took a particular liking to her because they had no children. They were concerned that her fate looked precarious if she remained where she was, and decided to help her escape. They put her into a box with air holes, hoisted it on to the back of their truck, and covered it with goods. In this way she successfully reached their home in Tientsin, where she could hide.

The rescue happened after she had been in the comfort station for two years and three months. A few months before the war ended, they sold their home in Tientsin and took her back to live with them in Korea. They had made enough money to buy a house and land in their native place. She was twenty-five.

In the autumn of that year she decided to visit her real parents. As she left, her foster-parents suggested she marry and bring her husband home to live with them. (This is an example of the traditional practice in Japan and Korea whereby parents, having only a daughter or foster-daughter, adopt her husband as a means of continuing the family line—an important Confucian principle.) But Chong Ja made no attempt to marry, because she has suffered poor health since her ill-treatment by the Japanese.

At home, she found that her father had been drafted by the Japanese. He had been so badly treated somewhere in the 'South Sea Islands' that he had died not long after returning home. So she had another reason for hating the Japanese. 'Cannot hate them enough,' she says.

When her foster-parents died, she was forty-three. Most of their property passed to relatives, since she had not been registered as a family member because of her failure to marry. She subsequently lived by casual work in the countryside. In recent times she has been receiving monthly welfare of the equivalent of about US$50, ten kilos of rice and two litres of barley. She has no money for even half-decent accommodation, and is in great need of any material compensation she can obtain. She is convinced her claim is a just one, although nothing can compensate her for a life ruined from the very eve of her planned wedding.

Other atrocities committed by the Japanese during the Pacific War, such as abuse of prisoners-of-war and massacre of civilian populations, were dealt with by the Tokyo war crime trials, and the perpetrators made to account for their deeds. Significantly, one

whole class of victims was totally ignored by everyone then and afterwards, when governments began negotiating wartime compensation with Tokyo. The comfort women were not unknown to the Allies, who had repatriated many. The United States Army had even,
as mentioned, made a study of a group of comfort women, and Allied soldiers had been known to take advantage of them. Only the
Dutch took action against the Japanese for forced prostitution—but
on behalf of Dutch women only. Indonesian women who were also
captured for comfort stations did not figure in the Batavia Trials, a
reflection of racist bias just as the failure of the Allies to try those
responsible for the comfort system is a reflection of sexism. There is
the niggling thought that the sufferings of the comfort women did
not matter enough for an issue to be made out of them.

Taiwanese activist Wang Ch'ing Feng noted that according to the
criminal code of Taiwan, a rapist gets seven years jail if his victim
commits suicide but only five if she does not. The logic seems to be
that what he has done is less of a crime if she is able to go on living
with it. No wonder it continues to be hard for women living in such
patriarchal societies to come forward and demand punishment.

It is possible to do what the Japanese Armed Forces did to the
comfort women if it is the belief that masculine needs have priority,
and that the prime duty of women is to serve men, surely the premise
of all patriarchal societies. As Japanese tradition has it, the woman
should walk two steps behind the man; as Confucianist philosophy
has it, a woman must obey first her father, then her husband and
finally her son. Nor are such attitudes confined to Asian societies.
Jan Ruff, who before the war had taken temporary vows as part of
the process of becoming a nun, was told after it that her horrific wartime experiences made her 'unacceptable' to the Church.

The central evidence that coercion and deception were used by the
Japanese military to recruit women for the comfort system comes, as
this book has shown, from the women themselves. At the time of
writing, there are no official documents to back up such evidence.
Nevertheless, their stories have been damning enough for the Japanese investigating team to be chary of interviewing the women, since
its official position was that the comfort system was voluntary.

In late July 1993, in a significant shift in position, the official investigating team interviewed sixteen Korean comfort women. Nine
women were selected as representative plaintiffs for the Tokyo lawsuit initiated at the end of 1991. Their cases were published by the

Association for Clarifying Japan's Postwar Responsibility, together with four others. Further interviews with five of the plaintiffs, and one of the others, were conducted by photo-journalist Ito Takashi, and published in a volume also containing interviews with seven women drafted for factory work. Ito, had been making intensive investigations of the forced draft of Koreans, and had earlier published accounts of labourers who had become victims of the atomic bombs, and those who had been abandoned on Sakhalin.

He describes the whole phenomenon as 'something that might logically have been expected to occur' in Japanese society in its totalitarian period. Although the women destined for factory work were distinguished by having some education or training which made them more useful, he notes that the line separating them from those drafted as comfort women was thin. One of his labour draft cases had originally been caught up in a comfort woman draft, but on arrival in Tokyo, was rejected as being too short. The draft order delivered to her home had been intended for her elder sister but, since she was in hiding, the younger had been taken instead. Ito's interviews include Mun Ok Ju (see Introduction) and Kim Hak Sun (see Chapter 7).

Women such as these have yet to receive a single yen of compensation from the Japanese government. The Tokyo lawsuit drags on, and may take years to reach a conclusion. In July 1994 the new Social Democrat Prime Minister, Murayama Tomiichi (in coalition with the Liberal Democratic Party), announced the final form of the 'measure in lieu of compensation' discussed by earlier Cabinets. He intended to present it on a visit to South Korea. The fund, amounting to $1.25 billion, would be used for 'women's support centres' and other measures for improved Asian relations. The proposal was, however, as on previous occasions, rejected by the Council for the Matter of the Comfort Women (now using the English title of 'Council for the Women Drafted for Sexual Slavery by Japan') whose general-secretary repeated its consistent demands for formal compensation of victims, a Diet resolution of apology and a search for the war criminals involved.

Meanwhile, throughout much of Asia, rape victims past and present are still considered defiled and shamed, as the traffic in women and children grows. If patriarchal Asian governments have shown a reluctance to come to terms with the emerging truth of the comfort women issue, the brutal reality is that they are not the only ones to blame. The vast comfort women system could not have survived without massive help from local collaborators. It has taken the rise of feminism among Asian women to bring the wider ramifications of the comfort women system to the world's attention. A solution involves improving the position of women world-wide.

Japanese responsibility

Professor Yoshimi in the introduction to his published collection of documents notes that the emergence of the comfort women issue in Japan is prompting parallel research in other countries. Ruthless exploitation of women and girls is by no means currently uncommon. A look at the modern prostitution racket in Asia is instructive. The traffic in women and young children is growing. In places like Thailand and the Philippines, prostitutes are getting younger and younger as men attempt to beat the odds on AIDS by picking on barely pubescent girls. When it comes to the needs of men, and when there is money to be made, anything goes. Governments stand indicted for complicity in the flesh trade by their failure to prevent it, or to take action to correct it when it happens.

The Japanese government also stands indicted for failing to take responsibility for its people's own history. For part of the fuel of the fire of the comfort women issue derives from official attempts to cover up, as well as from continued failure to inform and educate young Japanese on the less heroic aspects of the Pacific War. The inadequacy of education is such that one commentator described post-war generations as feeling themselves to be 'children of darkness', because they learn so little about the immediate past, either from their education or their parents. Overall, there is a pervasive—though not by any means complete—taboo on discussion of the war. The appearance to outsiders is of national amnesia.

At the individual level, the taboo suggests mass trauma arising from Japan's unique experience of modern history. European nations had experienced a major war every generation for many centuries, sometimes winning, sometimes losing, but adapting, while until the late nineteenth century, Japan had fought no civil wars for over two centuries and no external wars for nearly three. Then, jolted by Western imperialism and given impetus by British support, the country embarked on a series of ever-greater triumphs. Reckless opportunism finally ended in disaster. All this happened within the space of a single moderately long lifetime. Collective trauma is understandable.

The taboo appears in various forms at the official level. A once fairly conspicuous manifestation was the blank from the mid-1930s to 1945 in the *curriculum vitae* of older Japanese diplomats or international businessmen. Another is the scarcity of public memorials or museums recalling the war. The major exception is the Yasukuni Shrine to the war dead which, due to the Constitution's ban on government support for any religion, was viewed ambivalently until Prime Minister Nakasone's official visit. The War End Commemoration Day observances on 15 August each year, the principal one attended by the Emperor and leading members of the government, are purely occasions for mourning the Japanese dead. There are no expressions of sentiment, either positive or negative, regarding the war.

Most controversial and ultimately significant is the question of inadequate education. Treatment of the war is not entirely uniform because the Education Ministry does not have formal powers of censorship. Rather it has a screening and recommendation function, which can at times mean very limited flexibility. A survey of textbooks in relation to comfort women found, however, that the topic was mentioned only once.

The Ministry allowed Japanese aggression to be described in textbooks euphemistically as 'advance', rather than 'invasion'. Such evasiveness raises the general question of Japan's acknowledgement of its war guilt. From the contemporary Right-wing point of view, one prominent Diet-man publicly admitted that Japan had much to apologise for, but maintained that it should only apologise if the other former imperialist powers also apologised for their own past aggression. The Left wing for their part have nothing to apologise for: they were not players on the political scene before and during the war. Rather they were victims, along with the comfort women and Japan's other subjects.

When it comes to the comfort women issue, the question to ask is whether attitudes to women—and indeed to other 'races', like Koreans—have changed much in Japan since the war. One episode may be cited to suggest a persistence of attitudes which inspired the wartime comfort system. In December 1992, non-government relief agencies in Cambodia sent a letter of complaint about sexual harassment by United Nations troops to Akashi Yasushi, the Japanese

head of the Transitional Authority. He replied that it was natural for
hot-blooded soldiers who had endured the rigours of the field to
want to have a few beers and chase 'young beautiful beings of the
opposite sex'. It was as though the fact that the impulse was 'natural'
somehow made harassment acceptable, rather than a sign of indisci-
pline or lack of self-control. Judged by this response, women's
groups and the Left wing in Japan and Korea have good reason to
oppose the dispatch of Japanese troops on peace keeping operations
overseas.

In the final analysis, of course, the comfort women issue is about
the position of women in the world at large, not just in Japan. In a
survey done by the United Nations Development Program about the
position of women, half the human race, researchers were unable to
find any country which treated its women better than its men. And
Japan, which is first in the ranks of developed countries, is ranked
seventeenth on the treatment of its women.

Getting the world's attention

It has taken the rise of feminism among Asian women to bring the
comfort women issue to the attention of the world. It has taken
women to see the link between the wartime exploitation of their sisters and the contemporary exploitation of women in sex tourism in
parts of Asia including South Korea, the main source of wartime
comfort women. The issue is being spearheaded mostly by women
activists. In countries where the women's movement is relatively
inactive, or where there are no leading figures to espouse the cause,
comfort women remain a non-issue.

The absence of champions was responsible for the long lack of interest. Politics and governments remain male-dominated everywhere. Asian women may seem to have accepted their fate passively
for millennia—but those days are passing. The revolutionary idea
that women too are human, have rights and can demand justice is
taking hold. The energy and dedication with which the Filipinas
steamrollered their own reluctant government is an illustration of
the power of a cause over inertia and vested interests.

It is unlikely that the Japanese will be allowed to forget the comfort women. The injustice will live on to blot their history. And it was
not just the Japanese who have failed the human rights test. The Allies also failed, by not seeing that justice was done when they had the

power to enforce it. Their lapse reflects the poor record of mankind to womankind, especially in war.

Japan's abrupt change of role from long standing rival of the West in the Pacific to anti-Communist bulwark in East Asia, has made it expedient for both the Japanese and their anti-Communist allies to write off past rivalries, and concentrate on the present while conveniently overlooking issues of human rights. With the end of the Cold War, however, the international context has changed dramatically. Japan can no longer use its role as an anti-Communist bulwark as an excuse to sweep its human rights violations under its tatami mat. Japan's human rights record is certain to come under much closer international scrutiny. As a country which has ambitions to be accepted as a full member of the United Nations Security Council it will have to follow normal civilised standards which include acknowledgement of past crimes and the payment of compensation to the victims.

Besides the case of the comfort women and other victims of World War II, Japan is bound to be increasingly attacked for its treatment of domestic minorities such as Burakumin (low-caste Japanese), Koreans, Okinawans as well as both legal and illegal labourers from many Asian countries. No Western country of any importance practices the legalised racial discrimination which is the fate of Japan's long-settled Korean community. Racial discrimination, historical amnesia (a recent Minister of Justice argued that the 1937 Nanking Massacre was a 'fabrication') and therefore an unwillingness to attempt to right past and present wrongs will ensure that Japan remains an international outcast, an economic superpower which commands respect but which has few, if any, friends in either East or West.

Select annotated bibliography

The basic sources used are noted in this bibliography and in the more substantial cases, attribution is made in the text. However, many sources are of limited circulation and accessibility, being in the nature of pamphlets or special interest publications obtained through direct contact with activists. There are also a number of widely scattered press references.

Agora Editorial Council 1992, 'Jugun Ianfu Mondai ga tsukitsukeru mono' (What the military comfort women problem presents), *Agora* No. 174, 10 May, Tokyo. A special issue with articles about comfort women.

Allied Translator and Interpreter Section, Supreme Commander for the Allied Powers 1945, *Research Report: Amenities in the Japanese Armed Forces,* Tokyo. Two detailed sources on Manila and the North Burma front, with numerous extracts from other sources bearing on comfort women.

Brief van de Minister van Buitenlandse Zaken an de Voorzitter van de Tweede Kamer der Staten-Generaal, 's-Gravenhage 24 Januari 1994. Tweede Kamer, vergadejaar 1993–94, 23609 Nr 1 (Letter from the Minister of Foreign Affairs to the President of the Second Chamber of the States General, The Hague, 24 January 1994, session of 1993–94, 23609 No. 1). This document covers B. van Poelgeest's report to the Dutch Parliament.

Calica, Dan P. and Sancho, Nelia (eds) 1993, *War Crimes on Asian Women: Military Sexual Slavery by Japan during World War II,* Manila. The report of a task force on Filipina victims of military sexual slavery by Japan.

Chosenjin Jugun Ianfu Mondai o Kangaeru Kai (Association for the Study of the Korean Comfort Women Problem) 1992, *Chosenjin Jugun Ianfu Mondai Shiryoshu* (Reference Material on the Korean Comfort Women Problem), 3 vols, Osaka. Speeches, interviews and press cuttings compiled in support of the litigation campaign.

Chou, Wan-yao 1991, 'The Kominka Movement in Taiwan and Korea: Comparisons and interpretations', Paper for the Conference on the Japanese Empire at War 1937–45, Hoover Institute.

Dolgopol, Ustinia et al 1993, *Comfort Women: The Unfinished Ordeal,* Geneva. The preliminary report for the International Commission of Jurists.

Henriques, Fernando 1962–68, *Prostitution and Society: A Survey,* 3 vols, MacGibbon and Kee, London. The three volumes are: Primitive, Classical and Oriental; Europe and the New World; Modern Sexuality.

Ho Fang-Jiau (ed.) 1990, *Collection of Data on the ROC's taking-over of Taiwan (1945–49),* Taipei. A compilation of archival material in Chinese.

Huie, Shirley Fenton 1992, *The Forgotten Ones: Women and Children under Nippon,* Collins Angus & Robertson, Sydney. An account of the experiences of Dutch internees in Indonesia.

Hung Kuei-chi (ed.) 1985, *Jihpen Tsai-Hua Paohsing Lu 1928–45* (Record of Japanese Atrocities in China 1928–45), Kuoshih Kuan (National History Institute), Taipei. Direct references to comfort women from Japanese sources. Very fully covered to the date of publication.

International Public Hearing Executive Committee 1993, *War Victimisation and Japan,* Tokyo. Proceedings of the public hearing of 9 December 1992.

Ito Takashi 1992, *Jugun Ianfu. Joshi Kinro Teishintai* (Military Comfort Women and Women's Voluntary Labour Corps), Fubaisha, Nagoya. A collection of thirteen interviews, the most thorough of their kind, with commentary.

Japanese People's Movement 90s 1992, *Nihon Seifu Wa Tadachi Ni Sengo Hosho o Okonae* (The Japanese Government Must Pay War Compensation Immediately), Osaka. A report on Filipina comfort women.

Jugun Ianfu 110 Ban Henshu Iinkai (Editorial Committee for the Military Comfort Women Hotline) 1992, *Jugun Ianfu 110 Ban,* Tokyo. Wide-ranging interviews from the Tokyo hotline conversations.

Jugun Ianfu Mondai Kodo Nettowaku (Military Comfort Women Problem Action Network) 1992, *Jugun Ianfu Mondai Ajia Rentai Kaigi Hokokushu* (Reports of the Asia Solidarity Conference on the Comfort Women Problem), Tokyo. On the Seoul conference, August 1992.

Jugun Ianfu Mondai Uri Yoson Nettowaku (Compatriot Women's Network for the Military Comfort Women Question) 1992, *Kono 'Han' O Toku Tame Ni* (To Relieve This Rancour), Tokyo. Reports on meetings and press clippings.

Kim Hakusun-san no Shogen (Testimony of Ms Kim Hak-sun) 1993, Kaiho Shuppansha (Liberation Press), Osaka. In addition to an expanded presentation of Ms Kim's testimony, this volume contains the core portions of the 1992 reports by the governments of Japan and South and North Korea, with accounts of some private investigations.

Kim Il Myon 1976, *Tenno no Guntai to Chosenjin Ianfu* (The Emperor's Forces and Korean Comfort Women), San-ichi Shobo, Tokyo. The most comprehensive study of relevant war reminiscence literature, based on 75 substantial sources dated from 1942 to 1975.

Nihon Fujin Kaigi Osakafu Hombu (Osaka Prefectural Headquarters of the Japan Women's Council) 1992, *Jugun Ianfu 110 Ban Hokokushu* (Reports on the Military Comfort Women Hotline), Osaka.

Nihon no Sengo Sekinin o hakkiri-saseru Kai (Association for the Clarification of Japan's Postwar Responsibility) 1992, *Sojo* (Plaint), 2nd edition,

Tokyo. The plaint enlarged to cover the additional plaintiffs 1991–92, of the Asia-Pacific War Korean Victims Compensation Claim Case.

——1991–92, *Hakkiri Tsushin* (Clarification Reports), Nos 1 (1991) to 4 (September 1992) Tokyo. News, articles and documentation.

Nishino Rumiko 1992, *Jugun Ianfu* (Military Comfort Women), Akashi Shoten, Tokyo. An extensive collection of materials assembled through the author's Association for War Studies and Tokyo women's groups.

Senda Kako 1992, *Jugun Ianfu to Tenno* (Military Comfort Women and the Emperor), Kamogawa Shippan, Kyoto. A synopsis of the author's early pioneering investigations, with comments on the current outlook.

Suzuki Yuko 1991, *Chosenjin Jugun Ianfu* (Korean Military Comfort Women), Iwanami Shoten, Tokyo. A survey of then available material with a background sketch of modern Japanese-Korean relations.

——1992, *Jugun Ianfu Naisen Kekkon* (Military Comfort Women. Japanese-Korean Marriages), Miraisha, Tokyo. A very scholarly study of related political and administrative aspects and the assimilationist program in Korea under colonisation.

Takagi Ken'ichi 1992, *Jugun Ianfu To Sengo Sekinin* (Comfort Women and Postwar Responsibility), San-ichi Shobo, Tokyo. The Chief Counsel's account of the case to date.

Tomiyama Taeko 1992, *Kaeranu Onnatachi* (Women Who Do Not Return), Iwanami Shoten, Tokyo. A feminist artist's study of the cultural implications of the comfort women issue, with an account of the Kanita refuge settlement and Thai prostitutes in contemporary Japan. Paintings reproduced with poems.

United States Office of War Information 1944, *Japanese Prisoner of War Interrogation Report No. 49*, Ledo Stockdale, October.

Usuki Keiko 1992, *Gendai Ianfutachi* (Contemporary Comfort Women), Tokuma Shoten, Tokyo. South Korean studies on recollections of comfort women, sex tourism and prostitution at United States bases.

Van Poelgeest, Bart 1992, 'Tewerkgesteld in de Japanse bordelen van Nederlands-Indie' (Forced to work in the Japanese brothels of the Netherlands Indies), *NRC Handelsblad, Zaterdags Bijvoegsel*, p. 3, 8 August.

Yamane Masako 1991, *Matsushiro Daihon'eiato o Kangaeru* (Study of the Remains of the Matsushiro General Headquarters), Shinkansha, Tokyo. An account of the bunker complex constructed at the time of the leadership's last retreat, including the surviving comfort station.

Yoshida Seiji 1983, *Watakushi no Senso Hanzai: Chosenjin Kyosei Renko* (My War Crimes: The Forced Draft of Koreans), San-ichi Shobo, Tokyo. An account of the slave-raid type expeditions to draft labourers and comfort women.

Yoshimi Yoshiaki 1992, *Jugun Ianfu Shiryoshu* (Reference Material for Military Comfort Women), Otsuki Shoten, Tokyo. This outstanding source includes a detailed introduction followed by a collection of 106 documents and other references, including all significant parts of the Japanese government's 1992 report, together with all known United States and Australian sources.

Yun Chung-mo, trans Kashima Setsuko 1992, *Haha Jugun Ianfu* (My Mother a Military Comfort Woman), Gakusei Seinen Senta (Student and Youth Centre), Kobe. This translation of the Korean original published in 1982 is a well researched fictionalised treatment set in wartime Philippines and post-war Korea.

Yun Chung-ok et al 1992, *Chosenjin Josei ga mita Ianfu Mondai* (The Comfort Women Issue As Seen By Korean Women), San-ichi Shobo, Tokyo. This work reproduces Professor Yun's seminal studies in Korea, with a very comprehensive range of testimonies and background studies.

Index